DISCARDED

Democracy Delayed

Democracy Delayed

The Case of Castro's Cuba

Juan J. López

The Johns Hopkins University Press
Baltimore and London

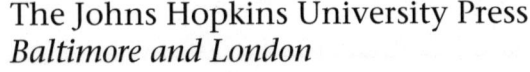

© 2002 The Johns Hopkins University Press
All rights reserved. Published 2002
Printed in the United States of America on acid-free paper
9 8 7 6 5 4 3 2 1

The Johns Hopkins University Press
2715 North Charles Street
Baltimore, Maryland 21218-4363
www.press.jhu.edu

Library of Congress Cataloging-in-Publication Data

López, Juan J. (Juan José)
    Democracy delayed : The case of Castro's Cuba /
Juan J. López.
    p. cm.
Includes bibliographical references and index.
    ISBN 0-8018-7046-1 (hard : alk. paper)
    1. Democratization—Cuba. 2. Cuba—Politics and
government—1959– 3. Authoritarianism—Cuba. 4.
Communism—Cuba. 5. Cuba—Relations—United States.
6. United States—Relations—Cuba. 7. Post-communism.
I. Title.
    JL1010.L67   2002
    320.97291—dc21
2001007990

A catalog record for this book is available from the British
Library.

*To Myrna and Juan Carlos, my wife and son,
for all their support*

Contents

Preface and Acknowledgments		*ix*
Introduction		*xiii*
1	The Castro Regime and Political Transition	1
2	Civil Society and Repression	29
3	Political Efficacy and Independent Communication	55
4	Assistance to Civil Society	85
5	U.S. Policies toward Cuba	110
6	The Economic Embargo	125
7	Conclusions	159
	Notes	*182*
	References	*217*
	Index	*227*

Preface and Acknowledgments

As I was revising my dissertation on the political economy of Argentina to submit it to a publisher, momentous developments were taking place in Cuba. Civil society was being re-created after a long period of near extinction. The Castro regime showed signs of weakness. It faced a severe economic crisis and had lost its Soviet patron. Communism seemed doomed to be swept away by the international wave of democratization. For the first time in over three decades, the Castro dictatorship seemed extremely vulnerable. When the Castro regime endured, contrary to expectations, explaining its ability to survive became a burning question. As I read the explanations in the scholarly literature, I realized how inadequate they were. I was already well acquainted with the literatures on transitions to democracy and on the Eastern European transformations. I saw the existing academic lacunae and the theoretical importance of explaining non-transitions in cases where many of the underlying conditions seemed to favor a regime change. I started by writing an article about the implications of the U.S. economic embargo for a political transition in Cuba. And then my research and writing on the non-transition in Cuba snowballed into this book.

In explaining the non-transition in Cuba, I analyze the conditions in Cuba since the 1990s, when many expected communism in Cuba to fall. Consequently, I look at the regime type under the rule of Fidel Castro. However, the relevance of this book goes beyond Castro's tenure. This is so for a number of reasons. Fidel has indicated that his younger brother, Raúl, will succeed him. If Raúl becomes the strongman in Cuba, the current regime might continue in its basic form or its nature could change. If the latter occurs and the regime becomes an authoritarian dictatorship, key factors that I identify as fostering a transition to democracy would remain important: independent communication, resources in the hands of the opposition, public protests, and economic pressure on the autocracy. A standard conclusion in the study of transitions

x *Preface and Acknowledgments*

from dictatorial rule, whether in Latin America or in Eastern Europe, is that almost all regimes faced serious pressures prior to the transitions. In the typical analyses of transitions to democracy developed from the experiences of Latin America and Southern Europe in the 1970s and 1980s, the pressures faced by authoritarian regimes tended to result in splits in the ruling bloc between hardliners and softliners, with the latter gaining the upper hand and implementing political liberalization as a strategy intended to save the dictatorships

I argue in this book that a transition to democracy is possible under the regime headed by Fidel Castro. Given the nature of the regime, only a transition by regime collapse seems plausible, that is, a transition initiated and pushed by civil society and the population at large, what Mark R. Thompson has called a democratic revolution. Yet this possibility depends on the strategic choices pursued by key actors in the drama. Thus, whether a transition will take place remains uncertain. I show that in the regime led by Fidel Castro, he and other hardliners dominate and adamantly oppose political liberalization. Consistent with theoretical observations about the relationship between types of dictatorships and possible transition paths, a transition in Cuba in which regime elites initiate and negotiate a political transition is extremely unlikely under the Fidel Castro regime.

If Fidel Castro dies or becomes incapacitated to rule and the regime changes in such a way that a negotiated transition ensues, there will be scholars who will affirm that a political transition in Cuba required the "biological solution," that Fidel had to die before change could happen. Cuba will be compared with Spain, Fidel with Franco. Spain rather than Eastern European countries will be seen as the model that was relevant for Cuba all along. And a deterministic construction of history will appear. But all of these arguments would be true only by default. It would be false to claim that such outcomes had to happen. This book will serve to deconstruct history and point to missed historical possibilities that did not materialize due to strategic choices adopted by main actors.

The relevance of this book also transcends the case of Cuba. The work uses the Cuban case to evaluate a number of hypotheses in the literature on transitions and on the effectiveness of economic sanctions as a policy instrument. Moreover, in explaining the non-transition in Cuba, I generate hypotheses that can be applied in accounting for other cases of non-transition from communism, such as China, Vietnam, and North Korea. A book I am co-authoring with Mark Thompson and Steven Saxonberg will build upon this one and will

test hypotheses presented here. For example, in trying to explain the endurance of communist regimes outside Europe, one could argue that communist regimes in countries such as Cuba, China, and Vietnam were established after national revolutions or that these regimes enjoy strong support out of feelings of nationalism. I argue that such factors are not important in accounting for the endurance of the Castro regime.

In the present book, I compare Cuba with East Germany, Czechoslovakia, and Romania. I follow a most-similar systems design. According to the regime classifications developed by Juan Linz and Alfred Stepan in their book *Problems of Democratic Transition and Consolidation,* I find that these Eastern European countries under communist rule had regimes quite similar to the Castro regime. In broad terms, all four countries are cases of hardline regimes. The comparison of transitions with non-transitions can provide a fuller understanding of these phenomena than solely comparing cases of transition. Yet the tendency in explaining the political transformations in Eastern Europe at the end of the 1980s was to draw comparisons with previous transitions in Southern Europe and Latin America.

This is the first scholarly, empirically based comparison between Cuba and Eastern Europe. These comparisons yield two results. One is to offer a better explanation for the endurance of the Cuban dictatorship. The other is to show that some factors in Eastern European transitions are more important than is usually recognized in accounts of the fall of communism in that region. Doing so adds to the relevance of this book beyond the Cuban case. I suggest what are necessary and what are sufficient conditions for transitions from communism by regime collapse. This book explains why the Castro regime has endured. I address the question using a combination of theory, comparative analyses, and available data. By becoming aware of reasons for the survival of the Castro regime, one can infer conditions that may bring about its demise. Hence, besides its contribution to scholarship, this book has policy implications. It combines a theoretical orientation with an unprecedented amount of data on the political, social, and economic circumstances in Cuba at the turn of the millennium.

The Eastern European transitions showed the critical importance of international factors as determinants of these processes even though the impetuses for these political transformations were internal to each case. The importance of international factors in transitions from communism goes beyond the Eastern European cases. The realization that international factors are important in

xii *Preface and Acknowledgments*

transitions calls for analyses to determine the ways in which these factors affect the probabilities of transitions. This book embraces this task.

An adequate explanation for why the Castro regime has endured since the end of communism in Eastern Europe requires consideration of U.S. policies toward Cuba. This book analyzes the Cuba policies of the Clinton administration. It was during the Clinton years at the White House that for the first time it became possible to topple the Castro government without an armed invasion. Another question in regard to U.S. policy that the book addresses is whether the economic embargo helps or hinders the prospects for a transition to democracy in Cuba.

I received excellent and detailed comments on the whole manuscript from Rasma Karklins, at the Department of Political Science of the University of Illinois at Chicago, and from Juan M. del Aguila, at the Department of Political Science of Emory University. I am very grateful to them. Several individuals provided me with data. Their assistance was invaluable. Orlando Gutierrez and Rafael Artigas from the Center for the Study of a National Option (Centro de Estudios para una Opción Nacional—CEON), a think tank based in Miami, allowed me to use very valuable interview data that the Center collected from focus groups of opposition activists inside Cuba. Carl Gershman, from the National Endowment for Democracy, sent me copies of all of NED's annual reports. Ernesto Betancourt, former director of Radio Martí, helped me obtain data about Radio and TV Martí and sent me the report of a major survey that he and others conducted among Cubans recently arrived to the United States. Scott G. Michael, from the Office of Cuba Broadcasting, sent me almost all the reports of audience studies for Radio and TV Martí. Roberto Rodríguez-Tejera, director of Radio Martí, also helped me obtain some very useful information about the station. Martins Zvaners at Radio Free Europe/Radio Liberty informed me about technical aspects of RFE/RL broadcasts before the fall of communism in Eastern Europe. And Pavol Salamon and Susie Kerekes, at the Open Society Archives of the Central European University, mailed me data on surveys of Czechoslovaks about Radio Free Europe. Finally, I want to thank my wife Myrna and son Juan Carlos for all their support and understanding while I worked to bring this project to fruition.

Introduction

In the immediate aftermath of the fall of communist dictatorships in Eastern Europe, a widespread expectation emerged that the domino effect would reach the Caribbean without much delay. As the Castro dictatorship nonetheless endured, explanations for its staying power proliferated. Despite the profusion of hypotheses for Cuba's non-transition, when one evaluates the explanations from a comparative perspective and in light of available data from Cuba, one finds that these hypotheses are wrong or inadequate. It has become increasingly important to formulate a sound explanation for the non-transition. There are other cases of non-transition from communism, such as those in China, Vietnam, and North Korea. While I do not include these cases in this book, a detailed analysis of the Cuban case can serve to better understand other instances of non-transition from communism.[1]

Models of transitions from communism based on the experiences of Latin America and Southern Europe showed limitations. Guillermo O'Donnell's observation that revolutionary paths from dictatorships do not lead to democratic regimes became outdated by the experiences of East Germany and Czechoslovakia.[2] Mark Thompson has cogently argued that transitions in these countries were democratic revolutions.[3]

A transition to democracy in Cuba under the regime of Fidel Castro could result from progressively larger and repeated protests, as in East Germany, Czechoslovakia, and Romania. To explain the non-transition in Cuba one has to answer the question why continuous mass demonstrations developed in Czechoslovakia, East Germany, and Romania and not in Cuba. I agree with the logical argument that a transition has not taken place in Cuba because Cuba is different from Eastern Europe. But in the literature on Cuba the differences that have been posed are the wrong ones. The fundamental obstacle to a transition in Cuba is that most people feel incapable of inducing a political transformation. Large-scale participation in protests that demand democratization

xiv   *Introduction*

have not occurred in Cuba mainly because the majority of the population thinks that their participation in opposition activities would be ineffective in achieving change. Unless people believe that their participation in acts of opposition can bring about political changes, there are no mass demonstrations in the streets and hence no transition by regime collapse. What really matters for mass demonstrations is what people in the general population think. While courageous civil society activists defy the regime, without repeated, large-scale demonstrations by the general population, those who thus far are not involved in any independent or opposition activities, there cannot be a transition from below. Democratic activists comprise a small percentage of the population and therefore cannot by themselves produce mass protests of the magnitude that brought about the collapse of regimes in East Germany, Czechoslovakia, and Romania.

The Cuban case points to the crucial importance for a transition by collapse of two factors: (1) a widespread belief in the population that change is possible; and (2) the ability of independent sources of communication to reach a large percentage of the people regularly. Independent means of communication are vital to development of a sense of political efficacy among citizens. In Cuba, in contrast to the Eastern European cases at the end of the 1980s, these two factors are missing.

The unwillingness of the Clinton administration to promote a political transition in Cuba was the key reason for the absence of effective channels of independent communication in the island. It remains to be seen if the administration of George W. Bush will help make independent sources of information available to most of the population in Cuba. By mid-2001, President Bush had stated that he is willing to implement policies that would quickly undermine the government of Fidel Castro. Yet, as of January 2002, there was no evidence that the Bush administration was doing anything new to foster a transition in Cuba. What he has done is to show stronger support than President Clinton did for the continuation of the economic embargo.

As Przeworski observes, questions about possibility are theoretical and necessarily involve propositions that are counterfactual.[4] Counterfactuals play a key role in evaluating causal hypotheses in political science. Scholars refer to counterfactual cases in which the postulated cause is assumed to be absent. Arguments to support a hypothesis using counterfactuals gain credibility from theories that have some independent empirical support and from historical facts relevant to the counterfactual case. In his discussion of counterfactuals,

James Fearon indicates that a counterfactual assertion is judged to be true if: (1) arguments in support of a causal hypothesis have credibility from theories and facts, and (2) the actual occurrence of the counterfactual causal factor would not preclude the initial conditions used to draw the inference. In my explanation for the Cuban non-transition, I argue that there are missing factors, such as effective channels of independent communication, that would be necessary for a transition to take place. These can be seen as counterfactual causal factors. Their occurrence would not preclude the underlying conditions, like widespread discontent with the dictatorship, that are also important components for a transition by regime collapse. Fearon argues that the validity of a counterfactual assertion is more likely to hold for small causes, such as specific policy decisions.[5] As I indicate, the missing factors explaining the Cuban non-transition are fundamentally due to policy decisions of the U.S. government.

I address the question of why a transition in Cuba has not occurred by using a combination of theory, comparative analyses, and available data. I also look at why the Castro regime has endured, despite all the serious problems it faces, while similar regimes, with analogous difficulties, fell in Eastern Europe. Another task of this book is to determine whether a number of general hypotheses about causes of transitions hold true for the Cuban case. Thus, I use the Cuban case to test general hypotheses about transitions and specific hypotheses about the non-transition in Cuba. Also, I generate hypotheses that could be applied to other cases of non-transition from communism. For example, Samuel Huntington, in *The Third Wave*, presents a list of causes of transitions to democracy.[6] Which ones are suitable in the Cuban case and which ones are not? Some of the questions I address are: (1) does poor economic performance increase the probability of a transition, or is it robust economic growth that does so?; (2) are economic sanctions effective in changing policies or regimes in target countries?; (3) are international norms in favor of democracy and respect for human rights a key cause of the demise of dictatorial rule?; (4) does the Catholic Church push for democratization?

The comparison of transitions with non-transitions can provide a fuller understanding of these phenomena than solely comparing cases of transition. Yet the tendency in explaining the political transformations in Eastern Europe at the end of the 1980s was to draw comparisons with previous transitions in Southern Europe and Latin America.[7] It is important to include "negative" cases in comparisons. Comparing just cases of transitions implies choosing

cases on the dependent variable and incurring selection bias. Comparing transitions and non-transitions introduces variance in the dependent variable and provides a better estimate of the underlying causal pattern than just comparing cases of transition. One view is that it is impossible to assess causal hypotheses without considering negative cases.[8]

A comparison between Cuba on the one hand and Eastern European countries on the other is valuable as long as it is theoretically informed and empirically grounded, two requisites that are often missing in these comparisons. My comparison of Cuba and Eastern European cases yields two results. One is to offer a new explanation for the endurance of the Cuban dictatorship. The other is to show that some factors in Eastern European transitions are more important than is usually recognized in explaining the fall of communism in Europe.

Following the classification of dictatorships in the work of Juan Linz and Alfred Stepan, East Germany and Czechoslovakia had frozen post-totalitarian regimes and Romania had a mixed type of totalitarianism and sultanism. I classify the regime in Cuba as a mixture of frozen post-totalitarianism and sultanism. Thus, of the types of communist regimes in Eastern Europe, the regime in Cuba is most similar to those in East Germany, Czechoslovakia, and Romania. In comparing Cuba with these Eastern European cases, I use the most similar systems design. The dependent variable, that is, the occurrence of political transition, differs between cases and thus differences in independent variables across the cases are presented as the explanatory factors. That is, those factors that Cuba has in common with these three countries cannot account for the non-transition in Cuba. Only differences that are theoretically relevant and empirically substantiated can be considered as plausible explanatory causes for the non-transition. As is common in comparative studies following a most similar systems design, it is always possible to find differences between the cases and claim that such differences account for the variation in the phenomenon to be explained.[9] After a thorough review of the literature on Cuba, I have found that the differences that have been drawn with Eastern Europe to account for the non-transition offer inadequate explanations. Yet, methodologically, it is impossible to avoid the complaint that I have missed a difference that really matters. But, I believe that the burden of proof is on the critic. If a difference is posed to account for the non-transition in Cuba, it is necessary to also point to the empirical validity of the difference, what exactly the difference implies (for example, that the dictatorship resulted

Introduction xvii

from a nationalist revolution can imply support for it among citizens at large and/or among regime cadres), and what the theoretical significance of the alleged difference for explaining (non)transitions is.

Some explanations for the non-transition in Cuba point to supposed differences between Cuba and Eastern European countries. Most arguments along this line disregard the empirical validity of the differences and/or their theoretical relevance to account for political (non)transitions. One difference that has been posed is that, in contrast to countries in Eastern Europe, members of the Communist Party in Cuba remain loyal to the Party, indicated by the fact that massive resignations have not occurred.[10] This argument is problematic and quite inadequate to explain the endurance of the regime. For one thing, large-scale defections from the communist parties did not take place until the very end of the dictatorships in East Germany and in Czechoslovakia, and not at all in Romania. Steven Saxonberg indicates that in the late 1980s, membership in the Czechoslovak Communist Party was increasing while survey data suggested that party members were fairly critical of the system.[11] The other difficulty with the party-loyalty hypothesis is that there is evidence of discontent among regime cadres in Cuba. (I will present the data later.) Moreover, in Cuba the number of party members who have turned in their party cards or otherwise ceased their membership in the Party may be larger than is assumed. According to one account, during 1996 in only two municipalities, there were 2,385 cases of resignations or "lost" membership records.[12] The Union of Communist Youths (Unión de Jóvenes Comunistas— UJC) has problems functioning as a recruitment channel for the Communist Party. Only between 32 percent and 43 percent of the members of the UJC go on to become members of the Party, and the UJC has difficulty getting youngsters to join.[13] Most of the focus groups in Cuba that participated in the Center for the Study of a National Option (Centro de Estudios para una Opción Nacional—CEON) study (described below) report that since 1990 the Party is having greater difficulties recruiting members, in comparison to previous times. Moreover, all but one of the groups in the CEON study maintain that people join the Party to get the most desirable jobs, to have access to higher education, or to try to avoid trouble with the authorities.

Being a member of the Party in Cuba is a requirement to be eligible for important material benefits, such as jobs in the tourist industry, where workers have access to dollar earnings, something very important in the current economic environment. Also, membership in the Party can provide some protec-

xviii   *Introduction*

tion from prosecution. This can be useful since stealing government property from one's workplace has become normal behavior. Party members apply for visas to emigrate to the United States.[14] Hence, being a member of the Party does not necessarily imply ideological commitment. Clearly, belonging to the Party does not mean that the person is a "true believer." One indication of the ideological decay in Cuba is the concern the government shows about the paucity of ideological fervor. In July 2000, the government launched a campaign to build "political culture," maintaining that the "battle of ideas" will be fought every day.[15]

In contrasting Cuba and Eastern European countries to explain the non-transition, some argue that an important difference lies in the origins of the dictatorships. In Cuba the regime resulted from a national revolution while in Eastern Europe communism was imposed by Soviet power. I call this the homegrown hypothesis.[16] As in Cuba, communism gained power in the Soviet Union after a national revolution; yet the overwhelming rejection of the Soviet regime was evident in the political transition in that country. The case of Nicaragua also suggests the inadequacy of this hypothesis in accounting for non-transitions from communism. In Nicaragua, the Sandinistas lost the presidency in a free election in 1990 and, as of 2002, have not won that post under a democratic regime. But what exactly does the homegrown argument imply? It assumes that because the regime had an origin in a national revolution, the dictatorship enjoys a high degree of legitimacy in the population and/or among cadres. (I will present evidence of discontent among cadres.) With respect to the common folk, one hypothesis for the endurance of the Castro regime explicitly states that the Castro government still enjoys considerable support among the population.[17] The homegrown argument assumes that the degree of legitimacy among citizens is important in explaining why dictatorships last.

Przeworski has lucidly argued that to use the notion of popular legitimacy to account for the survival of autocracies is tautological. Under a dictatorship there are no reliable survey data to measure the degree of popular support that the regime has. So if the dictatorship survives one can claim that it does because it enjoys popular legitimacy, and if the dictatorship falls one can say that it lost popular legitimacy. Autocracies can endure without any popular support, just by coercion.[18] Nevertheless, it is unreasonable to assume that the Castro regime enjoys a significant degree of popular support. It is impossible to measure discontent or support in methodologically sound ways. But vari-

Introduction   xix

ous indicators, such as repeated waves of rafters desperately risking their lives to leave Cuba, show pervasive aversion toward the regime. Moreover, the very poor economic performance in Cuba since the beginning of the 1990s has increased the grievances of the population. Although there may still be a percentage of the population that genuinely supports the Castro government, most likely such a percentage is very small. If analogous cases can serve as proxies of support for communism in the Cuban population, one can be fairly certain that the Communist Party in Cuba would be unable to win a majority in free elections. The electoral strength of communist parties (or their reincarnations) after transitions to democracy in Poland, Hungary, Czechoslovakia, and East Germany was minuscule. From the perspective of all the civil society groups that participated in the CEON study, the majority of the population does not support the regime. One group estimates that more than 80 percent of the population is against the government.

Another angle to consider in assessing the inadequacy of the homegrown argument is that in Cuba, although Castro came to power riding a wave of popular support, the quest of the Cuban revolution was to establish a democracy, not a Marxist-Leninist dictatorship. Before 1959, and in the early period of the revolutionary government, Castro portrayed himself as a democrat, pledging to restore the 1940 Cuban constitution. Thus, popular support for the struggle against Fulgencio Batista, the pre-1959 dictator, was support for democracy. As in the case of the Russian revolution, in Cuba the Communists hijacked the revolution to impose their dictatorship.

An additional argument for the non-transition in Cuba, similar to the legitimacy one but not quite the same, holds that the Castro regime enjoys a significant degree of support due to nationalism. For example, hostile policies on the part of the United States toward the Cuban government, such as the economic embargo, help Fidel Castro to stay in power by fostering support for the regime out of nationalism.[19] With respect to Eastern Europe, Valerie Bunce argues that nationalism (the quest for national liberation) was a fundamental factor in bringing down communist regimes in the Soviet Union and in Soviet bloc countries.[20] While republic-level nationalism in the Soviet Union and resentment against Soviet imperialism in Eastern European countries played a role in fostering opposition to communist regimes, the crucial importance that Bunce gives to this factor is questionable. Bunce seems to imply that if a communist regime enjoys national legitimacy, it should endure. But one cannot explain why the Castro government has survived by saying that the

regime enjoys substantial support due to nationalism. Although it is true that the Cuban government uses unfriendly U.S. policies to try to stir up nationalism, the effectiveness of these efforts is quite doubtful.[21] Just because a dictatorship equates itself with the flag does not mean that support for the regime will be forthcoming. Reports from Cuba and interviews with recent refugees show that the majority of the people do not pay attention to nationalist appeals from the Cuban government based on confrontation with the United States.[22] One of the nicknames for Fidel Castro in Cuba is "Armando Guerra Solo," literally "Fighting War Alone." In Romania, Ceauşescu tried to use nationalism as a pillar of support for his government, but this appeal was depleted and came to fall on deaf ears.[23] In the CEON study, some civil society activists believe that nationalism has some importance in generating support for the Cuban government, but 80 percent of the responses in the study maintain that nationalism is not a major source of support for the Castro regime.

Part of the explanation for the failure of nationalist appeals by the Cuban government in its attempt to bolster popular support is the disjunction between the government and nationalism due to "tourist apartheid" and the privileged treatment given to foreign investors. Cuban citizens who are not part of the ruling elite are barred from resorts and hotels serving tourists because of the mere fact that they reside in Cuba. Cubans who live abroad and visit the island can enter these resorts and hotels, but their relatives living in Cuba cannot.[24] There are also "health tourists," people who travel to Cuba to receive upscale medical treatment at facilities closed to the general population. Consequently, there is a strong resentment among people in Cuba about these discriminatory practices of the Cuban government against its own citizens.[25] Also, foreign capitalists are given generous concessions to do business in Cuba while the possibility for Cubans to develop their own private enterprises is severely restricted.[26] Castro and other hardliners oppose going beyond limited market reforms in Cuba's internal economy as they open the country to enclaves of foreign investment.[27]

Another explanation for the endurance of the Cuban government holds that for most people politics is a leisure-time activity, and due to the hard struggle of daily life in Cuba, for example, to get food and to commute, most people are too busy surviving to organize the politics of opposition.[28] This argument is not a viable one in accounting for the non-transition. It assumes that transition processes are normal political phenomena. The hypothesis dis-

Introduction   xxi

regards the fact that in East Germany, Czechoslovakia, and Romania, only a small fraction of the population joined dissident groups. The surge in mass protests that brought down communism in those countries was rapid and short-lived. People who had never belonged to opposition groups decided to demonstrate. Moreover, in Cuba, the number of political prisoners (425 according to one conservative estimate) and the large number of independent groups now in existence show that many people find the time, courage, and energy to participate in opposition activities.[29]

Another explanation for the non-transition in Cuba maintains that people do not want to be subject to extra surveillance by participating in civil society groups.[30] This contention seems logical because most people are constantly breaking laws in order to survive, for example, by stealing from the state or engaging in illegal market transactions. I would raise the same objections to this attempt to account for the endurance of the Castro government as I do for the "too busy" hypothesis. Another problem for the keep-a-low-profile argument is that for a large percentage of the population individual actions offer no satisfactory solution to the difficult living conditions that have persisted since the 1990s.[31] At the level of the general population, there is a positive association between the deterioration of the economy on the one hand and discontent and criticism of the Cuban government on the other. Many acts of opposition to the regime have resulted spontaneously (like food riots) as people have reacted to deprivation and unresolved grievances.[32] While dealing in illegal markets may enable people to fare better in the struggle to acquire basic necessities, those who do so are always vulnerable to government persecution for their illegal activities. The majority of the population continues to be dissatisfied with the political and economic status quo, which raises the question of why citizens do not attempt to change the regime.

Repression is frequently cited to account for the endurance of the Castro government.[33] Of all the hypotheses in the literature trying to explain the endurance of the Castro regime, repression is the only one that is sound. The repression in Cuba is certainly intense and widespread; it is an important constraint in any attempt to achieve a political transition. If repression were abandoned or drastically reduced, the regime would fall. A fundamental question is whether the regime in Cuba can maintain itself by the use of repression under all possible situations. In other words, does the repressive apparatus assure the survival of the regime? I argue that it does not.

xxii   *Introduction*

Closely related to the view that repression is a cause of the endurance of the Castro government is the argument that civil society in Cuba is very weak.[34] Repression in itself is insufficient to explain the shortcomings of civil society. Analyzing civil society is crucial for assessing the possibility of change under the Castro regime because the only likely path of transition under the current regime type is one pushed by civil society and the general population.

In fact, civil society in Cuba is similar to those in East Germany and Czechoslovakia at the end of the 1980s in terms of numbers of groups and activists. By these criteria, the strength of civil society in Cuba does not preclude a transition from below. Unlike the Eastern European cases, civil society activists in Cuba cannot earn a living legally, due to greater economic repression, and have less resources to produce and distribute samizdat literature. However, these limitations do not constitute insurmountable problems for a transition because material assistance from abroad could readily ameliorate these difficulties. Thus far, civil society groups in Cuba have received little humanitarian assistance and resources for the production of samizdat.

Saxonberg argues that in the late 1980s civil society groups in Eastern Europe, including Solidarity in Poland, were too weak to bring down the dictatorships. He conceives the weakness of civil society in terms of numbers of groups and members and the groups' organizational capacity.[35] While I agree that civil society groups by themselves did not topple communist regimes in Eastern Europe and would not do so in Cuba either, I maintain that civil society groups can play important roles in fostering transitions, including transitions by collapse.[36] Democratic activists can help organize the citizens into non-political groups, such as farmers' cooperatives or neighborhood associations with social aims. Although the original intent of these groups is non-political, they can channel their members into activities to push for democratization at some point in time. And civil society groups can foster a sense of political efficacy in the population.

A belief that political change is possible does not necessarily mean that people expect to achieve a transition to democracy. The expected change could be only political liberalization in a hardline regime. There is no necessary contradiction in the claims that people who participated in mass protests in East Germany, Czechoslovakia, and Romania at the end of 1989 felt that their behavior could bring about political change and that they were surprised by the extent of the changes that occurred. The outcomes may have far exceeded their expectations.

Introduction xxiii

With the exception of Romania, where open dissent was practically nil, civil society activists in many Eastern European cases carried out acts of opposition that served to develop a sense of political efficacy among the people. In the case of Romania, the population received news and information about opposition activities in neighboring countries. Thus, one can say that civil society activists in other Eastern European countries contributed to the formation of a sense of political efficacy among the Romanian population.

Civil society activists by their actions promoted a belief among the people that participation in public protests to demand political changes could succeed. The activities of civil society groups signaled that there were people willing to confront the authorities publicly to demand respect for human rights, even if some people were beaten or arrested. Activists also communicated to the population the need to overcome their fear and participate in actions to demand change. Moreover, after the Polish regime recognized Solidarity in 1988 and agreed to hold partially competitive elections, the idea that it was possible to achieve political change gained momentum throughout the region. The Polish example and glasnost in the Soviet Union started the domino effect on the Eastern European transitions, the essence of which was the development of a sense of political efficacy among citizens. Even if external indicators of the possibility of political change contributed to the development of political efficacy among the people, domestic events and activists also promoted such belief. For example, once acts of popular opposition took place in Timisoara, the mass protests spread throughout Romania because people found out about the events there through foreign broadcasts. The sense of political efficacy in Eastern Europe was something that developed at the end of the 1980s. Survey data show that before then people thought that the dictatorships could not be changed. I argue that in the Cuban case, civil society groups and activists inside the island can generate a sense of political efficacy among enough people to make possible the eruption of popular protests along the lines of East Germany and Czechoslovakia. Therefore, the strength of civil society as well as their strategic behaviors are quite relevant in assessing the prospects of transition in Cuba.

An explanation for the presence or absence of mass demonstration is incomplete if one only takes into account whether a belief in political efficacy is widespread in the population of a country. One also has to explain why. I do so in this book. The overall explanation for the occurrence of popular protests involves the consideration of a number of factors, including the role played by

xxiv   *Introduction*

international actors. Independent means of communication are vital to generating a sense of political efficacy among citizens. Samizdat publications and foreign radio and television broadcasts served as means of communication in Eastern European countries. It is not just a matter of independent sources of communication being able to reach a large percentage of the population regularly. The content of the communication matters. As I will show, in Cuba civil society activists lack the ability to convey news and information regularly to the majority of the population. Concomitantly, there is a very low degree of political efficacy in the population. I contend that these factors are fundamental to understanding why a political transition has not taken place in Cuba.

While I wrote this book before reading Saxonberg's The Fall: A Comparative Study of the End of Communism in Czechoslovakia, East Germany, Hungary and Poland, we both reach the conclusion that communication is a crucial determinant of mass protests against communist regimes as well as in transitions from other non-democratic regimes.[37] Saxonberg says that communication was the most important collective-action problem of pro-democracy revolutionaries in Eastern Europe, even before the political transformations at the end of the 1980s, such as in the Hungarian revolution of 1956 and in the workers' revolt in East Germany in 1953. Activists were concerned with reaching the populations with their messages to convince the people to participate in acts of opposition to the regimes.

In cases where political liberalization preceded transitions, such as in the Soviet Union and Hungary, the liberalization greatly facilitated the possibility of communicating information about activities and ideas contrary to the regimes. With liberalization, repression decreases (hence people are less afraid to participate in opposition activities), there is a surge of civil society groups and activities, and the number and ability of independent sources of communication able to reach the population increase. In Poland, Hungary, and the Soviet Union, criticisms of the dictatorships and news about activities of civil society even appeared in official news media and publications.[38] Foreign radio and television broadcasts were important as independent means of communication in all Eastern European cases, but in those countries where liberalization did not take place prior to transitions, foreign broadcasts were even more essential for the collapse of the regimes. Similarly, where no liberalization occurred, repression against the production and distribution of samizdat publications was greater. Therefore, help from abroad, or in the case of East Germany from

members of the Protestant Church, to those producing these independent publications was even more necessary than in countries that experienced liberalization. For example, equipment confiscated by the authorities in hardline regimes had to be replaced.

By the mid 1980s, scholars analyzing the transitions to democracy in Latin America and Southern Europe concluded that international factors were of minor importance in accounting for the transitions. Laurence Whitehead argued that in peacetime internal factors were of primary importance as determinants of transitions and international causes played a secondary role.[39] With the hindsight of more recent history, Whitehead acknowledges that international factors have played a more important role in other regions.[40] The Eastern European transitions showed the critical importance of international factors as determinants of these processes even though the impetuses for these political transformations were internal to each case. Indeed, the importance of international factors in transitions from communism goes beyond the Eastern European cases. The realization that these factors are important in transitions calls for analyses to determine the ways in which they affect the probabilities of transitions.

In transitions from communist dictatorships, the foreign policies of the Soviet Union and of the United States have been paramount, particularly in the respective backyards of these world powers. In Eastern Europe, the Soviet decision under Gorbachev's leadership to abandon the Brezhnev doctrine of saving communism in Soviet bloc countries through military intervention gave the green light for transitions in that region. The perception that the Soviets would not send tanks to prop up the dictatorships in Eastern Europe contributed to the confidence of civil society activists and of the general population that their pushing for democracy could succeed. Another international factor of great consequence in Eastern Europe was the diffusion or domino effect.

While international factors were important in the fall of communism in Eastern Europe, the international context did not make the Eastern European transitions unique and thus not comparable to cases of transitions or non-transitions in other parts of the world. Some scholars overemphasize "the Gorbachev factor" and assert that it made the Eastern European transitions sui generis, thus making attempts to compare Eastern Europe to other cases unsound. This argument is flawed. Inter-regional comparisons can be valid. Gorbachev's decision to terminate the Brezhnev doctrine lifted a crucial constraint

xxvi *Introduction*

on political transitions in Eastern European countries, but it was only a con-straint. As Przeworski argues, "The change in the Soviet Union did not propel transformations in Eastern Europe; what it did was to remove the crucial con-straint that had been blocking them. The constraint was external, but the im-petus was internal. This is why 'the Soviet factor' does not render invalid [inter-regional comparisons of transitions]."[41] In the case of Cuba, the Castro regime endures and yet no one can count on foreign tanks to come to the res-cue of Cuban communism.

Those who maintain that the Gorbachev factor made Eastern European transitions unique assert that Gorbachev pushed for political change in other countries of the region, and since he was powerful, his actions were a funda-mental cause of the political transformations. The implication is that since in Cuba there is no external actor that can decisively push for regime change, the current government endures. Bunce asserts that Gorbachev was crucial in the fall of communism in Eastern Europe because he pressed Eastern European leaders to imitate his reforms, undermining the power of hardliners and sup-porting reformers in the communist parties of those countries. She also states that Gorbachev, in many cases, also supported opposition forces in Eastern Europe.[42] The evidence does not seem to support Bunce's claims. According to Margot Light, although Gorbachev advised Eastern European leaders to im-plement economic and political liberalization, there is little evidence that the Soviet leadership interfered directly in East European domestic affairs. In the same vein, she sees no reason to believe that Moscow had a hand in Ceaușescu's violent end. Light argues that after 1985, the Soviet Union ceased using its veto power over policies and appointments in Eastern Europe. The system under which a decision taken in Moscow was binding on all members of the bloc came to an end.[43]

Saxonberg points to evidence that supports the observations of Margot Light. Saxonberg affirms that Gorbachev did not try at any time to promote or to stop political changes in Poland, Hungary, East Germany, or Czechoslovakia. He was basically passive. For example, Saxonberg indicates that, during Gorbachev's visit to Prague in 1987, he had the opportunity to show his support for reform, but re-fused to do so and instead spoke negatively about the Prague Spring. He made it clear that the Czechoslovak leadership did not have to follow his lead. When the ageing leader, Gustaf Husák, was going to step down, Gorbachev decided not to support the reform faction around Prime Minister L'ubomir Štrougal, and the conservative Miloš Jakeš was able to replace Husák as general secretary.[44]

Introduction xxvii

U.S. foreign policies also contributed to the transitions in Eastern Europe by sustaining and strengthening the broadcasts of Radio Free Europe (RFE) and Radio Liberty (RL) in the 1980s and by the material assistance that the National Endowment for Democracy (NED) provided civil society groups in the region. In Central America and the Caribbean, the loci of transitions and non-transition from communism in the Americas, U.S. foreign policies have been of central importance. Grenada had a transition by invasion. In Nicaragua, the high material and political costs that the Contras imposed (with U.S. assistance) on the Sandinista regime were fundamental in motivating the Sandinistas to allow competitive elections in 1990. Thus, one should expect that in the Cuban case U.S. foreign policies would be quite important in explaining the non-transition. I show that this expectation is supported by evidence.

A comprehensive analysis of the non-transition in Cuba must consider U.S. policies toward Cuba. On the one hand, some critics of the economic embargo argue that it hinders the possibility of a political transition.[45] For example, the embargo is blamed for giving the dictatorship excuses to repress opposition activists in Cuba. On the other hand, supporters of the embargo maintain that it helps to undermine the dictatorship by reducing its access to financial resources. Other policies of the United States, such as radio and television broadcasts to Cuba and aid to civil society groups, also affect the prospects for a transition. Radio Martí (RM)and TV Martí are controlled by the U.S. government, and the United States Agency for International Development (USAID) has a Cuba Program to provide resources to independent groups in Cuba. With the goal of regime change in mind, I address the question of whether the U.S. economic embargo against the Castro government and, in particular, the Cuban Liberty and Democratic Solidarity (Libertad) Act of 1996 helps, hinders, or is irrelevant for the probability of a political transition. I also analyze the impact of other U.S. policies toward Cuba.

The debate about the utility of the U.S. embargo on the Castro government has paid little attention to the scholarly literature on economic sanctions and on the political economy of transitions to democracy. I bring these two bodies of literature into the discussion of the embargo. In considering whether the embargo "works," I also evaluate the alternative policy of engagement with the Cuban government in terms of its effect on the possibility of helping to bring about economic, political, or social changes in Cuba.

This book provides an overview of U.S. policies toward Cuba since 1959 and focuses on policies during the Clinton administration. It was during the Clin-

xxviii   *Introduction*

ton years in the White House that for the first time since 1961 a political transition in Cuba was possible, this time without a U.S.-sponsored military invasion. The prevailing assumption in the scholarly literature is that President Bill Clinton gave priority in his Cuba policies to promoting a transition to democracy. This view was certainly supported by the rhetoric of the Clinton administration. Yet I argue that the Clinton administration actually sought to maintain the status quo in Cuba rather than promote a transition to democracy.

Foremost scholars who have studied transitions to democracy have not formulated a general theory. In the concluding volume of *Transitions from Authoritarian Rule*, after intensive analyses of the transitions in Latin America and Southern Europe in the 1970s and 1980s, Guillermo O'Donnell and Philippe Schmitter stated that they did not have a general theory of transitions. Huntington, in *The Third Wave*, with the perspective of a larger sample of transitions, maintains that there is no general theory to explain these phenomena across space and time. Thus, it would be foolish and pretentious on my part to try to formulate such a theory. What scholars have identified are some fairly common conditions in transitions and a number of patterns, paths, or modes of transitions. A list of paths or modes can be found in the work of Huntington just cited and in Linz and Stepan's *Problems of Democratic Transition and Consolidation*. In explaining the problems and prospects for a transition in Cuba, I discuss what conditions favorable to a transition are present or absent there. I conclude that some necessary conditions for a transition are missing and explain why this is so.

Studies of transitions from dictatorial rule, whether in Latin America or in Eastern Europe, typically conclude that the regimes faced serious pressures prior to the transitions. The difficulties could be poor economic performance, signs of popular discontent, social malaise, ideological decay, or a combination of various factors. In the typical analyses of transitions to democracy developed from the experiences of Latin America and Southern Europe in the 1970s and 1980s, the pressures faced by authoritarian regimes tended to result in splits in the ruling bloc between hardliners and softliners, with the latter gaining the upper hand and implementing political liberalization as a strategy intended to save the dictatorships.[46]

To partially substantiate my claim that a political transition is possible in Cuba, I will show that the Castro regime faces severe difficulties. Thus, why is it that the ruling bloc has not visibly split? The absence of noticeable divisions between political softliners and hardliners despite the strong pressures the

Introduction xxix

regime confronts is an indirect indication that the regime type is neither authoritarian nor mature post-totalitarian. In none of the Eastern European cases I use for comparison were there visible splits in the ruling elite before the onset of the mass protests that brought down the communist regimes. I will also present more direct evidence to support my classification of the Castro regime as a mixture of frozen post-totalitarianism and sultanism. Linz and Stepan classify the East German and the Czechoslovakian regimes as frozen post-totalitarian and the Romanian as a mixture of totalitarianism and sultanism. In these regime types, hardliners dominate and inhibit the possibility of softliners emerging and gaining sufficient power to last over time. Thus, the model of a split ruling bloc giving rise to political liberalization as a stage preceding the transition is not applicable to Cuba under Fidel Castro.

After analyzing the Eastern European transitions, Przeworski maintains that splits in the ruling bloc are important in explaining why transitions occur even when mass demonstrations take place before any visible division at the top of the regime. Part of the explanation for the absence of repression when large public protests occur is that the ruling bloc was divided.[47] Yet such reasoning does not explain why the mass protests occur in the first place, a fundamental factor in transition by collapse. Moreover, in transitions by collapse, splits in the ruling elite are not necessary to explain why those with guns do not shoot people in the streets. Przeworski maintains that in 1989 Eastern European dictators no longer controlled the guns.[48] Saxonberg argues that when mass protests took place in Czechoslovakia and East Germany in 1989, people were not massacred because decision making among the top regime officials became paralyzed.[49] Daniel Friedheim shows that the repressive apparatus in East Germany cracked at the local level.[50] Even if those at the top had given orders to shoot, the orders most likely would not have been obeyed by the rank and file. In the event that some units of the military or the political police actually shoot citizens in the streets, transitions by collapse may take place if other units join the people, as the Romanian experience indicates.

In the literature on transitions to democracy emerging from the experiences of military dictatorships in Latin America and Southern Europe in the 1970s and 1980s, a key factor in the dynamics of the transition processes was that rulers controlled the guns; thus there was always the danger that the transition process could be reversed by force if the rulers felt threatened.[51] Transitions in Eastern Europe demonstrated the limitations of this assumption. It is impossible to predict accurately what those with guns in Cuba will do. The un-

xxx   *Introduction*

armed opposition can be destroyed and the transition aborted by brute force if the regime succeeds in implementing the Chinese solution in the face of mass protests. However, there are indications that if large and continuous mass demonstrations take place in Cuba, the East German, Czechoslovakian, or Romanian scenarios could result.

Given the signs of discontent among regime cadres in Cuba, it is quite likely that groups or individuals inside the regime will defect if mass demonstrations to demand political changes take place. Since the regime in Cuba suppresses all dissent within its ranks, there could be latent softliners and even proto-democrats in the higher levels of the regime. Defections from and divisions inside the regime that become public as mass demonstrations take place would increase the prospects of a transition. Rasma Karklins and Roger Petersen have analyzed the dynamic interaction between public protests and defection of different groups inside communist regimes such as journalists and bureaucrats, with different groups having distinct propensities to defect.[52]

Many previous accounts for the non-transition have been based on little data, sometimes on impressionistic, short visits to Cuba, and on alleged differences between Cuba and Eastern European countries. By contrast, I rely on news and information from Cuba collected daily from 1995 to 2001. A major source of articles and commentaries from independent journalists in Cuba is CubaNet (www.Cubanet.org). CubaNet also compiles news on Cuba from newspapers in the United States and abroad, including sites from the official Cuban press. Other useful sites on the Internet have been Cuba Free Press (www.cubafreepress.org) and the dailies *El Nuevo Herald* and *Diario Las Américas*. I have also used a very comprehensive e-mail news service about Cuba called Cuba-L, which is provided by a team under the direction of Professor Nelson Valdés in the Sociology Department at the University of New Mexico.

In addition, I rely on several other data sets. One is a survey of 1,023 Cuban exiles who arrived in the United States between December 1998 and April 1999. This study, "Measuring Cuban Public Opinion: Project Report" (Gainesville: The University of Florida, 1999), was conducted by Churchill Roberts, Ernesto Betancourt, Guillermo Grenier, and Richard Scheaffer. The Office of Research of the International Broadcasting Bureau at the United States Information Agency (USIA) provided me with surveys of Radio Martí audiences conducted from the late 1980s to 1995.

Moreover, I have been fortunate to have access to a new and unprecedented data set, based on extensive interviews with members of opposition groups in-

side Cuba. This project was carried out by the CEON, a think tank based in Miami. I will refer to these data as the CEON data. A very comprehensive, open-ended questionnaire was constructed by CEON with expert advice and distributed among leaders of seven civil society groups in Cuba with the purpose of gathering data on the views of democratic activists about problems and prospects for the further development of civil society in Cuba and for the attainment of democratization. The questionnaire includes sets of questions on many of the most relevant issues facing independent groups. Some of the questions asked the activists for their views about attitudes and beliefs among the general public in Cuba. The groups operate in different regions of the country, all along the island. Each leader conducted a focus group with members of his or her organization to answer the questionnaire collectively. Members from two additional groups that were not included in the original sample joined one of the focus groups. Hence, the data used are from nine opposition groups in Cuba. The seven completed questionnaires were then sent from Cuba to CEON for analyses. The data were collected during the year 2000.

CEON could not gather direct survey data from the population, but perceptions of activists about what people think regarding civil society and issues related to political change are valuable as a proxy for public opinion because activists are sensitized to pay special attention to the beliefs, attitudes, and behavior of the population concerning civil society, their activities, and matters related to a regime change. Obviously, there are limitations to the inferences that can be made from the CEON data. The findings may not be representative of all the civil society groups in Cuba. It is true that only nine groups in Cuba participated in the focus sessions to answer the questionnaire, and that these groups were not selected randomly. It is impossible to draw a random sample of civil society groups in Cuba and then get those selected to answer an extensive questionnaire. Given the political context in Cuba, it is unreasonable to demand that a study of the nature carried out by CEON meet strict methodological standards. In practical terms, one has to make do with whatever information one can collect. And the data gathered by the CEON study are significant and fill in information gaps about civil society and its political context in the island. Moreover, this CEON study is the best, most comprehensive, and most systematic information currently available on the opinions of democratic activists in Cuba. What the data here suggest is closer to the truth about the beliefs and perceptions of civil society in Cuba than any other information at hand. The standard so far has been to make claims about the

xxxii   *Introduction*

opinions of activists in the island based on what one or a few activists say, usually in public statements.

Although one of my data sources taken in isolation could be questioned as being "soft," what makes the data I use robust is the consistency among the various sources. My arguments do not rest on a single data source. Rather, I consider multiple sources of information before drawing conclusions. So, it would be unfair to single out one source of data, find some flaw in it, and claim that my conclusions are invalid. One of the criticisms that can be made of the survey of Cuban immigrants conducted by Roberts et al. is that data provided by recent Cuban arrivals to the United States are unreliable. This survey is similar to those that were conducted in Eastern Europe before the fall of communism among travelers to the West or among immigrants from countries under dictatorial rule. This type of survey data was extensively used in Eastern European studies and proved to be more accurate than CIA and some scholarly analyses of what was going on under communist regimes in that region.

In the early 1950s, the Harvard Refugee Interview Project (HRIP) collected data from Soviet citizens living in the West. These data resulted in a number of publications and made precious contributions to the understanding of Soviet society. Later, the Soviet Interview Project (SIP) was implemented in the early 1980s. One of the reasons for doing so was to fill gaps in the available data on the Soviet Union. Information collected by the SIP led to an edited volume published in 1987 by Cambridge University Press.[53] Both the HRIP and the SIP confronted the crucial question of whether those interviewed, who could be considered hostile to the political system of the Soviet Union, could provide reliable information about Soviet society. Despite the numerous sources of bias in these studies, some common to all surveys and others arising from bias in the samples, as James Millar put it, students of Soviet life could not refuse to use this source of data. It was too valuable, and there was no alternative. But most important, the information gathered from interviewing unrepresentative samples of individuals proved to be accurate. The findings of the HRIP were widely accepted by the scholarly community and were corroborated by subsequent data from other sources.[54] Similarly, surveys of East German exiles before the transition to democracy closely correspond to data from a major retrospective survey among the East German population conducted by Karl-Dieter Opp, Peter Voss, and Christiane Gern after the transition. And there are indications that the data in the Opp et al. survey are highly reliable.[55]

Introduction   xxxiii

Summary

To explain the non-transition in Cuba, I compare Cuba with three cases of transitions in Eastern Europe, utilizing the most similar systems design. Although international factors, mainly the "Gorbachev factor, were quite important in the Eastern European transitions, these factors did not make the Eastern European context unique, and thus not comparable to transitions and non-transitions in other regions. My comparison of the non-transition in Cuba with transitions in Eastern Europe is justified.

Some explanations for Castro's staying power point to alleged differences between Cuba and Eastern European countries. Obviously, there must be some differences that matter in accounting for the non-transitions in Cuba. Yet in the literature on Cuba the differences that have been posed are the wrong ones. Many arguments pointing to differences disregard the empirical validity of the differences and/or their theoretical relevance in accounting for political (non)transitions. For example, some argue that, in contrast to countries in Eastern Europe, members of the Communist Party in Cuba remain loyal to the Party, pointing to the fact that massive resignations have not occurred. However, large-scale defections from the communist parties did not take place until the very end of the dictatorships in East Germany and in Czechoslovakia, and not at all in Romania. Moreover, there is evidence of discontent among regime cadres in Cuba. Personal gain seems to be the prevailing motivation for belonging to the Party. Being a member of the Party does not necessarily imply ideological commitment.

In contrasting Cuba and Eastern European countries to explain the non-transition, others contend that an important difference lies in the origins of the dictatorships. In Cuba the regime resulted from a national revolution while in Eastern Europe communism was imposed by Soviet power. This homegrown hypothesis is flawed. As in Cuba, communism gained power in the Soviet Union after a national revolution. The case of Nicaragua also suggests the inadequacy of this hypothesis. The homegrown argument assumes that because the regime originated from a national revolution, the dictatorship enjoys a high degree of legitimacy in the population and/or among cadres. Autocracies can endure simply by coercion. There are many indicators of widespread discontent in the population with the Castro regime. One should not forget that the Cuban revolution was made in the name of democracy and not of Marxism-Leninism.

xxxiv   *Introduction*

Others affirm that nationalism is an important basis of support for the Castro regime and hence a significant factor in explaining the endurance of the Cuban government. In this vein, unfriendly U.S. policies are blamed for helping Castro stay in power. Reports from Cuba and interviews with recent refugees show that the majority of the people do not pay attention to nationalist appeals from the Cuban government based on confrontation with the United States. Just as Ceauşescu in Romania, Castro's appeal to nationalism as a pillar of support has worn out. Part of the explanation for the failure of nationalist appeals by the Cuban government is the discrimination that the Castro regime practices against its own citizens and in favor of foreigners.

Of all the hypotheses in the literature trying to explain the endurance of the Castro regime, repression is the only one that is sound. The repression in Cuba is intense and widespread. If repression were abandoned or drastically reduced, the regime would fall. But I will argue in this book that the repressive apparatus does not assure the survival of the regime. If a popular uprising occurs and the regime responds by shooting protesters as the Chinese regime did at Tiananmen Square in 1989, it might collapse rather than survive. Given signs of discontent among regime cadres in Cuba, including members of the military, and the ideological decay, it is likely that groups or individuals inside the regime will defect if mass demonstrations to demand political changes take place. Even if those at the top give orders to shoot, the orders might not be obeyed. In the event that some units of the military or the political police actually shoot citizens in the streets, a transition by collapse may take place if other units join the people, as the Romanian experience indicates.

The numbers of groups and activists in civil society in Cuba are similar to those in East Germany and Czechoslovakia at the end of the 1980s. By these criteria, the strength of civil society in Cuba does not preclude a transition from below. I will show that repression in itself is insufficient to explain the shortcomings of civil society in Cuba. From the perspective of fostering a transition, the key shortcoming of civil society is insufficient material resources, and this problem can be largely ameliorated by external assistance.

Given the hardline Castro regime, which adamantly opposes political liberalization, a transition by collapse is the only plausible path. Analyzing civil society is crucial for assessing the possibility of regime change in Cuba because civil society activists can serve as catalysts in a transition by regime collapse. Civil society groups can foster a sense of political efficacy in the population. A fundamental question in explaining the non-transition in Cuba is why a pop-

Introduction xxxv

ular uprising has not developed, in contrast to what occurred in Czechoslova-kia, East Germany, and Romania. I maintain that the central obstacle to massive and repeated protests in Cuba is that most people feel incapable of inducing a political transformation. Most citizens in the population at large think that their participation in opposition activities would be ineffective in achieving change. I will show that for a transition by collapse to take place, two necessary factors are (1) a widespread belief in the population that change is possible and (2) the ability of independent sources of communication to reach a large percentage of the people regularly. Independent means of communication are vital to the development of a sense of political efficacy among citizens. In Cuba, in contrast to the Eastern European cases at the end of the 1980s, these two factors are missing.

An explanation for the presence or absence of mass demonstrations is incomplete if one only takes into account whether a belief in political efficacy is widespread in the population. One also has to explain why. The overall explanation for the occurrence of popular protests involves the consideration of a number of factors, including the role played by international actors. For example, the communication factor in the Cuban case is basically determined by U.S. policies. Radio and TV Martí are controlled by the U.S. government. Thus, why the Clinton administration did not implement the technical modifications in these stations to overcome the jamming by the Castro government is an important part of the explanation for the non-transition in Cuba. A comprehensive analysis of the non-transition in Cuba must consider U.S. policies toward Cuba, including the economic embargo since some of its critics argue that it hinders the possibility of a political transition. While this book provides an overview of U.S. policies toward Cuba since 1959, it focuses specifically on policies during the Clinton administration because it was during the Clinton years in the White House that for the first time since 1961 a political transition in Cuba was possible. The prevailing assumption in the scholarly literature is that President Bill Clinton gave priority in his Cuba policies to promoting a transition to democracy. Yet I argue that the Clinton administration actually sought to maintain the status quo in Cuba.

Democracy Delayed

CHAPTER 1

The Castro Regime and Political Transition

Major theoretical works on transitions to democracy concur that dictator-ships tend to fall when faced with crises. From the perspective of the model of transitions based on the experiences of Latin America and Southern Europe, Przeworski observes that splits in authoritarian power blocs are in-duced by signs of an imminent crisis, including indications of popular un-rest. Softliners, who emerge from the ruling elite, initiate political liberal-ization.[1] Huntington argues that when an authoritarian regime confronts seemingly unsolvable problems, usually of an economic nature, or when it resorts to greater repression, reformers within the regime are more likely to arise.[2] Even in cases where economic crises are not the main source of fac-tional conflicts between hardliners and softliners, deterioration of economic performance tends to widen cleavages in the ruling elite.[3] By contrast, when a dictatorship is perceived as successful in terms of economic performance, softliners are less likely to be able and willing to launch liberalization.[4] Thompson maintains that support for the regime among the political elite in China in 1989 was partly due to the fact that the economy was doing well at the time; thus there was approval of the decision to shoot protesters in

2   *Democracy Delayed*

Tiananmen Square and the regime survived.[5] From these observations, one should expect that the economic and ideological decay in Cuba, the social malaise, and the numerous signs of popular discontent are pressures that weaken the Castro regime.

Modernization theory holds that good economic performance fosters transitions to democracy. As countries reach higher levels of economic development, groups (such as workers, capitalists, or the middle class) emerge and acquire sources of power like wealth and/or organizational capacity independent from the state. Then these groups act against the dictatorships and transitions occur. From this perspective, advocated by supporters of engagement with dictatorships, to promote a transition in Cuba the U.S. embargo on the Castro government should end. It would be best if the Cuban economy prospered.

But empirical evidence shows no clear connection between increasing levels of development and transitions to democracy. In a cross-national statistical study involving 135 countries from about 1950 to 1990, Adam Przeworski and Fernando Limongi found that many dictatorships survive at all levels of economic development.[6] Przeworski and Limongi conclude that there are no grounds to believe that economic development causes transitions to democracy. They observe that what destabilizes regimes are economic crises.[7]

The connection between higher per capita incomes and transitions to democracy is more complex than modernization theory assumes, suggesting that other factors determine the effect economic development might have on the demise of autocracies. One intervening factor is whether the state controls the economy and does not allow wealth to be distributed among independent actors. Yet it should not be assumed that actors economically independent from the state under a dictatorship will necessarily want a transition to democracy. The long history of dictatorships and capitalism in Latin America should make this clear. Nina Halpern observes that in post-Mao China, economic independence among actors as a consequence of economic reforms apparently played a minimal role in motivating political action in 1989. Until the social protests of the spring of 1989, when most urban groups participated in demonstrations, urban entrepreneurs were generally politically inactive.[8]

Stephan Haggard and Robert Kaufman argue that dominant-party system dictatorships are more likely than military regimes to persist through economic crises. Yet the data they present show that the end of communist dictatorships in Eastern Europe was associated with economic crises.[9] In their data set of twenty-seven dictatorships, twenty-one experienced economic decline prior to

transitions. All communist dictatorships in the set (Poland, Nicaragua, Romania, Hungary, and Czechoslovakia) experienced economic deterioration or stagnant, low rates of growth in the years before their demise.[10] The economies of Czechoslovakia, Romania, and other Eastern European countries had a declining trend in average annual GNP growth from 1970 to 1990. In East Germany, average annual rates of growth went on a downward course from 1970 to 1980 and stagnated afterward until the collapse of communism.[11]

Scholars of Eastern European politics largely agree that a key factor underlying the pressures leading to the fall of communism was poor economic performance.[12] This does not mean that poor economic performance was "the" cause of the fall of communism in Eastern Europe. Declines in the populations' standard of living decreased people's tolerance for the regimes. As their situations grew worse, the populations became increasingly aware of the failure of their own regimes to provide an acceptable level of prosperity. The connection between deterioration of economic performance and transitions to democracy is also observed in Latin America, where economic decline and drops in standards of living predated the wave of democratization in the region during the 1980s.[13]

In Poland, the communist leadership realized that economic reforms were necessary to overcome the crisis and that they did not have popular support to implement socially painful reforms. Hence, the rulers sought negotiations with the opposition.[14] In Hungary, the drying up of external resources increased internal tensions and, as in Poland, economic decline led the regime to negotiate with the opposition out of fear of social upheaval.[15] Following the association between poor economic performance and the breakdown of dictatorships, it is interesting that the revolution in East Germany started in Leipzig, a city characterized by severe economic decay and pollution.[16] In the Soviet Union, the economic crisis contributed to the selection of Gorbachev as the first secretary of the Party; and the resistance to perestroika in the Party and in the bureaucracy led Gorbachev to implement glasnost.[17] The latter was an impetus for regime change not only in the Soviet Union but also in other Eastern European countries.

Two ways in which poor economic performance can contribute to the fall of dictatorships are (1) by fostering latent or active opposition to the regime among citizens and groups in civil society (people blame the government for their increased poverty and withdraw support or acquiescence); and (2) by reducing benefits to active supporters and coalition allies.[18] Linz and Stepan

4   *Democracy Delayed*

argue that in post-totalitarian regimes, government authorities increasingly resort to performance criteria as the basis of support.[19] From this perspective, a current weakness of the Castro regime is that economic performance and living conditions are quite poor in Cuba.

The decline of the Cuban economy at the macro level after 1990 made the standard of living of the population much worse than in previous times, with even greater shortages of food and fuel and a deterioration of means of transportation.[20] Survey data show widespread popular dissatisfaction with microeconomic conditions.[21] Carmelo Mesa-Lago estimates that in 1985 Cuba's GDP per capita was $334, similar to that of Haiti, and in 1996 the Cuban GDP per capita was $91, taking into account the official value of free benefits and subsidies provided to the population.[22] Moreover, since 1989, benefits and services granted by the government, such as education, health care, and rationed food, have deteriorated significantly.[23] The government is unable, or unwilling, to expend its scarce resources to assure that the basic needs of the population are met. It is obvious that the condition of economic decay, emphasized as an important cause of the breakdown of communist regimes in Eastern Europe, is quite prevalent in Cuba today. This fact shows that poor economic performance is insufficient to produce transitions from communist rule. Yet there are various indications that such conditions in Cuba weaken the Castro regime.

Some indicators of the decline in the quality of the health care system available to the common folk are an increase in the mortality rate of people 60 years of age and older (from 48 to 53 in 1989–93) and an increase in cases of tuberculosis per 100,000 inhabitants (from 6 to 12 in 1989–93).[24] People complain that the health care system is inefficient, is corrupt, and lacks the necessary technology and medications. Citizens perceive that there are two systems of medical care, a good one for government officials and foreigners and a poor one for the general population. This discrimination generates resentment in the population.[25] To cite one piece of evidence, a non-random survey conducted among 787 individuals in schools and work sites between December 2000 and January 20001 by two civil society groups in Havana shows overwhelming dissatisfaction with medical services. Negative responses range from 64 percent to 93 percent (with a mean of 83 percent) for ten indicators of health care quality.[26]

The availability of food through the government retail system for the general population has severely worsened; some basic necessities are simply un-

The Castro Regime and Political Transition   5

obtainable through this channel. In 1997, food rationing covered less than half of the monthly minimum food needs, forcing people to buy food at high prices in the black market or in government dollar stores.[27] Daily intake of calories per capita declined from 2,845 in 1989 to 1,670 in 1994. In 1993, there was an epidemic of optical neuritis caused by malnutrition and vitamin deficiency.[28] The difficulty in paying for imported oil has led to recurrent shortages of electricity, subjecting the population and industries to frequent blackouts and disrupting many sectors of the economy.[29] A consequence for the population of electrical blackouts is that food requiring refrigeration can spoil, without compensation from the government.

Over 60 percent of those receiving retirement pensions get less than 100 pesos (the equivalent of about $5) a month. With this amount, it is impossible to eat during the whole month.[30] Between 1989 and 1997, the average real pension decreased by 42 percent.[31] The average salary in Cuba is also meager. It is about 200 pesos a month, the equivalent of about $10. A survey of Cubans who arrived as exiles to the United States between 1998 and 1999 shows that in Cuba only 26 percent of the respondents got their food using their ration books (through the official supply system), only 25 percent obtained their medications at regular pharmacies (in contrast to pharmacies that sell in dollars), and none reported buying their clothes using ration books. People had to get their food, medicines, and clothing mostly at high prices in the black market, at dollar stores, at farmers' markets, or from their families and friends abroad.[32] Since salaries are insufficient to obtain basic necessities, people try to supplement their income by engaging in illegal activities, such as stealing government property and dealing in the black market.

The economic growth reported by the government since 1994 has not improved living conditions for the population. Carlos Lage, a vice president of Cuba's Council of State and the top official in charge of the economy, in a speech at the fifth plenum of the Central Committee of the Communist Party in March 1996 stated that despite the economic recovery ordinary Cubans should expect to continue living with the austerity characteristic since the collapse of communism in Eastern Europe.[33] The Central Workers Union (CTC), the government-controlled labor union, declared in September 1996 that the growth of the economy in 1995–96 had not meant a significant improvement in the consumption of basic foodstuff for the general population.[34] The disjuncture between official claims of economic recovery and the living conditions of the population continues.[35]

6   *Democracy Delayed*

Among the general population, one can note a positive association between deterioration of the economy on the one hand and discontent and criticism of the Cuban government on the other.[36] Citizens have reacted spontaneously to deprivation and grievances, participating in food riots, for example. People in neighborhoods have come together to demand collectively that the government provide them with resources to alleviate critical shortages of food, water, medical supplies, or other essential needs.[37] Government workers, as well as self-employed individuals, have resorted to collective action to defend their economic interests from government abuses.[38]

Besides confronting serious economic problems and the consequent popular discontent, the Cuban government rules over a population showing signs of significant social decay, related to poor economic conditions. Many graduates of colleges or professional schools do not find employment in their field. Those who find any employment at all earn miserable wages (from $3.25 to $9.00 a month). There is apathy among young people toward studying or working. Many engage in crime or prostitution to earn more money than they would through regular employment.[39] Havana has already been labeled the capital of sex tourism in the Caribbean.[40] Suicide and alcoholism are major problems.[41] The social malaise is an indicator of deep alienation from the regime.

The Performance of the Cuban Economy

As Gorbachev was partially implementing market-oriented reforms under the rubric of perestroika, the Cuban government was going in the opposite direction. From 1986 to 1989, the Cuban economy underwent a "rectification process" that moved it even farther away from market mechanisms. Economic growth in Cuba was negative or stagnant from 1986 to 1989. Then, with the fall of communism in Eastern Europe, the Cuban economy plummeted. Of all countries under communist rule before the political transformations in Eastern Europe in 1989, Cuba was the most dependent on Soviet subsidies. In 1989, Cuba received about $6 billion in economic aid from the Soviet Union, a typical amount of annual assistance from the Soviet Union.

The shock of lost Soviet subsidies was dramatic. For example, in 1989, Cuba's foreign currency revenue was $11,500 million, including Soviet aid. By 1993, the amount was $1,800 million.[42] From 1989 to 1993, Cuba's Global Social Product decreased by 45 percent.[43] By 1994, the tumble of the economy stopped. But the growth data are more indicative of the end of the free fall of

The Castro Regime and Political Transition   7

Table 1. Selected Economic Indicators for Cuba

	GDP growth rates[a]	Value of exports (in US$ m)[b]	Value of sugar exports (in US$ m)[c]	Index of total import capacity 1989 = 100[d]	Sugar production (in million metric tons)[e]	Estimate of net revenue from tourism (US$ m)[f]
1989	1.2	5,400	3,942	100	8.1	101
1990	−3.0	5,415	4,333	93	8.0	80
1991	−10.7	2,980	2,282	55	7.6	133
1992	−11.6	1,779	1,236	32	7.0	182
1993	−14.8	1,157	757	27	4.3	240
1994	0.7	1,331	759	29	4.0	280
1995	2.5	1,492	714	41	3.3	363
1996	7.8	1,866	976	47	4.5	455
1997	2.5	1,819	853	55	4.3	495
1998	1.2	1,540	601	59	3.8	545
1999	6.2	1,466	504	60	4.0	627
2000	5.6	n/a	n/a	n/a	4.1	n/a

[a] Pérez-López, "The Cuban Economy in Mid-1997," 2; Mesa-Lago, "The Cuban Economy in 1997–1998," 2; Maybarduk, "The State of the Cuban Economy 1998–1999," 1.

[b] Value of merchandise exports in Morris, "Interpreting Cuba's External Accounts," 146.

[c,d] Morris, "Interpreting Cuba's External Accounts," 146.

[e] Mesa-Lago, "The Cuban Economy in 1997–1998," 2; Mesa-Lago, "Assessing Economic and Social Performance in the Cuban Transition of the 1990s," 863; Alonso and Galliano, "Russian Oil-for-Sugar Barter Deals 1989–1999," 335; Armando H. Portella, "Concluye otra zafra pobre," *El Nuevo Herald*, May 28, 2000; Armando H. Portela, "Pronostican otra pobre zafra azucarera," *El Nuevo Herald*, October 16, 2000.

[f] Mesa-Lago, "The Cuban Economy in 1997–1998," 2–3; 1990–92 and 1999–200 are estimated based on gross revenue data form Morris, "Interpreting Cuba's External Accounts," 146 and Mesa-Lago's rate of 33 percent of gross revenue.

the economy than of actual growth, since the veracity of the statistics supplied by the Cuban government is quite doubtful.[44]

Sugar production, the traditional foreign-currency earner for Cuba, does not promise to be a solution to the economic quagmire because, as is typical of other sectors of the economy, it suffers from deteriorating infrastructure, inefficiency, and low labor productivity. The average annual output for 1981–90 was 7.7 million tons. Since then, production has declined and stagnated (see table 1). The production for the 2001 harvest was 3.5 million tons.[45] The earnings from sugar production are further reduced by the high interest rates that the Cuban government has been paying on foreign loans to finance the harvesting and processing of sugar. In 1996, Cuba borrowed $300 million at an annual interest rate of 16.6 percent and in 1997 $300 million at 16 percent interest.[46] Revenue from tourism has surpassed that from sugar (see table 1).

8   *Democracy Delayed*

Tourism has become an economic lifesaver for the regime. The end of the U.S. embargo would bust the revenues from tourism.

Before 1991, Cuba traded mostly with the Soviet Union. For example, in 1987, 72 percent of Cuba's trade was with the Soviet Union and 87 percent with countries in the Council for Mutual Economic Assistance. Since 1989, Cuba's trade with Russia has been mostly barter of sugar for oil at market prices. Cuba's trade with other Eastern European countries has practically ceased. The loss of Soviet bloc markets represented a sharp decline in Cuba's exports and imports. Since 1989, Cuba has had annual merchandise trade deficits. For example, in 1995, the trade deficit was $1.3 billion, and in 1997, it was $2.4 billion.[47] The trade deficit for 2000 was $3.2 billion according to Cuba's Central Bank.[48]

Cuba ceased servicing its hard-currency debt in 1986. At the end of 1998, Cuba's hard-currency foreign debt was $11.209 billion.[49] As a consequence of the foreign debt situation, Cuba's external financing is mostly in the form of costly, short-term loans. Cuba even has problems repaying its short-term debts with its trading partners. For example, in 2000, Cuba rescheduled short-term debts with Japan for $125 million.[50] In May 2001, the Castro government suspended payments on its debt with Spain despite having renegotiated the debt in October 2000. This suspension was part of a series of irregularities in the payment of that debt.[51]

One of the consequences of Cuba's foreign debt is disruption in trade. At times, firms in foreign countries have refused to continue trading with Cuba or have threatened to suspend deliveries to Cuba because of arrears in payments.[52] Among the essential goods Cuba needs to import are fuel and food. Cuba needs to import fuels to cover 50 percent to 80 percent of its needs.[53] The dependence on imported oil and the precarious financial situation of Cuba make the country very vulnerable to increases in the price of oil. For example, in 1999, the increase in the price of oil cost Cuba $92 million.[54]

An indicator that the revenues of the Cuban government are in dire straits are numerous reports, from sources such as Pax Christi in the Netherlands and independent journalists in Cuba, that the Cuban government commercializes humanitarian aid donated by foreign entities. Clothing in fair condition is sold to the population in dollar stores, called "shoppings," and clothing in poor condition is sold in pesos. Donated medicines are also sold to the population or used in health care facilities serving foreigners. Cuba has "health tourism," a government business that provides medical care to foreigners at at-

tractive prices.[55] The general population is excluded from medical facilities serving health tourists.

The loss of Soviet subsidies and the subsequent economic decline forced the Cuban government to implement some very limited economic reforms. One was to open the country to foreign investment, including the tourist sector, which has become a key source of foreign-currency earnings for the government. Yet all reforms have been tightly controlled by the government, preventing the spread of wealth in the population. Reforms in the domestic market, in contrast to those in foreign enclaves, have been implemented halfheartedly and even rolled back, as in the case of authorization for self-employment in some very small-scale, private activities. In 1993, the government allowed self-employment in some occupations. These private activities are constrained by regulations aimed at keeping the ventures small and preventing enrichment. For example, private restaurants are required to have no more than twelve chairs and to hire only family members. In June 1996, there were 208,500 registered private ventures, comprising 4.5 percent of the labor force. Then the figure dropped to 180,000 by the end of that year, when the government imposed heavy taxes on these entrepreneurs. By March 1997, the number declined even farther, to 171,861.[56] Since then, the state has cracked down on the self-employed in an apparent campaign to reduce their numbers even more, despite the problem of unemployment in Cuba. This is an indication of the anti-reform tendencies of the government.

Stories of crackdowns on the self-employed abound. To give some examples, at the end of 1999, a baker in Las Tunas was forced to destroy his oven where he made pastries for sale to public.[57] In 2000, the government implemented a wave of repression against private entrepreneurs all over the island. In March, there was a raid against more than one hundred personal and family businesses in Havana, imposing heavy fines, confiscating merchandise, and closing some businesses down.[58] In April, in the town of Sagua de Tánamo (province of Holguín), government officials took away the licenses from twenty individuals who made soap, a very scarce commodity among the population.[59] In May, in the province of Ciego de Avila, the same thing happened to numerous independent entrepreneurs.[60] In July, in the province of Villa Clara, the government suspended the licenses of more than one hundred individuals who smelted aluminum, employing more than 3,000 workers, paying high salaries, and producing good-quality products.[61] The campaign to drive entrepreneurs out of business, even against those holding licenses, con-

10 *Democracy Delayed*

tinues.[62] As the economy stabilized after 1994, the government has moved to crack down on private enterprise in the domestic market. This contradicts the argument that if the Cuban economy prospered, the Castro regime would implement more market reforms. The contrary is more likely to occur.

A question discussed among scholars is why the Cuban government has pursued a policy of severely limiting the opportunities for citizens to engage in private enterprise. Why has the Castro regime refused to follow the Chinese path of economic reforms? One explanation is the alleged ideological fervor of the ruling elite for Marxism-Leninism, especially Fidel Castro's. According to this argument, ruling elites take seriously the anti-capitalist aspects of the official ideology. I find this interpretation problematic. The government has shown pragmatism rather than commitment to ideology in fostering capitalist enclaves. Attracting increasing amounts of foreign investment has been a key goal for the regime. In the introduction, I referred to signs of ideological decay in Cuba among government cadres, even if officially the regime continues to pay lip service to ideology. I believe that the main reason for the policy of stifling private enterprise in the population is political. The government fears the spread of wealth and economic independence in the general population. Economic independence from the state can empower citizens. People whose livelihood is not heavily dependent on decisions of government officials can be less worried about participating in civil society groups and in activities promoting democratization. I do not think that individuals who are economically independent from the state will necessarily participate in opposition activities or even in nonpolitical civil society groups. But economic independence increases the chances that those who are predisposed to engage in such activities will do so. As I will explain in chapter 2, economic repression is one of the most effective tools in the hands of the government in its battle against civil society. The regime seeks to deprive democratic activists of all means of earning a living, condemning them and their families to misery. Members of opposition groups in Cuba argue that if people could have secure means of subsistence, the membership of these groups would increase. Apparently, the Cuban government does not think that the Chinese model of allowing private enterprise among its citizens while maintaining political control could work in Cuba or in China in the long run.

Note that the capitalism that the government promotes is basically in the form of ventures it can control. The market-oriented reforms that have been implemented have not spread wealth in the population to any significant extent. The state blocks the consequences of economic growth assumed by mod-

ernization theory. More foreign investment and greater economic prosperity would increase the revenues of the state rather than strengthening any social group independent from the state. Hence, when the state controls the economy to the extent that it does in Cuba, economic growth does not foster democratization as modernization theory predicts.

The Cuban government is in a dilemma regarding economic reforms. Poor economic performance tends to undermine dictatorships. The deterioration of the economy in Cuba since the 1990s has been accompanied by greater discontent with the regime among citizens at large and among regime cadres. Further economic reforms would improve conditions, including increasing the production of foodstuffs. The Castro government must recognize these facts. But apparently government elites consider that the negative political consequences of allowing private enterprise to flourish outweigh the favorable effects of better economic performance for regime survival.[63] Consistent with my argument that repression against private initiatives is better explained by calculations of what is best for the survival of the regime than by adherence to ideological canons, the Cuban government has prohibited doctors from prescribing medications that are freely available from the Catholic charity Caritas, even when the medicines are unavailable in government pharmacies. This government policy is contrary to the ideological claim that the population is entitled to medical care as one of the "social gains of the revolution."

When it came to power, the Castro government appropriated most of the land. State farms produced almost all the agricultural output. But these farms were an economic failure. Data from Cuba's Central Planning Board indicate that in 1989 Cuba imported 79 percent of the grains it consumed, 99 percent of beans, 21 percent of meat, 44 percent of fish, and 38 percent of dairy products.[64] From an already poor performance, agricultural output declined from 1989 to 1995. For example, the production of rice declined by 58 percent, milk production by 46 percent, and egg production by 47 percent.

In 1993, the government introduced reforms in the agricultural sector. Most state farms were converted into cooperatives called Unidades Básicas de Producción Cooperativa (UBPCs), "Basic Units of Cooperative Production." The state distributed the land to the cooperatives while retaining ownership. The cooperatives were to sell to the state about 80 percent of their crops at below-market prices; the rest of production could be sold in free farmers' markets established in 1994. However, most UBPCs also turned out to be quite inefficient. At the end of 1994, only 9 percent of the UBPCs were profitable and

12   *Democracy Delayed*

had increased their production. These cooperatives suffer from low labor productivity, waste, and lack of incentives.[65] According to the Cuban government, in 1999, 61 percent of the UBPCs producing sugarcane and 60 percent in other agricultural activities were unprofitable.[66]

Despite having fewer resources and being under the threat of government confiscation (hindering incentives to invest), private farms are more efficient than the UBPCs.[67] Reports about the productivity of small private farms and cooperatives, independent from state control, indicate that their performance is successful.[68] Yet small private farms have only 3.4 percent of the land. Independent cooperatives do not receive credits or other help from the government, and the government hinders the activities of private farmers, for example, by regulating commercialization and transport of products to markets. In some cases, the government has confiscated their property, forcing them to sell their cattle at prices set by the government and seizing their products.[69] Given the shortage of food in Cuba and the expenditures to import foodstuffs, the government policy to suppress private agricultural production shows that the regime has a strong aversion to economic reforms in the domestic market. Those who blame the U.S. economic embargo for the shortage of food in Cuba should take a close look at the policies of the Cuban government in the agricultural sector.

In 1989, the Cuban government began a campaign to attract foreign investment, mostly in the form of joint ventures in which state enterprises are the majority shareholders. Foreign investment has been allowed primarily in enclaves oriented toward exports and in the tourist industry.[70] Tourism accounts for a large share of all foreign investment and is the main foreign-currency earner for the government.[71] However, the tourist industry, as is true of other sectors of the economy, is inefficient. It costs the government 69 cents to make one dollar. Although those who work in the tourist sector must be members of the Communist Party, theft by employees is a problem that reduces government revenues.[72] This fact underscores the lack of strong ideological commitment among party members.

Using official figures, foreign investment "committed/delivered" as of August 1996 was about $752 million.[73] According to the U.S.-Cuba Trade and Economic Council, the total foreign investment committed/delivered as of March 1999 was about $1.8 billion.[74] Risk analyses published for foreign investors, such as Euromoney, rank Cuba as one of the riskiest countries in the world. Thus, private investment in Cuba must typically be in projects that re-

quire small investments, offer high profits, and make possible quick rates of return on investments. Ibrahim Ferradaz, Cuba's foreign investment minister in 1996, stated that more than 75 percent of joint ventures and economic associations with foreign firms in Cuba involved investments no larger than $5 million.[75] The business climate in Cuba inhibits a sufficient level of foreign investment to make a significant difference for economic growth. And foreign joint ventures employ only 1.3 percent of the working-age population.[76]

Yet foreign investment provides hard currency to the regime. The Cuban government is receiving about $212 million in annual income, including tax revenues, from foreign investment. In addition, the state collects about $361 million a year from wage confiscation of Cuban workers employed in joint ventures. Foreign firms cannot hire workers directly. The state provides the workforce through a special employment agency. On average, the state receives from foreign investors $450 a month per worker, while the government pays workers in Cuban pesos the equivalent of approximately $10 a month.[77]

Regime Types and Modes of Transition

To understand why the Castro regime has not fallen, and how it might do so, one should determine the feasibility in Cuba of different modes of transition. First, I turn to a discussion of the applicability of transition paths in which a split in the regime occurs and softliners negotiate a transition with members of the moderate opposition.

Linz and Stepan argue that the type of non-democratic regime is a key determinant of the available modes of political transition.[78] Negotiated/pacted transitions are possible in authoritarian regimes (the kind of dictatorships once found in South America and Southern Europe, for example) and in mature post-totalitarian regimes (the type of regime in the Soviet Union under Gorbachev and in Hungary before the fall of communism). According to the characteristics of regime types presented by Linz and Stepan, it is clear that the Castro dictatorship is neither an authoritarian nor a mature post-totalitarian regime. Negotiated transitions are impossible when there are no regime softliners (those who believe that some degree of political liberalization is necessary for the dictatorship to endure) with sufficient power and autonomy over time to restrain the regime hardliners (those who oppose any political changes in the dictatorial status quo) and conduct negotiations concerning political liberalization with members of the moderate opposition.[79] In frozen post-

14 *Democracy Delayed*

totalitarian and sultanistic regimes, if regime softliners emerge and show a willingness to negotiate with democratic moderates, they are quickly eliminated or demoted by hardliners.

Using the categories of Linz and Stepan, the Castro regime can best be classified as a mixture of frozen post-totalitarian and sultanistic regimes.[80] In a frozen post-totalitarian regime, there is persistent tolerance of some civil society critics, but almost all control mechanisms of the party-state endure and do not evolve (as in East Germany and Czechoslovakia in 1989). Also, a frozen post-totalitarian regime includes some limited spaces for a market economy; and the regime type has features associated with totalitarian regimes (but in a deteriorated form), such as an official guiding ideology and routine mobilization of the population.[81] The essence of sultanism is unrestrained personal rulership; the ruler acts according to his own unchecked discretion. Political power is directly related to the ruler's person, and all individuals, groups, institutions, and the economy are permanently subject to the sultan's unrestrained and despotic intervention. In sultanistic regimes, there is a tendency toward dynastic succession, and influential figures in the regime derive their importance from being on the sultan's personal staff. A dynastic feature of the current regime in Cuba is Fidel Castro's endorsement of his brother Raúl as his successor.[82] Another feature of sultanism in Cuba is the official promotion of a cult of Fidel Castro's personality. For example, as part of the celebrations of the forty-second anniversary of the victory of the Cuban Revolution in January 2001, *Granma*, the government newspaper, published a series of articles portraying Fidel as the preeminent Cuban of the twentieth century in all the branches of science, sports, culture, and political thought.[83] In sultanistic regimes, there is no space for regime softliners who might negotiate with democratic moderates for the sultan's demise.[84] In saying that the Castro regime has features of sultanism, I do not mean that the regime fits well into a pure sultanistic type.

Given the nature of the Castro regime, one should not expect the emergence of softliners with sufficient power over time to be able to negotiate a transition.[85] Hence, theoretically, a negotiated political transition in Cuba is impossible under the current regime. Consistent with theory, Fidel Castro and other hardliners dominate and adamantly oppose political liberalization. No regime softliners are visible. Here, I follow the standard conception of softliners in the literature on transitions to democracy, viewing them in terms of their advocacy of political liberalization, not as economic reformers. This clar-

The Castro Regime and Political Transition 15

ification of the term is important because some scholars in their attempt to demonstrate that there are moderates in the Cuban ruling elite say that advocates of market reforms (even if very limited ones) are "softliners." In a cogent example, Carlos Lage (Cuba's minister of economy) stated on September 2, 1999, that there is already a democracy in Cuba while at the same time advocating foreign investment.[86]

For years, peaceful dissidents have repeatedly asked the Castro government to start a dialogue with members of the opposition in Cuba concerning steps toward political liberalization. Dissidents have tried to convince members of the elite of the desirability of democracy and respect for human rights. They have requested amnesty for political prisoners, the right to form independent labor unions, and a national referendum on political liberalization.[87] The government has not responded positively to these requests.[88]

One example of the ineffectiveness of the petitions by democratic activists is the experience of Concilio Cubano at the beginning of 1996.[89] Concilio was an umbrella organization of over one hundred civil society groups in Cuba. It formally petitioned the Cuban government for permission to meet for its first national conference on February 24–27, 1996, appealing to a provision in Cuba's constitution that recognizes the right of free association. The government denied permission and launched an intensive campaign of repression against its members. A large number of dissidents were either detained or imprisoned.

Despite the serious pressures which the regime faces, no softliners have emerged, demonstrating that the Cuban dictatorship is neither authoritarian nor mature post-totalitarian. In authoritarian or mature post-totalitarian regimes facing serious problems, the ruling elite is supposed to split with the emergence of capable softliners. In Cuba, even if individuals inside the regime would like to advocate political reforms, they cannot make such views public. Doing so would result in demotion or elimination. I pose the hypothesis that there are latent softliners in the Cuban regime because of the economic crisis, social malaise, and other pressures. But these individuals cannot make their views public. Only if the regime collapses or changes to a mature post-totalitarian regime (maybe after the death of Fidel Castro) would latent softliners show their true position. In the Soviet Union, Mikhail Gorbachev was able to find allies within the Communist Party and the bureaucracy, people who supported glasnost. Yet these same people had been there in the pre-Gorbachev period, indicating that latent political reformers existed under the orthodox mantle of the pre-1985 period. A practical question is whether such covert po-

16   *Democracy Delayed*

litical reformers could help bring about the end of the Castro regime in the event of a political transition pushed from below. Intuitively, the answer is positive. When softliners emerge in authoritarian regimes, some are proto-democratizers who, upon confronting the choice between democracy and the status quo or an even more repressive dictatorship, prefer democracy. In the dynamics of regime collapse, members of the regime defect as mass protests emerge and spread. Some of these individuals who jump ship can help the process of collapse. For example, government journalists can start reporting what is truly happening or party members can grant access to resources (e.g., photocopiers) to democratic activists in the heat of democratic revolutions.

Some critics of the U.S. economic embargo maintain that tightening the embargo (as was done with the Cuban Democracy Act of 1992 and the Libertad Act of 1996) is detrimental for political reformers in the regime because a confrontational U.S. policy toward the Castro government gives hardliners in the ruling elite a convenient pretext to repress softliners. Thus, the U.S. policy is seen as hindering the possibility of a peaceful transition to democracy.[90] This argument is flawed, both theoretically and empirically. Indeed, hardliners have launched attacks on potential reformers since the Helms–Burton bill became law. The best-known assault by hardliners took place at the fifth plenum of the Central Committee of the Communist Party of Cuba in March 1996.[91] In his speech, Raúl Castro attacked academics in Cuba who have published with scholars in the United States. Raúl targeted specifically the Center for American Studies (Centro de Estudios de Américas) for allegedly falling into a trap laid by foreign Cuba experts. According to Raúl Castro, academics in the United States served the U.S. aim of promoting "fifth columnists" to generate subversion. He stated that "the party cannot tolerate officials who act on their own; . . . we must strive to maintain our revolutionary purity." After his speech, the Center's director was fired and replaced with an academic who had hardline credentials. Copies of the speech were distributed to all academic centers, and teams of "inspectors" were sent to other academic institutions mentioned in the speech.[92]

While one can observe attacks by hardliners on apparent softliners after U.S. measures strengthening the embargo, the causal relation between the two factors is spurious. When have hardliners in Cuba allowed softliners to flourish? Do hardliners need any externally generated pretext to crack down on reformers when they feel it is necessary? True to his sultanistic nature, Fidel Castro has through time repressed potential challengers within the regime. In the

The Castro Regime and Political Transition   17

1960s, Castro repressed members of the pre-1959 communist party, the Popular Socialist Party, during the "microfraction" crisis because he perceived Moscow-oriented Communists to be a potential challenge to his authority. After 1980, mechanisms of control were strengthened, and there were widespread substitutions of personnel as Castro launched a campaign to eliminate infringement on his authority.[93] In the mid-1980s, Fidel Castro launched an attack on individuals and ideas favorable to perestroika, resulting in the dismissal of high-ranking personnel.[94]

In the same vein as the argument about the negative consequences of the embargo for regime softliners, some opponents of the embargo claim that measures to strengthen the economic embargo have a negative impact on the strength of civil society groups in Cuba because such U.S. policies give the Cuban government a pretext to increase repression.[95] Yet the Cuban government has intensified repression whenever the regime has felt pressure from the opposition, regardless of whether measures to strengthen the U.S. embargo were in place. In 1991, neither the Helms–Burton law nor the Cuban Democracy Act of 1992 was yet enacted. Yet there was a surge of repression in Cuba against dissidents and human rights activists. In May 1991, in reference to the fall of communism in Eastern Europe, Fidel Castro declared that if a single concession is made to "reactionaries," all sorts of concessions are demanded until they ask for your head.[96] The regime did not need any pretext of U.S. policy to justify repression. The campaign launched by Castro in 1991 against opponents in civil society was motivated by a desire to avoid the experiences of Eastern European countries, rather than by an intensification of hostility on the part of the United States against the Cuban government. In May 1991, in an address transmitted over Radio Martí, President George Bush said that the United States had no aggressive intentions toward Cuba and pledged that the United States would not invade Cuba. Thereafter, until 1992, Bush systematically opposed bills introduced in Congress that would have tightened the U.S. economic embargo.[97]

The Possibility of a Transition from Below

Some other scenarios that have been conceived for a political transition in Cuba involve various ways in which the current dictatorship might change, opening the possibility for a split in the regime and the implementation of a transition from above. Such regime change might occur if: (1) Fidel is overthrown by a military coup or (2) Fidel is assassinated. These scenarios are highly improbable, given the tight security that surrounds him and the mechanisms

18   *Democracy Delayed*

in place to prevent a military coup.[98] After the natural death of Fidel Castro, something that could be a decade or more in the future, the type of dictatorship might change and the new ruler(s) might be willing to participate in a negotiated transition. This book is about the Castro regime, however, and does not speculate about what might happen after Fidel Castro. I argue that as long as Fidel Castro is alive, and thus as long as the current type of dictatorship endures, the only path of transition that is both theoretically and practically possible is a transition in which the initiative comes from civil society and the population at large, that is, a transition from below.[99] I argue that such a transition path is possible while Fidel Castro is still at the helm. I do not discuss possible transition scenarios after the death or incapacitation (physical or mental) of Fidel Castro. It is not obvious that when Fidel Castro dies a democratic transition from above will occur. His brother Raúl or one of the younger members of the Politburo could maintain the frozen post-totalitarian features of the current regime. Even if the Cuban government evolves toward an authoritarian or a mature post-totalitarian regime after Fidel is gone, many of the issues I discuss in this book will still be relevant. In transitions from these types of regimes, civil society and the general population can still play important roles. Pressure from below is what moves the processes of transition forward toward democratization. Thus, topics I address here, such as the strength of civil society groups, decisions by citizens to participate in mass protests, and the role of independent communication, are relevant no matter what type of non-democratic regime one finds in Cuba.

Following the work of Linz and Stepan, the most likely path of regime transition in frozen post-totalitarian regimes is mass uprising, and the most likely domestic cause for the demise of a sultanistic regime is assassination of the sultan or revolutionary action by armed groups or civil society.[100] O'Donnell concurs with Linz and Stepan in perceiving the unavailability of a negotiated mode of political transition from dictatorships characterized by unrestrained personal rule.[101] In O'Donnell's view, caudillos-führers are highly paranoid and have a compulsion to eliminate any source of power independent of their whims, particularly softliners. Softliners may emerge, but they cannot move too far toward liberalization without being removed from their leadership positions by the caudillo. The only possible modes of political transition are the death of the supreme leader or the leader's overthrow.[102]

A transition to democracy in Cuba could result from massive and repeated protests, as in East Germany and Czechoslovakia, or the transition could be

The Castro Regime and Political Transition 19

similar to the popular revolt that ended the Ceaușescu regime. In East Germany and Czechoslovakia, popular protests grew larger and, over a relatively short period, rendered the repressive apparatuses inoperative. The military remained neutral, and the dictatorships collapsed rather peacefully. Members of the repressive forces beat people in the initial demonstrations, but that was the extent of the violence. In Romania, the military and most of the security forces sided with the population.

The claim that a transition from below can take place in Cuba has been questioned. Some scholars object to the idea that a transition in Cuba could follow such path because, supposedly, (1) civil society is too weak and (2) repression is too strong.[103] Other scholars assume that a split in the ruling elite is a prior requirement for a transition by collapse, but this claim is empirically incorrect.[104] There were no visible splits in the ruling elites in East Germany, Czechoslovakia, or Romania before the mass demonstrations started the process of collapse. I discuss this issue at greater length later in this book. In subsequent chapters, I support the hypothesis that a transition from below in Cuba is possible and discuss why such a transition has not taken place.

A Synopsis of Transitions in the German Democratic Republic, Czechoslovakia, and Romania

Since Romania, Czechoslovakia, and the German Democratic Republic (GDR) had transitions from below and their regimes were similar to the current one in Cuba, it is helpful to recall some key events in the fall of the communist dictatorships in the three countries. This synopsis of their transition provides a background for the discussions in succeeding chapters on the problems and prospects for a transition from below in Cuba.

Cuba and the Eastern European cases have "underlying" conditions for a political transition in common. In Cuba, East Germany, Czechoslovakia, and Romania, communist regimes faced serious domestic pressures, such as poor economic performance, social malaise, widespread discontent in the population, and signs of social unrest. Some scholars claim that these were the "actual" causes of the fall of communism in Eastern Europe. Although these problems weaken autocracies, including the Castro government, the Cuban case shows that they are not sufficient causes for a transition. Transitions by regime collapse do not take place if there are no mass protests that spread and continue over time. Underlying problems and discontent are not sufficient to bring about large-scale demonstrations. Again, the Cuban case is testimony to

20   *Democracy Delayed*

this observation. Mass demonstrations are necessary but not sufficient for a transition. Once popular revolts emerge, whether a transition takes place depends on whether the regime successfully implements the Chinese solution at Tiananmen. If people are massacred and no units of the military and/or the political police side with the people and a Romanian scenario endues, then the dictatorship wins and no transition takes place. (The to shoot or not to shoot issue in the Cuban case will be addressed later.)

Presenting an overview of how popular protests developed in the three Eastern European countries serves to indicate the roles of independent communication and of civil society activists, the dynamics of the emergence and spread of the demonstrations, and the collapse of the repressive capacities of the regimes. In Romania, the revolt occurred despite the fact that there was no civil society and only a handful of dissidents. The diffusion effect made possible by foreign broadcasts substituted for the absence of a civil society, incorporating in it the actions of civil society groups in neighboring countries. Thus, in a sense, the role of civil society groups in helping to bring about transition was "imported" in the Romanian case. The Eastern European cases present a model of how mass protests could develop in Cuba and what factors are necessary for such events. I argue, contrary to many scholars, that the so-called weakness of civil society in Cuba is not an impediment to a political transition. What can be seen from the Eastern European cases is that, in contrast to Cuba, independent sources of communication, mainly foreign radio broadcasts, had a wide reach. I will discuss this and other related variables at greater length in chapter 3. In addition to foreign radio and television broadcasts, democratic activists in East Germany and Czechoslovakia disseminated their messages through samizdat publications. Civil society groups in Cuba do not have the resources to do so. The case of East Germany points to the positive role that the Protestant Church played. The Catholic Church in Cuba has refused to play a similar role.

Although sectors inside the Ceauşescu government, members of the Communist Party and of the Securitate, seem to have played important roles in its overthrow, the initiative came from below. Mass uprisings triggered the actions regime cadres took against the Ceauşescu dictatorship.[105] The mass demonstrations came first and the splits in the regime followed. In December 1989, in the city of Timisoara, the police went to evict a popular Hungarian priest from his church. He was an outspoken defender of human rights, and had asked his parishioners days before the scheduled eviction to protect him. A crowd of about a thousand had gathered outside the church to protect the priest the day the po-

lice came to get him. The priest's call had been broadcast by foreign radio. The police assaulted the people, giving rise to demonstrations and riots. A spark caused an explosion under propitious conditions.

Nicolae Ceauşescu ordered the political police and the army to shoot. Initially, the orders were disobeyed by the internal affairs minister and the defense minister, the two officials responsible for internal security. The general in charge of the army in Timisoara did not issue live ammunition to the troops in the streets. Subsequently, Ceauşescu placed the secretary of the Central Committee of the Party in charge of carrying out the crackdown in the city. Security forces and army soldiers fired on the population, and about seventy people were killed on December 17, 1989.[106] When protests began again in Timisoara on December 20 and orders were given to the army and the security forces to shoot, individual soldiers refused and joined the demonstrators. Units of the security forces also defected. By the evening on that day, several tanks were in the possession of the demonstrators, the army had returned to the barracks, and about 100,000 protesters had gathered in the center of the city.[107] In a regime with the appearance of a monolith, at least some military officers, rank-and-file soldiers, and whole units were unwilling to shoot the people to save the regime. In Cuba, with numerous signs of discontent in the military, it is not unreasonable to think that the same thing could happen.

The news of the events in Timisoara spread throughout Romania via foreign radio and television broadcasts. On December 21, Ceauşescu held a rally in Bucharest to have people show support for the regime. At the rally, people started to demonstrate against Ceauşescu, chanting "Ceauşescu assassin." That event was being shown on Romanian television and signaled to the population throughout Romania that Ceauşescu was vulnerable. The Securitate tried to arrest the protesters and started shooting.[108] That day, Ceauşescu ordered his minister of defense, General Milea, to have the army fire on the crowds. But General Milea ordered army commanders not to shoot demonstrators and committed suicide. When the news of his death was broadcast, it was assumed that he had been killed on Ceauşescu's order, and the event encouraged the army to join the people.[109]

On December 22, thousands of people stormed government buildings. The uprising was spontaneous.[110] Ceauşescu and his wife fled the city by helicopter. The revolt spread across the country—and this was a crucial factor. Ceauşescu ordered the political police to terrorize the population. Units of the security forces fired on people in the streets, but the security forces could not

22   *Democracy Delayed*

handle the situation alone. The army did not shoot. Army troops and most units of the Securitate joined the people on the anti-Ceaușescu side.[111] A confrontation ensued between the army and some units of the political police. The forces supporting Ceaușescu were defeated, and Ceaușescu and his wife were captured by the army, given a show trial, and executed.

Czechoslovakia had not experienced political liberalization when its velvet revolution began.[112] There was no visible split in the ruling elite before the regime started to collapse in November 1989. Even before the collapse of the East German regime, the previous domino to fall, there were fairly large protests. For example, in March 1988, several thousands gathered with candles for prayer and a silent demonstration in support of religious freedom and human rights. On August 21, 1988, the twentieth anniversary of the Soviet invasion of Czechoslovakia, about 10,000 demonstrators, mainly young people, marched in Prague chanting slogans in favor of freedom. Some of their demands were democratic elections, the abolition of censorship, and the rehabilitation of the victims of political persecution. Another demonstration took place on October 28, 1988, in which about 5,000 chanted "freedom."[113] In December 1988, on the fortieth anniversary of the declaration of human rights, dissident groups in Prague organized a public meeting in which dissidents spoke to an audience of between 3,000 and 5,000 for one and a half hours.[114] Other demonstrations occurred in January 1989. In the months before November 17, 1989, additional demonstrations took place, with the number of participants varying from approximately 2,000 to 10,000. These are examples of opposition activities in which civil society activists took part and which sent a message to the population that there were many people willing to defy the regime to demand democratization. The population received the message directly at the protest sites and through Radio Free Europe and other foreign radio stations. These actions must have increased the belief among people that political change was possible. (I use the term *political efficacy* to refer to this belief.) Moreover, these were actions carried out by domestic actors. Although advances toward democratization in Poland, Hungary, and the Soviet Union certainly fostered this sense of political efficacy in neighboring countries, domestic actors also helped develop and spread this belief among their fellow citizens. I argue that in Cuba civil society groups can, with greater resources and the ability to communicate with the population, cultivate a sense of political efficacy among the people.

In January 1989, representatives of independent groups were arrested, in-

The Castro Regime and Political Transition   23

cluding Vaclav Havel. The arrests triggered daily, spontaneous demonstrations for four days. The demonstrators demanded the release of those arrested and the democratization of society. In all these demonstrations, the police repressed the participants with water cannons, dogs, tear gas, and beatings. Some people were arrested.[115] In January, a number of artists signed a letter to the government demanding Havel's release, democratization, and the start of a dialogue between the government and the opposition. A second letter, from 670 members of the academic and scientific community (later endorsed by 2,000 other intellectuals), expressed the need for an open dialogue, access to information, and democratization. This marked the defection of the intellectual community from the regime.[116]

In 1989, students pushed for self-administration, to be outside the Socialist Union of Youth. About 12 percent of the student body signed the petition, and some faculty members also supported the demand. The campaign for this demand led to the formation of the Independent Student Organization (STUHA—meaning "Ribbon") with the aim of struggling against communism. Reformers in the Prague City University Students Council (USC) of the Socialist Union of Youth gave the independent student organization access to their publishing facilities. Reformers in the Prague City USC and STUHA organized the demonstration of November 17. Fliers convoking participation for the demonstration and disclosing the meeting place for the march were printed at the student press.[117] This action, organized by a civil society group, became the immediate cause (the triggering event) of the regime collapse.

The turning point in Czechoslovakia occurred on November 17, 1989. Afterward the regime collapsed rapidly. On November 17, with the permission of the government, a student march took place to honor a student killed by the Nazis fifty years earlier. About 50,000 people (mostly students) participated. People were beaten by the police, which ignited public anger.[118]

After November 17, protests, strikes, and large demonstrations erupted, leading to demands by both official and unofficial organizations that the communist leadership resign. On November 18, a group of students, joined by intellectuals and artists, called for boycotts in universities and for a national general strike set for November 27. Industrial workers supported the strike call. The adherence to the strike spread across the country in twenty-four hours. On the same day, the Civic Forum (an umbrella organization) was formed by both dissident and governmental groups to demand political changes. The Civic Forum organized mass demonstrations and published a program calling

24   *Democracy Delayed*

for free elections and democracy. On November 19, 200,000 people demonstrated in central Prague to protest the police violence on November 17. The crowds continuously occupied Prague for the next three days. By November 23, the number of demonstrators had grown to over 300,000.[119]

The Communist Party crumbled, with thousands of party members leaving the Party and government organizations abolishing themselves.[120] In November, the bulk of the media revolted and their reporting became increasingly open.[121] On November 20, the Youth Union of the Communist Party, whose chairman sat in the Central Committee, turned its office facilities over to the strike committees. This is an example of how, as a dictatorship is collapsing, those who defect from the regime can help the process along. On November 22, the police of the northern district of Prague sent a statement to the leadership of the Communist Party saying that the police could no longer be used as an alternative means to finding a political solution to the situation of the country. Militias met in mass meetings and voted themselves out of existence.[122] The coercive ability of the regime melted away. The Communist Party Presidium and the Secretariat resigned on November 24. In two meetings of the Central Committee, all leaders associated with the policies of the previous twenty years were forced to resign, changing the structure of the party leadership.[123]

Mounting public pressure culminated in a general strike on November 27. Six thousand strike committees had been established prior to the general strike. On November 29, the Federal Assembly abolished the constitutional principle of the leading role of the Communist Party. Government officials repeatedly met with representatives of the opposition and accepted virtually all their demands. The government had not acquiesced to negotiations until forced by mounting pressure after November 17. The Civic Forum used its strength of mobilization in the streets to press the Communist Party for more and more concessions. Vaclav Havel was elected president by the communist Federal Assembly on November 29. The Communists also yielded to the formation of a new government with a communist prime minister but with a non-communist majority. Free elections were set for June 1990.[124]

East Germany is another case in which neither political liberalization nor a visible split in the ruling bloc occurred before the regime started to collapse. Before the fall of 1989, there had been some demonstrations but participation was not large. For example, on January 15, 1989, a few hundred demonstrators demanded the right of freedom of expression as well as other rights. Eighty people were arrested, and the demonstration was dissolved violently.[125]

The Castro Regime and Political Transition 25

Since 1982, people had come to the Nikolai Church every Monday at 5:00 P.M. for a peace prayer. In 1988, would-be emigrants started to see the peace prayers as a forum to express their concerns. Attendance increased dramatically, up to a thousand, and the peace prayers became highly political.[126] It became general knowledge that at a certain place and time people critical of the regime came to these prayers. It was also known that after the Mass service, a number of people went to the city center. All this knowledge served to coordinate the mobilization of people. Opp, Voss, and Gern argue that the demonstrations surged spontaneously and that the peace prayers were a necessary condition for the coordination of the protests. Thus, if people were critical of the regime and wanted to meet with like-minded individuals, they would either go to the prayers on Mondays at 5:00 P.M. or go near the Nikolai Church at about 6:00 P.M.[127] Hence the tradition of the peace prayers served as a mechanism of communication among people, but the crucial element was communication.

There are indications that activists served as catalysts for the protests. At the end of 1988, peace activists set up a podium in the courtyard of the Nikolai Church in Leipzig where anyone could speak while the peace prayers were being held inside the church. In this "speaker's corner," activists read protest notes, passed resolutions, and addressed issues that were precluded from discussion inside the church. The audience was initially comprised mainly of would-be emigrants. Eventually, the focus of attention of the participants in the peace prayers shifted from the church service to the outside courtyard, and the peace prayers gradually came to be seen as a prelude to public protests.[128] Thus, in East Germany, as in Czechoslovakia, activists served as catalysts for the protests that resulted in democratic revolutions. This is not to say that the revolutions can be explained solely in terms of what activists did, but the activists played an important role.

The first mass demonstration occurred on September 25, 1989, after one of the peace prayers at the Nikolai Church. People gathered outside the church, and someone led the crowd in a march. About 5,000 people participated. Then, participation in demonstrations snowballed. On Monday, October 2, another church also held a peace prayer. On that day about 20,000 people participated in a demonstration after the peace prayers. In all the demonstrations before October 9, there were clashes with the security forces as these forces tried to disperse the demonstrators. Many people were taken into custody. On Monday, October 9, about 70,000 demonstrated following peace prayers. On

26   *Democracy Delayed*

that day, the security forces did not try to repress the demonstration. The repressive apparatus stopped working, and the regime disintegrated in a matter of weeks. Massive demonstrations continued in Leipzig every Monday night after church services, and the number of participants skyrocketed. Many of the demonstrators came from areas surrounding Leipzig. The demonstrations spread to other cities as well.[129] In early November 1989, the government and the Politburo resigned and the Berlin wall was broken down.

In East Germany, loyalty to the repressive apparatus disintegrated.[130] Before the demonstrations reached the turning point on October 9, 1989, some members of the political police had already refused to follow orders. At the local level, orders to repress were disregarded. Mielke, the head of the Stasi, ordered the police chief in Leipzig to use force on October 9, but the police chief refused because the crowds were too large. On that day, three party leaders in Leipzig signed a proclamation, played on the city's loudspeakers and the radio, calling for a peaceful dialogue between the people and the regime.[131] Friedheim, by interviewing former members of the repressive apparatus in East Germany, found that by the fall of 1989 many were unwilling to use force against protesters because they no longer believed in their own legitimacy to rule.[132] Opp, Voss, and Gern argue that as the number of people participating in demonstrations increased, it became evident that it was "the people" and not just small opposition groups that were demanding change; slogans chanted at demonstrations in the GDR, for example, "no violence" and "we are the people," most likely also decreased the willingness of those with guns to repress the protests violently.[133]

Conclusions

The relationship between economic growth and the demise of dictatorships has been a major controversy in comparative politics. The issue is whether growth or decline undermines autocracies. Transitions in Eastern Europe and in many cases in Latin America took place when dictatorships faced economic distress. It is obvious that the condition of economic decay, emphasized as an important cause of the breakdown of communist regimes in Eastern Europe, is prevalent in Cuba today. Yet poor economic performance is not sufficient to cause regime changes. If it were, the Castro regime would have fallen already. What economic problems seem to do is to weaken dictatorships. In the Cuban case, one observes an association between the economic quagmire since 1990 and increasing signs of discontent with the regime among citizens and regime

cadres. Dissatisfaction with economic conditions has induced citizens to show their grievances in public spontaneously and to engage in collective action to demand resources from the government. If news about these actions were disseminated in the population, it would help generate a sense of political efficacy, as I will explain in chapter 3. Thus, discontent with economic conditions is not only a latent motivation that can induce people to join demonstrations to demand political changes once the numbers of citizens in the streets is large. Unhappiness with the economic situation can also act as a catalyst in the onset of protests.

"Modernization theory" assumes that economic development distributes resources, which can be converted into power, among individuals independent from the state. This is not necessarily so. The empirical verdict seems to be that there is no justification for the argument that transitions to democracy occur as levels of economic development increase. If the state tightly controls the economy and does not allow wealth to be distributed among independent actors, economic growth strengthens the dictatorship and not independent groups who might at some point in time demand democracy. Economic growth in Cuba would strengthen rather than weaken the Castro regime. The market reforms that the Cuban government was forced to allow because of the loss of Soviet subsidies and the subsequent economic decline have been very limited and controlled by the state, preventing the spread of wealth in the population. As the economy has stabilized, the government has moved to curtail private entrepreneurship in the population. This is an indication of the anti-reform tendencies of the government and contradicts the argument that if the Cuban economy prospered the Castro regime would implement more market reforms. The refusal of Fidel Castro to follow the Chinese model of "market Leninism" seems to be based on political calculations rather than on commitment to the anti-capitalist aspects of official ideology. The government seems to fear the political empowerment of citizens that can result from the spread of wealth and economic independence in the general population. That is, the Castro regime seems to be committed to preventing exactly what the advocates of modernization theory assume would occur automatically with economic prosperity.

To assess how and under what conditions a transition could take place in Cuba, it is necessary to determine the plausibility of different transition paths. Knowing which is the most likely mode of transition under the Castro regime provides us with an understanding of what factors are necessary for a regime

28   *Democracy Delayed*

change. If some necessary factors are missing, we then are better able to explain why the dictatorship endures. Following the association between regime type and mode of transition presented by Linz and Stepan and looking at the nature and behavior of the Castro regime, the only plausible transition from that regime is one pushed from below, a transition by regime collapse. Such a transition path is possible while Fidel Castro is still at the helm. The "underlying" conditions for a political transition, such as poor economic performance and widespread discontent in the population, are common to Cuban and the Eastern European cases I use for comparison. Some scholars claim that these underlying conditions were the "actual" causes of the fall of communism in Eastern Europe. Although these problems weaken autocracies, including the Castro government, the Cuban case shows that they are not sufficient causes for a transition.

Transitions by regime collapse do not take place if there are no mass protests that spread and continue over time. Discontent is not sufficient to bring about large-scale demonstrations. It is necessary to understand why mass demonstrations have not taken place in Cuba to explain the non-transition in that country. I argue that there are some necessary elements for a transition from below to occur that are missing in Cuba. But these missing conditions can be created by key actors in the drama. The histories of how popular protests developed in the three Eastern European countries that experienced transitions by collapse show the importance of independent sources of communication, the catalytic role civil society activists played, and the collapse of the repressive capacities of the regimes. The claim that a transition from below can take place in Cuba has been questioned. Some scholars object to the idea that a transition in Cuba could follow such path because, supposedly, (1) civil society is too weak and (2) repression is too strong. I will address these objections in chapter 2.

Mass demonstrations are necessary but not sufficient for a transition. Once popular revolts emerge, whether a transition takes place depends on whether the regime successfully implements the Chinese solution at Tiananmen. If people are massacred and no units of the military and/or the political police side with the people and a Romanian scenario endues, then the dictatorship wins and no transition takes place. The shoot or not to shoot issue in the Cuban case will be addressed later.

CHAPTER 2

Civil Society and Repression

Two objections to the argument that a transition from below is possible in Cuba are that, in contrast to Eastern European countries, civil society in Cuba is too "weak" and government repression is too strong. These objections are usually presented as two sides of the same coin, with the alleged weakness of civil society explained in terms of the degree of repression. Since I believe that a transition from below is possible in Cuba, I have to address these hypotheses that challenge my argument. They are best evaluated by a comparative analysis. Are civil society "weaker" and repression stronger in Cuba than in East Germany, Czechoslovakia, and Romania, where communist regimes collapsed? If the answer to both questions is negative, then these hypotheses cannot account for why a transition from below has not taken place in Cuba. Yet some characteristics of civil society and repression might differ between Cuba and the Eastern European cases. And these differences might partially account for the non-transition in Cuba. Hence, I have to be more discerning in my consideration of various aspects of civil society and of repression than simply looking at them as "weak" or "strong."

30   *Democracy Delayed*

In the brief overview of the mass protests in the Eastern European countries provided in chapter 1, I indicated that civil society activists in East Germany and Czechoslovakia played a catalytic role in these popular demonstrations. By their messages, in words and actions, activists helped to foster a sense of political efficacy among citizens in their respective countries and thus encouraged people to participate in protests. Some scholars maintain that before the onset of the large protests that developed at the end of 1989 in East Germany and Czechoslovakia, the names of activists, such as Havel, were not widely known among the people. Even if this is true, what is important for the growth of political efficacy in the population is not the knowledge of the names of activists. Rather, what is important is the dissemination of signals (e.g., that many people were publicly defying the regime to demand democratization) that change was possible. A question I address in this chapter is whether civil society groups in Cuba are playing such a role. If they are not, the reasons are part of the explanation for the non-transition.

I conceive civil society as being comprised of groups that emerge and are maintained independently of the state. One can evaluate the strength or weakness of civil society in terms of the size of the membership in these groups, the number of groups, and the resources the groups have available. In the Cuban context, and with the goal of regime change in mind, an important factor to consider is the extent to which groups in civil society are able to induce individuals in the general population to participate in independent or opposition activities. Participation depends on the predisposition of citizens to do so. Citizens can be influenced by the actions and messages of groups in civil society. But this means that civil society activists must be able to communicate with the population, something that might be beyond their control. The predisposition of citizens to participate would also depend on the purpose(s) of the activities and whether citizens support such objective(s).

In terms of the number of activists and the number of independent groups, civil society in Cuba at the end of the millennium is stronger than it was in Romania just before the end of the Ceauşescu dictatorship and similar to those in East Germany and Czechoslovakia in the summer of 1989. Civil society in Cuba has experienced a significant rebirth since the mid-1990s. This development seems to be the result of two processes in the evolution of totalitarian regimes toward post-totalitarianism, what Linz and Stepan call detotalitarianism by decay and by societal conquest. The first term refers to the decay of the regime's structures and erosion of the cadres' ideological be-

lief; the second is the creation of spaces that resist or escape totalitarian control.[1] As the Castro regime has changed, civil society groups have emerged from informal networks and shared goals among groups of citizens. As Rasma Karklins has argued, these networks and shared goals form the nuclei for the emergence of civil society in Soviet-type systems.[2] Civil society in Cuba today not only has the potential to play a catalytic role in fostering the mass protests necessary for a transition, but also is strong enough to provide interlocutors to regime elites to negotiate a transition once the regime starts to collapse. Just as Havel and other democratic activists negotiated the exit from power of communist rulers in Czechoslovakia at the end of 1989, so activists in Cuba are capable of playing this role. The presence of actors in the opposition with whom to negotiate and the ability of civil society groups to fill the power vacuum created by a disintegrating regime substantially increase the likelihood that the transition process will end up in a democracy. Note the case of Romania. Without a civil society to fill the power vacuum once the Ceaușescu government fell, members of the old elite took over and established another type of dictatorship.

In terms of resources and the ability to induce participation by the population in independent or opposition activities, civil society groups in Cuba are weaker than their counterparts in East Germany and Czechoslovakia. But, as discussed below, these shortcomings can be surmounted by U.S. government policies and, to some extent, by more material assistance to activists in Cuba from Cubans in the United States. The absence of these policies and of greater assistance inhibits the ability of civil society to develop a sense of political efficacy in the population. Hence, these facts help explain why the dictatorship has endured. In Eastern Europe, the diffusion effect was important in building the belief in political efficacy among the populations in the region, particularly in Romania, which had no civil society that could help develop a sense of efficacy among its own people. Since the Eastern European contagion effect did not extend to Cuba, the task of civil society activists in cultivating political efficacy among the Cuban population is even more crucial for the prospect of a transition in the island. What is important for the development of a sense of political efficacy are messages of popular defiance and of partial successes against autocratic regimes. In principle, these messages do not have to be diffused from abroad; they can come from sources and events internal to a particular country. In East Germany and Czechoslovakia, for example, there were numerous smaller demonstrations before the big ones took place. In Cuba,

32   *Democracy Delayed*

civil society activists frequently defy the government and achieve partial successes. But the inadequacy of independent sources of communication prevents the general population from knowing about these activities. With more resources, democratic activists and groups could do much more. Therefore, poor communication and meager resources in the hands of civil society are particularly important factors accounting for the non-transition.

In Romania, before the start of the revolt that toppled Ceauşescu, the opposition was minuscule. According to one estimate, there were about twelve overt dissidents.[3] In June 1989, there were only two independent organizations, neither of which had publicly known leaders.[4] Dissidents worked alone or almost alone.[5] Yet a political transition took place. The absence of a civil society in Romania was compensated by the ability of the population to receive foreign broadcasts with information on the successes on the road toward democratization in neighboring countries.

In the GDR, one calculation is that as of 1988, there were about 200 active independent groups, in and out of the church, with each group having an estimated 20 to 100 members.[6] According to the Ministry of State Security (Stasi), as of June 1989, there were approximately 160 dissident associations with membership ranging from 3 to 39; the hard core of the opposition consisted of about 60 individuals.[7]

In Czechoslovakia, the foremost dissident group was Charter 77, a small, mostly intellectual group isolated from the mass public. The issues it addressed were frequently abstract, removed from the daily concerns of the average citizen.[8] However, a number of groups emerged in 1988 and 1989. By the summer of 1989, the hard core of dissident groups consisted of about 60 people, with approximately 500 supporters and collaborators.[9] By 1989, there were about 40 opposition groups.[10] None of the groups formed in 1988 and 1989 could be considered an organized political opposition.[11]

It is estimated that in Cuba there are about 150 independent groups, counting the independent libraries as one group. (There are seventy-three independent libraries, each established by the initiative of a few individuals.) Despite the constant repression against independent journalists and other members of civil society groups, new groups continue to emerge, even if others break up or disintegrate.[12] Groups are of numerous types, including political, environmental, professional, advocates of human rights, and peasants' cooperatives. The variety of civil society groups in Cuba parallels the heterogeneity of groups in the civil societies of East Germany and Czechoslovakia at the end of the 1980s. In

Czechoslovakia, as of mid-1989, some independent groups focused on monitoring human right abuses, some had explicit political aims, others were concerned with the ecology, and others offered legal protection to citizens.[13]

In Cuba, from 1995 to 1997, the number of independent news agencies grew from one to 8 and the number of reporters from a handful in Havana to several dozen around the island.[14] In 1998, 18 new independent entities emerged.[15] During 1999, 30 new institutions were formed, and in 2000 52 new ones were established.[16] Fifty percent of the groups in the CEON study report that democratic activists are helping to organize the population in independent grassroots associations such as farmers' cooperatives and neighborhood libraries.

There has also been an increase in opposition activities in the provinces, outnumbering those in the city of Havana, the initial center of such activities. Yet the number of opposition activities in Havana has not decreased.[17] Another indicator of the development of civil society is the number of acts of civic resistance (e.g., marches, demonstrations, fasts, and vigils) over time. In 1997, there were 44 recorded actions, in 1998, 100, in 1999, 227, and in 2000 444.[18] Most of these actions are organized by civil society activists. For example, in 2000, 88 percent of the actions were planned. The rest, such as work stoppages, were carried out spontaneously by citizens.

In terms of the number of activists, various sources estimate that there are several thousand.[19] Although there is no information on the membership size of groups, the strength of civil society in terms of the number of activists can be assessed by these estimates of the total number of activists. Whatever the correct figure for Cuba today, there are now more overt dissidents in Cuba than there were in Romania, and possibly about the same number as in Czechoslovakia and in East Germany, at the end of the 1980s.

One achievement of civil society in Cuba has been the collaboration among groups in implementing specific activities. Attempts to form a broad umbrella organization of independent groups have failed. However, the ability of groups to work together in carrying out projects is more important for the capacity of civil society to struggle for democratization than is the formation of an umbrella organization. In the GDR and Czechoslovakia, umbrella organizations were not created until the communist regimes were collapsing. In Cuba, the cooperation among groups increased since the end of the 1990s. This coordination of efforts can make the activities of these groups more effective in confronting the Castro government. Although there is room for greater collaboration among civil society groups, it is false that these groups

34   *Democracy Delayed*

are disorganized. Let me first refer to attempts to form umbrella organizations, and then I will point to evidence of coordination of group efforts.

One attempt to establish a broad umbrella organization was the creation of Concilio Cubano in October 1995. Concilio was not an unstructured cooperation mechanism. It was a group in itself, with a Secretariat (having 5 to 9 members), a National Coordinating Council (made up of 26 to 30 individuals), and 130 affiliated groups of various types.[20] Its central goal was to push for a peaceful transition to democracy. The eventual disintegration of Concilio cannot be attributed only to the repressive crackdown against its leadership in February 1996. After the wave of repression, Concilio leaders declared their desire to maintain the organization and were optimistic about doing so. In April and December 1996, Hector Palacio Ruiz maintained that Concilio was growing in terms of affiliated groups and geographic representation, arguing that the future of Concilio was very promising.[21] In May 1997, Leonel Morejón Almagro declared that Concilio was not dead and that difficulties could be overcome.[22] Yet Concilio disintegrated, due at least in part to problems within Concilio itself, particularly disagreements among its leaders.[23]

On July 17, 1997, the formation of the Alianza Nacional Cubana, a new umbrella organization, was announced. Among its leaders was Leonel Morejón Almagro, a founder and leader of Concilio Cubano, who said that it was a new project to unify the opposition.[24] In July 1999, those who had fasted for forty days at Tamarindo 34 (a street address) in Havana, to ask the government to respect human rights and free political prisoners, announced the formation of a new umbrella organization at the end of the fast. The new organization was called the Foro Tercer Milenio (Forum Third Millennium). Initially, it was comprised of the five groups represented by the participants at the fast in Tamarindo 34, with the intention of bringing into it many other independent groups.[25] The declared purpose of the Forum was to coordinate the activities of opposition groups to push for a nonviolent political transition by asking the population to participate in street demonstrations to demand democracy.[26]

The unification efforts of the Forum eventually faltered. When it was first announced, one of the affiliated groups was the Lawton Foundation of Human Rights, whose leader, Dr. Oscar Elías Biscet, had participated in the Tamarindo 34 fast. At the beginning of September, Dr. Biscet and William Herrera, two of the founders of the Forum, had a serious fight.[27] In October, there was a meeting to formalize the creation of the Forum. It was announced then that twenty-three groups were affiliated with the Forum, including William Herrera's

Civil Society and Repression 35

group. The Lawton Foundation was not among them, and Dr. Biscet did not attend the meeting.[28] By November 1999, the Forum consisted of twenty-four opposition groups.[29] After the end of 1999, the Forum seems to have come to an end. There has not been any news about it since.

Although many democratic activists in Cuba believe that unity among opposition groups would strengthen the pro-democracy movement, the establishment of a broad umbrella organization is very unlikely before the regime starts to collapse in the face of continuous mass protests. Before then, divisions among civil society groups and government repression hinder the formation and endurance of an umbrella association. The government is very afraid of the unification of independent groups and would quickly move to decapitate such an organization. That was the experience of Concilio Cubano in 1996. But failures to form broad umbrella organizations do not represent a serious obstacle for the goal of achieving a political transition. East Germany's dissident umbrella organization, New Forum, was not formed until September 1989, one month before the collapse of the regime. It was the mass protests that propelled the New Forum rather than vice versa.[30] In Czechoslovakia, the umbrella organization, Civic Forum, was not formed until November 18, 1989, when the regime was already collapsing.[31] In Romania, there was no umbrella organization of opposition activists before the end of the Ceauşescu government.

Despite failure in maintaining a broad umbrella organization, the ability of independent groups in Cuba to cooperate with each other and the vitality of civil society were shown by the 40-day fast in June–July 1999. The stated purpose of the fast was to demand respect for human rights and freedom for political prisoners. Democratic activists from different groups started the fast in Havana. In solidarity with those in Havana, 54 other sites of fasting were established throughout the island. One hundred and forty-three independent groups in Cuba declared their support for the fast. About 2,000 activists and 136 individuals from the general population visited the Havana site during the period of the fast. Across the island, 6,288 individuals signed visitors' registers at the fasting centers. In the late 1990s, civil society groups increasingly coordinated their efforts in carrying out activities. Of 100 acts of civic resistance recorded in 1998, 31 involved the participation of more than one independent group in Cuba.[32] In 1999, more than one group participated in 60 percent of the 227 acts of civic resistance recorded.[33] All responses to the CEON questionnaire affirm that civil society groups are willing to cooperate with each

36   *Democracy Delayed*

other in carrying out activities. At the end of 2000, groups were forming coalitions or united fronts. Rather than being widely encompassing umbrella organizations, each of these narrower coalitions combines about a dozen groups.[34] As leaders of the democratic movement in Cuba have indicated, there is room for greater coordination among groups in civil society. But the opposition in Cuba is not "atomized," as some in the United States argue.[35] Evidence from various sources shows that civil society groups have organizational capacity and coordinate their efforts among themselves.

Yet groups face a number of obstacles to greater cooperation. One is a tendency for self-promotion among some leaders who think that they are better or more important than the rest. This type of behavior is called *protagonismo*, connoting a self-delusion of grandeur. Another is government repression, since the ruling elite tries hard to disunite the opposition. There is not much that can be done about these impediments. But another obstacle to greater coordination can be surmounted. This hindrance is scarce resources to establish regular communication among groups, especially among those geographically distant from one another. Activists need money for transportation and fax machines, among other things. International sources can provide groups in Cuba with more material assistance. Another impediment to greater cooperation among groups is disagreements about strategies. However, some opposition groups in Cuba and abroad are trying to build consensus in the pro-democracy movement regarding strategies. Every group in Cuba that participated in the CEON research project believed that reaching greater consensus on a strategy, tactics, and short-term objectives is very important in their struggle for democracy. Eighty percent of the groups in the study believe that it is possible to reach greater consensus among civil society groups.

Further evidence of advances in organization among civil society groups is increasing ability over time to take advantage of events that place Cuba in the international spotlight. When the pope visited Cuba in January 1998, civil society groups missed the opportunity to communicate their demands for democratization to the population in Cuba as well as to the international community. There was a heavy presence of foreign news media, the regime relaxed its repression, and there were large gatherings of people for religious events. Only isolated, individual acts of opposition to the dictatorship took place while the pope was in Cuba. This missed opportunity for democratic activists was probably due to the enduring disorder of the opposition movement caused by the crackdown in February 1996 against civil society leaders affili-

ated with Concilio Cubano. Some opposition leaders were imprisoned for extended periods and many others were pushed into exile. Moreover, according to observations by independent journalists, the discord among civil society leaders following the wave of repression also disrupted the operations of the movement. The setback to the organizational capacity of independent groups lasted well past January 1998.[36]

By contrast, for the Ibero-American Summit, held in Havana in November 1999, the opposition movement was better prepared to take advantage of the event. Months before, democratic activists announced that they would hold meetings concurrent with the Summit.[37] Although government repression prevented the parallel opposition summits, the international publicity and contacts with foreign heads of state prior to the Summit led to an unprecedented level of attention given to the internal opposition in Cuba by foreign dignitaries and the foreign press. Many foreign government officials met with members of the opposition. Yet the Cuban government was able to maintain tight control of the streets, showing that the opposition movement has not been able to promote large-scale protests.

Objectives and Strategies of Opposition Groups

The CEON data show a number of agreements and disagreements among opposition groups in Cuba. There is wide consensus on objectives. Every group in the sample wants transitions to democracy and to a market economy. The Cuban opposition, both inside and outside the island, is not revisionist. They want to get rid of communism, not reform it. Hence their goal is a complete political transition. With respect to strategies, all groups favor a peaceful transition. Another issue on which all but one of the groups agree is that a transition is possible while Fidel Castro is still alive.

While no group in the data set has a comprehensive view of how a transition can be attained, the groups in the study are on the right track. The factors they think are necessary for a transition would actually help bring it about. In their responses to the question, "How does your group think that a transition to democracy will be achieved?" they mention: (1) in a peaceful manner, (2) with cooperation or unity among opposition groups to pressure the government, (3) with international solidarity for the internal opposition, (4) with international pressure on the Castro government, (5) communicating to the people what it is like to live under a democracy, (6) with the creation of a consciousness of change in the population, and (7) with the population express-

38   *Democracy Delayed*

ing what they really feel. Two groups state that with pressure on the government, a split in the government would occur, with a sector defecting from the dictatorship and joining the push for democracy. All the groups in the sample support the idea of promoting mass demonstrations, at some point, to peacefully demand democratization. Some groups mention necessary conditions before this strategy can be implemented: (1) the creation of "subjective" conditions, (2) greater coordination among opposition groups, and (3) greater international support for the internal opposition. The CEON data show that the strategic views of the opposition groups do not constitute an obstacle to a transition. Thus, what is holding back a transition in Cuba is not the time frame of opposition groups.

Some opposition groups in Cuba think that the way to achieve a transition is by convincing the Cuban government to establish a dialogue with members of the opposition about the implementation of political changes. Groups seeking a dialogue with the government try to avoid confrontations with it and adopt some positions taken by the Castro government in its confrontation with the United States. For example, these groups oppose the embargo, wanted Elián González returned to Cuba, and oppose material assistance from the U.S. government to civil society groups in the island. Reports in the news media show that the Party of Democratic Solidarity (Partido Solidaridad Democrática), the Socialist Current (Corriente Socialista), the Liberal Democratic Party (Partido Liberal Democrático), and the Cuban Democratic Project (Proyecto Demócrata Cubano) favor seeking a dialogue with the government.[38] But the position of trying to avoid confrontations with the government is a minority position within the opposition and is not a serious obstacle to the possibility of a transition from below.

Two groups in the CEON study envision softliners (political reformers) inside the regime playing a role. Softliners could gain power and, with pressure from below, the political reformers would negotiate a transition. Other groups want to push for changes regardless of what the government does. Given the current regime type in Cuba, it is unreasonable to expect that it would be willing to pact a transition or that softliners could constrain hardliners and conduct negotiations with the opposition.

What is important in fostering a political transition by regime collapse is not that some groups think that the transition should be negotiated. A negotiated transition does not depend on the existence of civil society groups alone, but on the emergence of softliners in the regime with enough power to

constrain hardliners over time and to carry out negotiations with members of the opposition. In East Germany, for example, there were dissidents who sought negotiations with the communist government. What is important for transitions in hardline regimes is what civil society groups do to foster a feeling of political efficacy in the population so that mass protests develop. In Cuba independent groups are willing to carry out activities that can generate pressure from below. Groups want to convey messages to the population that could build a feeling that change is possible.

The Struggle for the Streets

Despite the achievements of civil society, the Cuban government has been able to maintain tight control over the streets. The relevancy of the transition paths of East Germany, Czechoslovakia, and Romania for Cuba is shown by the paranoia of the Castro dictatorship about the possibility of losing control of the streets. Even small acts of public defiance are routinely repressed. This behavior on the part of the Cuban government indicates that it considers the development of mass protests to be a serious threat to regime survival. The absence of mass demonstrations also shows that opposition groups have not succeeded in fostering these events despite the fact that many activists see such development as desirable in the quest for democracy. Public protests have taken place, but the numbers of participants have been small. As I have indicated, explaining the lack of large-scale protests to demand democratization is fundamental to understanding why a transition has not taken place.

Opposition activists would like to see large numbers of people participating in protests to demand democratization. Leonel Morejón Almagro, the former president of Naturpaz, an independent environmental group, declared in February 1999 that the time of meetings in houses and of writing was over, that now it was time to take to the streets to force the government to negotiate with the opposition.[39] At the press conference to mark the end of the forty-day fast in July 1999, William Herrera, the president of the Liga Civica Martiana (an opposition group), argued that one of the main objectives of the current efforts to achieve political change should be to develop the capacity for mobilization of the population.[40]

One way in which opposition groups hoped to take advantage of the international attention connected with the ninth Ibero-American Summit in Havana in November 1999 was by calling for a demonstration in a Havana park to ask for the release of political prisoners and to denounce human rights

40   *Democracy Delayed*

abuses by the government.[41] The demonstration was prevented by government repression. Only about ten activists were able to arrive at the park and they were beaten and arrested by the political police and other repressive forces.[42] In a clear display that there is a struggle for the streets, members of the repressive forces yelled, while confronting the opposition activists, "The streets belong to Fidel [Castro]."[43]

Activities in public places—marches, ceremonies, protests (e.g., in front of courtrooms in which opposition leaders are being prosecuted), and symbolic acts (e.g., placing flowers at a monument or throwing them in the sea)—are regularly repressed.[44] Whenever opposition groups have announced their plans to hold public activities or have publicized meetings to be held on certain dates, such as the anniversary of the universal declaration of human rights, the government routinely arrests a number of activists and posts members of the repressive forces in front of the homes of others (to prevent them from leaving their homes). Also, repressive forces are deployed at the protest sites to arrest, harass, and/or beat up activists who manage to make it to the sites.[45] Such tactics were implemented with particular intensity by the government at the time of the ninth Ibero-American Summit in Havana, when over 200 activists were arrested throughout Cuba.[46]

In contrast with public opposition activities, indoor activities by independent activists are less likely to be repressed. Examples of indoor activities that civil society activists have carried out are fasting (to commemorate or to petition something), operating independent libraries, holding educational seminars, and having symbolic acts in churches (e.g., observing a minute of silence to honor victims of the dictatorship).[47] But on occasions, even indoor opposition activities have been repressed. Government agents have gone inside the homes of activists to detain them or to beat them up.[48]

The dictatorship has effectively controlled public spaces because: (1) only activists have participated in public acts of defiance organized by opposition groups; consequently the numbers of demonstrators have been small; and (2) the larger protests that have occurred as people in the general population (independently from opposition groups) have reacted to deprivation and grievances have been ephemeral and localized, lasting at most a day. On rare occasions, some citizens, unaffiliated with any civil society group, have joined public protests led by democratic activists. But again, the numbers of people in organized demonstrations have been very small.[49]

Civil Society and Repression   41

A crucial shortcoming of opposition groups in their attempt to achieve democratization has been their inability to induce the participation of sizable numbers of people in public protests. The government realizes this and does not expect large numbers at protests called by the opposition. The size of the repressive forces that the government deploys at the sites of public protests is rather small. For example, opposition groups announced that they would commemorate the fiftieth anniversary of the universal declaration of human rights at Butari Park in Havana on December 10, 1998. The day of the event, the government arrested some activists, prevented others from leaving their homes, and sealed access to the park with a force of about 200 men.[50] In August 1999, Naturpaz called for a public ceremony at Lenin Park in Havana in favor of protecting the environment. The government deployed a force of a few dozen men to prevent activists from gathering at the park.[51]

In the battle for the streets, the government has counteracted opposition tactics that initially were effective. On August 27, 1998, dozens of people shouted pro-democracy slogans in front of the Popular Provincial Tribunal of Havana, where democratic activist Reynaldo Alfaro García was being tried for his political activities. The foreign press covered the protest, constituting a success for the opposition. On November 27, 1998, the same thing happened in front of the Tribunal, as opposition activists protested the trial of independent journalist Mario Viera. Several activists were beaten by a government-organized mob and the foreign press covered the disturbance. On December 17, 1998, for the trial of Lázaro Constantín Duval, an opposition activist, the government preemptively arrested a number activists and, with about 100 members of the repressive apparatus, blocked access to the area around the building where the trial was to take place.[52] This government tactic has been repeated ever since. It was reiterated at the trial of the four authors of "The Fatherland Belongs to All of Us" in March 1999. Before the trial, about 100 opposition activists were detained, and the area around the building where the trial was held was completely sealed, preventing all but close family members of the accused from getting close to the building.[53] More recently, for the trial of Oscar Elías Biscet, about fifteen opposition activists were arrested beforehand to prevent their potential presence at the trial.[54]

In contrast with public acts of defiance in which only opposition activists participate, when the general population has committed rebellious acts, the government has not been able to repress them easily or has refrained from doing so. In these protests, the numbers of participants have been much larger

42   *Democracy Delayed*

than in the cases in which only members of the opposition try to gather for public protests. The regime seems to be vulnerable to the development of mass demonstrations as occurred in East Germany and Czechoslovakia, hence the importance of popular participation in confronting the regime for the possibility of a transition from below.

Citizens have participated in acts of defiance out of rage caused by hardships and injustice. The largest protest occurred on August 5, 1994, triggered by police brutality. Approximately 3,000 people protested in various areas of Havana for many hours. Protesters chanted "down with Fidel" and "assassins" and engaged in violent acts like throwing stones at tourist stores (an indication of popular resentment against tourist apartheid). On May 27, 1998, more than 500 people marched through the Plaza of the Revolution in the funeral procession of Yuset Ochotorena López, a young man murdered by the police. Mourners carried the coffin on their shoulders. When the police tried to take the coffin away from them and place it in a funeral vehicle, the mourners beat back anti-riot policemen and agents of State Security. In July 1999, about 1,000 people protested against the dictatorship and in favor of democracy in the city of Puerto Padre (province of Holgín). The spontaneous protest erupted when members of the Cuban Coast Guard tried to apprehend a small boat in which residents of Puerto Padre were trying to leave for the United States. The repressive forces did not use violence to disperse the crowds.[55] In December 2000 in the city of Havana, about 1,500 people, some with sticks and stones, prevented police and housing authorities from evicting a family from their home.[56] In none of the spontaneous protests have members of the security forces or the police shot demonstrators, which indicates that regime leaders might fear that giving orders to shoot is likely to backfire.

Repression and Regime Cohesiveness

Civil society activists cannot hope to win the battle for the streets without the participation of hundreds or thousands of people. When there are large numbers of people in the streets, a two-sided dynamic takes place. Here, I am following the model of the development of mass protests and regime responses delineated by Karklins and Petersen.[57] The two aspects of the process are (1) the tendency for the numbers of protesters to grow continuously once a certain point is reached and (2) the tendency for the regime, including its repressive capacity, to collapse as the numbers of demonstrators increase. People feel safer acting publicly against highly repressive regimes when they are part

Civil Society and Repression   43

of a large crowd. As the number of protesters increases, the power of the regime to punish any single individual decreases. When people feel protected, they are more likely to express their true anti-regime attitudes by participating in public protests. The larger the numbers of protesters, the more secure people feel and the more individuals decide to go on the streets. When the number of protesters passes a certain point (a societal threshold), a bandwagon effect is triggered and no one wishes to be seen as supportive of a regime without a future. A concomitant process of defection from the regime occurs as the numbers of protesters grows. Similarly, individuals in the regime, such as bureaucrats, journalists, policemen, and members of the military, are more likely to defect as the numbers of people in the streets increase. Members of the regime make a cost-benefit calculus. The larger the number of demonstrators, the more likely the regime will not survive and the more rational it is to jump ship. Huntington argues that normally opposition to the regime has to be widespread before the military deserts the regime.[58]

Large numbers of protesters also tend to undermine the effectiveness of repression. Light repression is insufficient to stop the demonstrations and harsh repression backfires by generating a feeling of outrage and solidarity in the population that results in a surge in the numbers of people participating in protests. Acts of violence on the part of the regime become the focus of anti-repression (which become anti-regime) protests.[59] Also, the larger the number of people in the streets, the more obvious it is that it is "the people" and not just some opposition activists who are demanding political change. The more people participating in demonstrations, the harsher the repressive measures that the regime would have to apply to stop the protests, most likely resorting to a massacre as the Chinese did in 1989. As Opp, Voss, and Gern indicate, the probability that the security forces may disobey orders to repress is greater the harsher the sanctions demanded by the regime and the less legitimate the repression appears.[60] In East Germany and Czechoslovakia, the repressive apparatus disintegrated as continuously large-scale protests developed.

In East Germany and Czechoslovakia, as long as the numbers of people participating in public acts of defiance were small, basically civil society activists alone, the protesters got beaten and/or arrested. These were the experiences in 1988 and early 1989 in these countries. The regimes were able to control the streets. One observes the same thing in Cuba at the turn of the millennium. But when the numbers in the streets became large in these Eastern European countries, the dynamics described above ensued and communism fell. In

44   *Democracy Delayed*

Cuba, events have hinted at the relevancy of the Eastern European example. In the few cases where spontaneous demonstrations have involved fairly large numbers of people, as in Havana in 1994 and in Puerto Padre in 1999, the Castro regime has had difficulty controlling the streets or has let the protests fizzle out, refraining from using repression.

Since the most likely path of political transition in Cuba is a transition from below, mass demonstrations to demand democratization is a key factor in making it possible. Hence, it is important to determine why in Cuba popular participation in opposition activities is low. In the literature on Cuba, one can find various hypotheses for such phenomenon. Fear of repression is the key explanation.[61] The repression in Cuba is certainly intense and widespread. Given the various indications of the pervasive discontent in the population and the decay of the legitimacy of the Castro government (both ideological and based on appeals to nationalism), the fundamental pillar of the regime is repression. That communist dictatorships rested on repression rather than popular support was amply demonstrated in Eastern Europe, including the Soviet Union with its "homegrown" regime and Romania, where Ceauşescu appealed to nationalism. Whenever repression decreases, there is a surge in civil society activities to demand democratization. Since the street is the only channel in which to press demands on an autocratic regime, popular discontent turns into popular mobilization.[62] And if repression ceases to function, the surge in the number of people protesting in the streets is dramatic. Such was the case in East Germany and Czechoslovakia when repression ended toward the end of the communist regimes. At that stage in the process of regime breakdown, fear evaporates and more people feel free and secure enough to express their opposition.

The degree of repression in Cuba today does not make a transition from below impossible. Repression is not the main explanation for the low level of popular participation in public, independent activities. The connection between actual repression and propensity to engage in dissident activities is not necessarily inversely related. Individual experiences of repression can backfire for the government and foster more opposition rather than less. Based on interview data from the Soviet Interview Project, Karklins found that Soviet emigrants who had experienced repression personally or in their family had a greater propensity to engage in dissident activities.[63] Karklins argues that instilling fear, rather than actual repression, is an effective means of coercion.[64] Moreover, the more severe forms of repression, like long imprisonment, are only

Civil Society and Repression   45

applied selectively in Cuba. A similar experience was observed in the Soviet Union. As Karklins indicates, sending dissidents to labor camps in the Soviet Union required trials, which were costly in two ways. Trials indicated that the KGB had failed to do its work of generating fear. In addition, the Soviet Union had to pay a political price for trials in terms of international publicity of its human rights violations.[65] The Castro government also pays in international censure whenever a democratic activist is sentenced to a long prison term.

Repression in Romania before the fall of Ceauşescu seems to have been harsher than in Cuba today. In Romania, dissidents often "disappeared," a sign that they had been executed. In Cuba today, political opponents are not routinely killed, as was done in the 1960s. In Romania, organized political dissent appeared in the 1970s, but by the 1980s most of the dissidents were dead, in prison, in psychiatric hospitals, or involuntary exiled abroad. Political activism was minimal and largely focused on the desire of some citizens to emigrate to the West. Periodically, a lone individual or two carried out isolated, symbolic acts in public and arrests predictably followed.[66] In Romania, there was infrequent eruption of working-class unrest that tended to be spontaneous and leaderless, with the government restoring order and control.[67]

There is not a great difference between the degree of repression in Cuba and in East Germany and Czechoslovakia prior to the fall of 1989. In the GDR, the Stasi increased its size and surveillance efforts after Gorbachev started implementing reforms in the Soviet Union.[68] The East German regime responded to pressures and demands for liberalization with repression.[69] Protests against the regime were almost absent. When small protests occurred, they were crushed immediately.[70] Almost all collective activities prior to October 9, 1989 (the day that repression stopped), were dissolved violently.[71] People were imprisoned or expelled from the country for trying to demonstrate or unfold banners calling for democratization.[72] In Czechoslovakia, up to the eve of the collapse of the communist regime, the degree of repression was also high. According to one account, the level of repression there was similar to that in East Germany.[73] Efforts to mount demonstrations or other public protests were quelled by the security apparatus.[74] The government response to increased activism after the second half of 1988 was repression in the form of harassment and preemptive arrests.[75]

A difference between repression in Cuba and repression in Czechoslovakia is that in the latter detentions of dissidents were mostly short-term, such as a few hours or days, while in Cuba some opposition activists have been impris-

oned for much longer periods (e.g., a year or more).[76] Also, economic repression in Cuba is more severe than it was in Czechoslovakia. In Czechoslovakia, dissidents who were fired from their jobs because of their political activities could still hold jobs of lesser status with the government.[77]

In Cuba, dissidents are systematically dismissed from their jobs, are not allowed to work in any other state institution, including joint ventures with foreign capitalists, and are denied licenses to work as independent entrepreneurs.[78] All groups in the CEON study say that if a person is fired from his or her job for political reasons, the individual has a very hard time making a living. In such cases, people can: (1) engage in illicit economic activities, providing the government an additional reason for repression; (2) depend on assistance provided by family members or friends—who typically do not have much themselves; or (3) depend on assistance from abroad. One group mentions that economic repression is effective in decreasing membership in civil society groups—people refrain from joining or end their membership. More people would join civil society groups if sustenance for them and their families would not be in jeopardy. According to another group, the economic situation of activists hurts them more than the repressive apparatus. Yet the effectiveness of the economic repression against democratic activists can be undermined by humanitarian aid to activists from abroad. The problem is that such assistance is meager. All groups in the CEON study mention that the economic assistance sent to independent groups is scarce and unsystematic. Civil society activists in Cuba receive little humanitarian assistance and very little resources, such as money and equipment, with which to carry out their political work.

One question in the CEON questionnaire asked, "What do independent groups need to be more effective in achieving their objectives?" Sixty-six percent of the groups mentioned material assistance from abroad, including equipment, money, and humanitarian aid. The same number of groups also said that they need information or advice, such as help in determining a strategy, knowledge about the methods that the repressive apparatus uses in dividing the opposition, and educational materials about civic struggles against autocracies. Groups mention that the assistance they have received has helped them to do their work and has relieved the basic needs of activists who have been fired from their jobs, their families, and the families of political prisoners.

Communication among civil society groups is necessary to better coordinate their activities, something that can increase the effectiveness of the

Civil Society and Repression 47

democracy movement in Cuba. One question in the CEON study asked, "Could it be possible to establish an effective communication network among independent groups?" Every group in the study maintains that it would be possible to establish an effective network. All the groups, except one, argue that in order to create such a communication network the groups need resources (e.g., faxes, cell phones, computers, modems, money, and printers).

In Cuba, on several occasions, people have shown their ability to overcome fear of repression. One example is participation in spontaneous protests as people have reacted to hardships and injustice. A participant in the protest of August 5, 1994, in Havana described his experiences at the protest in an interview with an independent journalist. He said, "I had already received many blows [from members of the repressive apparatus] . . . but I was more resolved than ever . . . I returned home and went to bed. The contusions all over my body were hurting, but I was happy."[79] Also, there have been numerous acts of solidarity in the general population with members of dissident groups. Citizens have defended opposition activists when the latter were attacked by government repressive forces.[80] In a meeting of leaders of the Committees for the Defense of the Revolution (CDRs), some participants stated that the population had attacked the Committees.[81] Citizens are also becoming bolder in criticizing the regime in public. For example, in Havana's Central Park as of 2001, groups of citizens gather regularly to discuss political affairs openly, including criticizing the Castro government for such things as corruption and the violation of human rights.[82]

If there are mass demonstrations, the regime will confront the issue of whether to shoot people in an attempt to suppress further mass protests and save the dictatorship. It is impossible to predict with certainty what those with guns will do. But there is reason to think that at least some units of the security forces in Cuba would refuse to fire on the population if ordered to do so. Friedheim, interviewing former members of the repressive apparatus in East Germany, found that by the fall of 1989 many were unwilling to use force against protesters because they no longer believed in their own legitimacy to rule. The coercive apparatus was comprised not only of the security forces (e.g. the Interior Ministry), but also of party members who oversaw the security forces and some other government officials.[83] If the loyalty of members of the security apparatus depends on the degree to which they believe in the official ideology, their loyalty in Cuba today is questionable. Belief in the official ideology has decayed considerably, both among the population and among gov-

ernment cadres. Some members of the political police have provided information to and helped dissident groups.[84] Anecdotal evidence indicates that some members of the security apparatus in Cuba are already taking into account, when they deal with members of the opposition, their personal well-being in a post-transition period.[85] Members of the intelligence apparatus and of the military have gone into exile abroad or have been apprehended trying to leave Cuba illegally.[86] And the pervasive corruption in the government, reaching into top ranks, strongly suggests that ideological fervor is dead or moribund.

Inside the Cuban military, there are signs of discontent, and government elites have shown concern about the loyalty of military officers. These observations contradict the view in the literature on Cuba that the military shows little signs of disloyalty or anti-regime sentiment.[87] Some authors have argued that the military remains loyal to the government out of material interests since military officers have acquired positions as managers of joint ventures with foreign capitalists, enjoying privileges and high incomes. While some high-ranking officers have become part of a "red-bourgeoisie," not all officers have such privileged positions. Some high-level officers might be ready to give orders to fire on the population to save the regime, but their orders might not be followed by junior officers and/or rank-and-file soldiers. At least some officers might join the people if a massacre takes place, with a Romanian-type scenario.

In Cuba, the military as an institution is not involved in the repression of civil society. Therefore, it is likely that the military will remain neutral or will side with the population if repeated mass demonstrations develop. Domingo Amuchastegui, a former official of the Cuban government who was a chief intelligence analyst and professor at the National Defense College, argues that it is very unlikely that the Cuban armed forces would fire on the population in the event of mass demonstrations.[88]

The regular armed forces are the Revolutionary Armed Forces (FAR). The political police are under the direction of the Ministry of Interior (MININT) and have armed troops. Units of the MININT would be more likely than units of the FAR to fire on the population. Sixty-six percent of the groups in the CEON study say that there is some involvement of members of the regular armed forces in repression. But every group in the CEON study reports that neither opposition groups nor general citizens perceive that the regular armed forces as an institution is responsible for the repression.

One of the questions in the CEON study asks whether civil society activists and citizens in the general population believe that people would be shot in the streets if large, peaceful mass demonstrations take place. Activists in 60 percent of the groups do not think that those with guns will fire on the people if mass demonstrations occur. The other 40 percent of the groups believe that people would get shot. Regarding the perception of activists about what the general population thinks concerning the likelihood of people getting shot in mass protests, the responses are evenly split. Half of the groups reports that people are afraid that those with guns would fire and the other half affirms the opposite. These responses indicate that it should not be assumed that fear of a massacre in the event of mass protests is widespread in the population. Since the Castro regime faced the economic problems and growing discontent that developed in the 1990s, whenever large, spontaneous protests have taken place, like the one in Havana in August 1994, people have not been shot in the streets. This evidence and the responses to the CEON questionnaire suggest that fear of a massacre among citizens is not a key in accounting for the absence of mass protests to demand democratization.

With the deterioration of the Cuban economy in the 1990s, a key role for the Cuban military has been to run agricultural and business enterprises, including department stores and tourist resorts.[89] According to Marine General Charles Wilhelm, a former head of the U.S. Southern Command, the size of the Cuban armed forces has been reduced by about half, most of their equipment is unusable, and about 70 percent of the armed forces' effort is devoted to their own self-sustainment.[90] A Cuban government official disclosed that 50 percent of the armed forces is dedicated to agricultural activities. A colonel in the Cuban air force, who defected to the United States in 1994, declared that there is growing discontent among officers in the Cuban military because they have been forced to work in the agricultural sector. The view of this defector is consistent with other evidence of problems of morale and disillusionment with the regime in the armed forces.[91] A report from Cuba at the end of the 1980s maintains that many military officers were unhappy with the increase in corruption among high-level government officials and with the technological backwardness of the country.[92] Indications of widespread corruption among government officials abound.[93]

The situation in the Cuban armed forces parallels that of the armed forces in East Germany and Romania. By 1989 in East Germany, about 10,000 soldiers were used as cheap labor in factories or farms. Within the army, about

50   *Democracy Delayed*

half of those involved in the security apparatus believed by 1989 that the communist regime did not have the right to rule.[94] In Romania, military disaffection was fostered by Ceauşescu's policies, which weakened military professionalism and corrupted the officer corps.[95]

Title II of the Helms–Burton law calls for the U.S. government to prepare a plan of assistance to transitional and democratic governments in Cuba. Following this directive, the Clinton administration disclosed in January 1997 a plan entitled "Support for a Democratic Transition in Cuba." The document pledges the U.S. government to help Cuba in various ways, for example, by providing technical and financial assistance. In addition, the document states that the United States is willing to return to a democratic government the naval base at Guantanamo (a carrot to Cuban nationalism) and that the armed forces in Cuba could play a positive role in the transition. In reference to militaries in former communist countries, the document makes the point that their core professional interests need not be threatened by democracy and that the armed forces in such countries have withdrawn from non-military functions like internal security and economic activities. Moreover, the document offers military-to-military cooperation of the U.S. armed forces with a Cuban military that is supportive of a civilian democratic government. After President Clinton made public the "Support for a Democratic Transition in Cuba," the Castro government conducted a national campaign to have military officers sign a document supporting the Castro regime and repudiating U.S. policies toward Cuba.[96] Contingency plans for the death of Fidel Castro, disclosed in a document of the Cuban government, called for the arrest of more than one hundred military officers who were under investigation.[97]

In East Germany and Czechoslovakia civilian cadres of the dictatorships defected as mass demonstrations developed.[98] In Cuba, there are signs that the support for the regime among its cadres and professionals who remain inside government institutions has eroded. This evidence contradicts the argument of some scholars that the regime is internally cohesive because all its members have a stake in its long-term survival.[99] A significant number of independent journalists in Cuba were former employees of the government mass media. This parallels the fact that in Eastern Europe the members of the government news media were the first ones to defect.[100] Some Cuban government officials provide information to independent journalists.[101] In February 1992, nineteen university professors were expelled from their jobs for signing a petition demanding democratic reforms, respect for human rights, amnesty for political

prisoners, and university autonomy. During the 1999–2000 academic year, one hundred teachers were fired from their jobs for opposing policies of the Ministry of Education; most of the teachers refused to continue teaching courses with political content in favor of the government. Abel Prieto, former minister of culture and currently the president of the Union of Writers and Artists in Cuba, in an interview in December 2000 stated that writers in Cuba are discarding self-censorship and adopting a more autonomous position in addressing "social contradictions" in Cuba.

A report from the Central Commission of Cadres (Comisión Central de Cuadros), created to help the Council of Ministers evaluate the work of the top levels of the nomenklatura, stated that problems with salaries impair the motivation of cadres.[102] In meetings to discuss the Party's platform for the fifth national congress held in the fall of 1997, Communist Party members in Havana reported that a surprising number of cadres openly criticized the platform. Traditionally, such meetings had been devoted to rubber-stamping. Members said that the platform did not mention solutions to the economic problems that Cubans face every day. According to one party member, "People are saying they do not see the government admitting anything wrong or taking any real steps to get us out of our crisis; they are at the end of their ropes, depressed."[103] A series of reports indicates that corruption and lack of discipline are widespread among members of the Communist Party and that many members of the Communist Youth Organization are refusing to become members of the Party.[104] The regime also has had problems with the motivation of the Committees for the Defense of the Revolution. In a meeting held in Santiago de Cuba in April 1997, CDRs leaders were criticized by the national leader of the CDRs for abandoning their mission of maintaining surveillance of their blocks and neighborhoods.[105] Members of the opposition in Cuba report a sharp deterioration in the role of the CDRs as informants for the regime. On September 27, 2000, in the city of Manzanillo, about thirty members of the CDRs defended a political dissident who was attacked by an agent of the repressive apparatus as the dissident was returning to his home from an opposition activity.[106]

The CEON data provide further evidence of the widespread discontent and corruption among government personnel. Every group mentions that there is discontent among government cadres. Half of these groups emphasize that there is discontent among the vast majority of government officials. Respondents cite as evidence of discontent defections abroad, retirement from public

52   *Democracy Delayed*

life, corruption, trying to live outside Cuba, and anonymous letters critical of Fidel Castro and the regime sent to high government officials. Eighty-three percent of the groups affirm that corruption among government officials is pervasive, in all branches of the government and at all levels, from ministers to the lowest officials.

Conclusions

Neither the strength of civil society nor the degree of repression by the Castro government in Cuba is a fundamental impediment to a transition from below. At the turn of the millennium, in terms of the number of activists and the number of independent groups, civil society in Cuba is stronger than it was in Romania just before the end of the Ceauşescu dictatorship and similar to those in East Germany and Czechoslovakia in the summer of 1989. In Cuba since mid-1995, despite the continuous repression and the inadequate material resources in the hands of the opposition, civil society has continuously grown, established networks to coordinate efforts among groups, and incrementally increased acts of defiance. Democratic activists are not "atomized" and have become a constant thorn in the side of the regime. Opposition groups have made some progress in organizing the population independently of the state and in demonstrating to citizens that there are people willing to confront the regime. These are beginning steps toward freedom. But there is a long way to go.

Neither the objectives, nor the strategies, nor the timing that many opposition activists have in mind appear to be obstacles in the development of a transition process. There is wide consensus on the need to move toward democracy and a market economy. The vast majority of the opposition in Cuba is not revisionist. With respect to strategies, groups want to demand changes peacefully and have a fairly clear idea of what has to be done to achieve a transition. Many believe that a transition is possible while Fidel Castro is still in power. They are not waiting for him to pass from the scene.

Regarding repression, it was harsher in Romania under Ceauşescu than in Cuba today. The degree of repression in Cuba seems to be similar to that in East Germany and Czechoslovakia prior to the fall of communism. Although there is substantial fear of repression in the Cuban population, people have shown that they can overcome their fear and confront the regime. An important difference in Cuba is that economic repression against dissidents is particularly harsh. It hinders the growth and effectiveness of civil society activists.

It drains the time and energy of dissidents as they try to find sustenance for themselves and their families. People who would otherwise join civil society groups refrain from doing so to avoid being placed in a highly precarious economic situation. But the effectiveness of the economic repression of the Cuban government could be undermined with more humanitarian assistance sent to democratic activists from abroad. The problem is that such assistance has been meager. Other types of material assistance, such as money and equipment, would greatly help civil society groups carry out their activities. For example, they would be better able to coordinate their actions and communicate with the population.

In the Eastern European countries that experienced transitions by regime collapse, civil society activists played a catalytic role in the development of popular protests. By their messages, in words and actions, activists helped to foster a sense of political efficacy among a large percentage of the population in their respective countries and thus encouraged sizable numbers of people to participate in protests. What was important was the dissemination of signals that change was possible, messages of popular defiance and of partial successes against autocratic regimes. In principle, these messages do not have to be diffused from abroad; they can come from sources and events internal to a particular country. In Cuba, civil society activists frequently defy the government and achieve partial successes. Civil society in the island has developed the potential to play a catalytic role, but the realization of that potential is frustrated by the absence of effective independent channels of communication. This is an issue that I will elaborate in chapter 3. In Eastern Europe, the diffusion effect was important in building the belief in political efficacy among the populations in the region. Since the Eastern European contagion effect did not extend to Cuba, the task of civil society activists in cultivating political efficacy among the Cuban population is even more crucial for the prospect of a transition in the island.

The regime has been winning the battle for the streets because the numbers of protesters in public acts of defiance organized by opposition groups have been small and because the larger protests that have occurred as people in the general population have reacted to deprivation and grievances have been ephemeral and localized. With more material resources and the ability to communicate regularly with the population, civil society in Cuba could foster a sense of political efficacy among citizens. The fact that thus far this has not occurred is part of the explanation for the non-transition. But these shortcomings can be surmounted by U.S. government policies.

If large and repeated protests develop, the Castro regime might collapse, as the East German and Czechoslovak communist regimes did. In Eastern Europe, when repeated, large protests developed, regime cadres jumped ship and the repressive capacity of the regime disintegrated. The Cuban government shows signs of internal weakness. The ideological legitimacy of the regime has crumbled and appeals to nationalism seem to fall mostly on deaf ears. The pervasive corruption among government officials is a sign of the decay. There are numerous indications of discontent among cadres, including officers in the Revolutionary Armed Forces and even members of the political police.

In contrast with public acts of defiance in which only a small number of opposition activists participate, in the few cases when the Cuban government has been confronted with a relatively large number of citizens who have spontaneously defied the authorities, the government has not been able to easily repress the people or has refrained from doing so and has allowed the protests to fizzle out. The regime seems vulnerable to the development of mass demonstrations. Moreover, people have not been shot in any of the spontaneous protests, which indicates that regime leaders might fear that giving orders to shoot is likely to backfire. The survival of the Castro regime appears to depend on its ability to prevent large and repeated peaceful demonstrations to demand political change.

It is impossible to predict with certainty what those with guns will do if large demonstrations challenge the regime. Will one see an East German scenario or a Romanian one? If one has to believe in something to pull the trigger, few if any shots will be fired. The worst-case scenario is likely to be the Romanian one and not the Chinese. Units of the regular armed forces, or even of the political police, could very well join the people.

CHAPTER 3

Political Efficacy and Independent Communication

Political Efficacy and Transitions

The concept of political efficacy was introduced to political science by Angus Campbell in 1954.[1] It has been defined as "the feeling that individual political action does have or can have an impact upon the political process."[2] There is strong empirical evidence supporting the association between a feeling of efficacy and political participation.[3] Much of the evidence comes from studies conducted in democracies, linking a sense of efficacy and voting. Yet the concept of efficacy is also relevant in explaining political participation in contexts where individuals engaging in such activities might suffer harsh repression. Numerous theoretical and empirical works support this assertion. I argue that a widespread sense of political efficacy among the population is necessary for mass protests to occur under dictatorships, especially in hardline ones like the communist regimes in East Germany, Czechoslovakia, Romania, and Cuba.

The importance of a sense of personal political efficacy among the population for them to participate in political activities that challenge the political

56   *Democracy Delayed*

power structure has been recognized in various studies of unconventional political behavior, that is, behavior that can lead to punishment by the authorities. Alan Marsh found that a belief in the effectiveness of protest behavior (e.g., demonstrations and invasions of property) in Britain had a strong positive impact on the likelihood that people would engage in such behavior.[4] Mitchell Seligson obtained evidence in his study of land invasions by peasants in Costa Rica supporting previous findings that a high sense of personal efficacy is necessary to participate in such activities; discontent is insufficient.[5] Consistent with these previous studies, a survey conducted by Opp, Voss, and Gern in Leipzig after the fall of communism shows that a sense of political efficacy in the population was the key to participation in the demonstrations that took place there before the collapse of the communist regime.

Opp, Voss, and Gern conducted a large number of interviews among residents of Leipzig soon after the fall of communism. They found that the vast majority of those who participated in demonstrations up to October 9, 1989 (when the repressive apparatus ceased to function), believed that it was very likely that they would suffer severe sanctions (e.g., being arrested or injured by the security forces) for participating in public protests. With each passing demonstration before October 9, the percentage of those who feared repression increased, with fear being most prevalent on October 9.[6] Before October 9, there were rumors that the government was going to implement a "Chinese solution" and troops were deployed. But fear of repression did not stop people from marching. On October 9, 70,000 people gathered at or near the Nikolai Church in Leipzig for a protest march.[7] The interview data collected by Opp, Voss, and Gern also show that feelings of personal political efficacy among a significant percentage of the population was an indispensable factor for massive protests. People believed, even before the turning point on October 9, that extensive protests could produce political changes and that personal participation would be influential in achieving that goal.[8] These findings not only support my argument about the importance of a widespread belief in personal political efficacy for mass demonstrations but also undermine the idea that fear of repression in Cuba explains the very low level of citizen participation in opposition activities. Their findings suggest that people can surmount their fear of repression if they think their actions can bring about political change.

The validity of the survey done by Opp, Voss, and Gern is indirectly supported. There is consistency between its findings about the importance of political efficacy in explaining participation in mass protests and theoretical ar-

Political Efficacy and Independent Communication   57

guments on the relationship between these two variables in the Eastern European transitions. In turn, these theoretical formulations embody empirical observations. Przeworski, in talking about the strategic behavior of actors involved in processes of transitions from authoritarian rule, emphasizes that expectation of success in changing the regime is a pivotal determinant of such behavior. Actors behave rationally, and in transition their expectation of what strategies will be successful are based on signals such as economic crises or manifest loss of regime legitimacy indicated by mass unrest.[9] Anthony Oberschall uses a rational choice model of collective protests to explain individual decisions to participate in the 1989 demonstrations in Leipzig; a key variable is each individual's expectation of the contribution that his or her participation would make in obtaining the collective good sought.[10] Karklins and Petersen argue, with the cases of Czechoslovakia and East Germany in mind, that a factor involved in people's decision to participate in demonstrations was their prediction that their participation would lead to political change.[11] Mark Thompson makes the point that the 1989 rebellion in East Germany was a kind of self-fulfilling prophecy. East Germans came to believe that their participation in protests could succeed in bringing about political change and this belief was a key cause of the success of the demonstrations.[12] Numerous scholars argue that by the end of the 1980s, Eastern Europeans believed that by participating in demonstrations they could achieve political change in their respective countries.[13] After the fall of communism in Czechoslovakia, Saxonberg interviewed former members of the opposition. He found that in 1989 dissidents came to believe that political change in Czechoslovakia was possible.[14] Other scholars make the same point for the general population in Czechoslovakia. They affirm that, before the large demonstrations that brought about the collapse of the dictatorship, the general population felt that political change in their country was possible after observing the transformations in East Germany and in other Soviet bloc countries.[15]

A common hypothesis in the literature on the fall of communism in Eastern Europe is that the contagion or diffusion effect was a central factor in explaining the transitions. The transitions in Poland and Hungary, Gorbachev's decisions to implement glasnost in the Soviet Union, and his signals that the Soviets would not intervene militarily to save communist regimes in Eastern Europe supposedly generated a feeling of political efficacy among citizens in other Eastern European countries.[16] Przeworski refers to the sequence of transitions in Eastern Europe as a domino effect and argues that as the process of

58   *Democracy Delayed*

transition took place in one country people elsewhere updated their probabilities of success in toppling their own dictatorship.[17] The implication is that people developed a sense of efficacy.

The spread of political efficacy among Eastern European populations was not entirely a matter of diffusion across countries. Although advances toward democratization in Poland, Hungary, and the Soviet Union certainly served to foster a sense of political efficacy in neighboring countries, domestic actors also helped develop and spread this belief among their fellow citizens. In principle, these messages do not have to be diffused from abroad; they can come from sources and events internal to a particular country. What is important for the development of a sense of political efficacy are signals that change is possible, such as popular defiance and examples of partial successes against autocratic regimes. In East Germany, the mass exodus of 1989, which can be considered an internal development, triggered the demonstrations that toppled the dictatorship.[18] The population in East Germany knew about the setbacks that communist regimes had already suffered in Poland, Hungary, and the Soviet Union. But despite knowledge of these external events, it was not until the exodus in East Germany that its political transition got under way. Some authors point to the large exodus of East Germans in 1989 as an element contributing to the development of political effectiveness among people in the GDR. The inability of the East German government to stop the outflow, despite having a policy of strict control of migration, was a signal of regime weakness.[19] Moreover, initial demonstrations in East Germany, Czechoslovakia, and Romania fostered further protests in each of these countries. Saxonberg's interviews of individuals who had been dissidents under communist rule in Czechoslovakia indicate that their rising expectations of change were not only influenced by what had happened in neighboring countries but also by internal factors in Czechoslovakia, such as poor economic performance and signs of regime weakness.[20]

According to Saxonberg, civil society activists did not expect the regime to collapse as it did. They thought that hardliners would be replaced by softliners, who would then implement political liberalization.[21] There is no necessary contradiction in the claims that: (1) people who participated in mass protests in East Germany, Czechoslovakia, and Romania at the end of 1989 felt that their behavior could bring about political change and (2) people were surprised by the extent of the changes that occurred. The outcomes may have exceeded their expectations.

Political Efficacy and Independent Communication   59

It is commonly thought that in the GDR and Czechoslovakia dissident groups had a limited role in organizing protests and in mobilizing the population.[22] Nevertheless, pronouncements from democratic activists directed at the population, information about activities of opposition groups, and news about the initial demonstrations must have been crucial in generating widespread feelings of political efficacy among citizens. Saxonberg observes that in the East German and the Czechoslovakian democratic revolutions of 1989, dissidents acted as catalysts for the mass demonstrations by starting protests. These initial protests provided a model for people to follow. The main problem for dissidents in promoting protests among people was communication; "they had to spread the news of what was happening."[23]

There are indications that civil society activists served as catalysts for the protests in East Germany and Czechoslovakia. There were numerous smaller demonstrations before the large ones took place. These opposition activities, in which civil society activists took part, sent a message to the population that there were many people willing to defy the regime to demand democratization. The population received the message directly at protest sites and through Radio Free Europe and other foreign radio stations.

At Nikolai Church in Leipzig, the birthplace of the East German revolution, civil society groups, especially the opposition group Arbeitskreis Gerechtigkeit (AKG), adopted the cause of the would-be emigrants as a potential source of protests. When church leaders banned opposition groups and would-be emigrants from the peace prayers at the end of 1988, opposition activists set up a podium in the courtyard of the church, where anyone could speak while church services were being held inside. In this "speaker's corner," activists read protest notes, passed resolutions, and addressed issues such as the demands of those who wanted to emigrate. The audience was initially comprised mainly of would-be emigrants, but eventually the focus of attention of the participants in the peace prayers shifted from the church service to the outside courtyard. And the peace prayers gradually came to be seen as a prelude to public protests. On September 25, 1989, the first of the Monday demonstrations that finally led to the collapse of the regime, opposition groups instigated the demonstration that followed the church service.[24] The demonstration of November 17 in Czechoslovakia organized by reformers in the Prague official student organization and the independent student group STUHA became the immediate cause of the regime collapse. The students distributed fliers encouraging participation in the demonstration and disclosing the meeting place for the march.[25]

60   *Democracy Delayed*

If by the end of the 1980s people in Eastern Europe had come to believe that their participation in protests could be successful in attaining political change, before that time this was not the case. This difference in the belief in political efficacy across time indicates that such a feeling is created under some conditions. Data and observations suggest that populations in Eastern Europe before the end of the 1980s were characterized by a low sense of political efficacy. At the end of the 1970s, the population in Czechoslovakia was characterized by passivity, escapism, and servility toward the regime.[26] The Romanian population was described as "meek," willing to endure the dictatorship.[27] During 1983–84, travelers from Czechoslovakia, Poland, and Hungary to Western Europe were asked in a survey, "What do you think the rest of the eighties will bring for your country?" Only 4 percent of Czechoslovaks, 9 percent of Hungarians, and 15 percent of Poles thought that under pressure from the people the dictatorships under which they lived were going to experience fundamental change. By contrast, 41 percent of Czechoslovaks, 30 percent of Hungarians, and 31 percent of Poles thought that pressure for more freedom was going to decline as more and more people pursued their own interests.[28] Thus, if someone argues that citizens of Eastern European countries believed or did not believe in the efficacy of their anti-regime participation, it is necessary to specify the time period of reference.

The Dearth of Political Efficacy among the Cuban Population

The Cuban case points to the crucial importance of a widespread belief in the population that political change is possible and to the critical role of independent sources of communication in developing such belief among people. These two factors are necessary for a transition by collapse, but they are missing in Cuba. Independent means of communication are either absent or effectively jammed by the government. Poor communication and meager resources in the hands of civil society are significant factors accounting for the non-transition.

I argue that in Cuba civil society groups could, with greater resources and the ability to communicate with the population, cultivate a belief of political efficacy among the people. Since the Eastern European contagion effect did not affect Cuba, the task of civil society activists in cultivating political efficacy among the citizens is of utmost importance for a political transition. In Cuba, civil society activists frequently defy the government and achieve some successes against the Castro government, such as getting the government to

Political Efficacy and Independent Communication   61

partially meet socioeconomic demands. But the inadequacy of independent sources of communication prevents the general population from knowing about these activities.

Large-scale protests to demand democratization have not occurred in Cuba mainly because the majority of the citizens in the population at large who thus far are not involved in any independent or opposition activities think that their participation in opposition activities would be ineffective in achieving political change. While courageous civil society activists defy the regime, without repeated, large-scale demonstrations by the general population there cannot be a transition from below. The dearth of political efficacy in the population is a crucial obstacle to a transition under the Castro regime. If a sense of efficacy were widespread in Cuba, then a transition along the paths of the East German or Romanian transitions could occur.

That most citizens feel politically impotent against the Castro government is a legacy of decades of totalitarian rule. Cuba under the Castro government has had a long experience of harsh repression and failed attempts to topple the regime. Almost since the very beginning of the dictatorship, especially during the 1960s, many Cubans, inside and outside the island, tried to overthrow the dictatorship by force of arms. All these attempts ended in failure. Thousands who opposed the government, through either violent or peaceful means, were killed. According to a recent data source, as of early 2000, the Castro government was responsible for 20,400 extrajudicial killings, that is, executions or murders in prison by guards.[29] Thousands of Cubans have been political prisoners, at one time or another, since 1959.

Numerous reports by independent journalists in Cuba indicate that the vast majority of the population perceives that the only solution to their gloomy existence is to leave the island. Most people see only two choices: to emigrate (exit) or to endure their plight (indicating resignation rather than loyalty).[30] Voice, to push for a transition, is not considered a viable alternative by most.[31] A survey conducted in 1997 by the National Council for Civil Rights in Cuba (an independent organization) shows that the foremost wish for the near future of 41 percent of the respondents was to leave the country; only 18 percent of respondents wished to see political changes in Cuba. A more recent study by the independent Cuban Center for Social Studies on values among young people, conducted between 1986 and 1999, shows that youths are hopeless about the future and have no desire to engage in political action to bring about change, even though they dislike the regime.[32] The document,

62   *Democracy Delayed*

"Cuba, Its People and Its Church Facing the Beginning of the Third Millennium," published by clergy from the dioceses of Santiago de Cuba, Holguín, Bayamo-Manzanillo, and Guantanamo in July 1999, characterizes the population in Cuba as having a sense of "induced hopelessness" regarding their ability to put an end to the dictatorship.[33]

The CEON study posed a series of questions about why more people are not participating in public opposition activities. From the perspective of the activists, there are three fundamental reasons, each mentioned by 83 percent of the groups in the study: (1) insufficient communication between civil society groups and the population, (2) fear of repression, and (3) a sense of political inefficacy among citizens, that is, people do not think that their participation in these activities will lead to political changes. As one group put it, "a lot of people believe that nothing is going to change [by their participation], only that they will get into trouble with the government." Another group stated that if people believed that their participation would be effective, they would be willing to go to the streets to demand democratization. The CEON questionnaire asked which was more important in explaining the low degree of popular participation in public acts of opposition, fear of repression or a sense of political inefficacy. Sixty percent of the groups said that both factors are equally important and 40 percent think that political inefficacy is more important.

A question in the CEON study asked how a belief in political efficacy could be developed in the population. Sixty-six percent of the groups believe that the key is greater communication between civil society activists and the population. Three of the groups also mentioned that in order to build a sense of political efficacy in the population it is necessary for civil society groups to be more effective in their work. These three groups argue that the work of civil society activists would be more effective if groups had greater resources and coordinated their work among themselves.

An alternative explanation for the low level of participation by the Cuban population in opposition activities is fear of political and economic changes. The survey conducted by Roberts et al. among recent Cuban arrivals to the United States asked about the biggest fear Cubans have about the future. The most frequent responses were as follows: (1) that exiles would return to take away their homes, 40 percent; (2) the end of free education up to the university level, 24 percent; (3) the end of free health care, 32 percent; (4) unemployment, 30 percent; and (5) chaos and killings during the transition, 51 per-

cent. However, 68 percent of the individuals interviewed thought that capitalism would be the best economic system for Cuba.[34] Fears do not seem to preclude a desire for fundamental change. This conclusion is also supported by the fact that, in the Roberts et al. survey, 88 percent said that both political and economic changes are necessary in Cuba.[35]

The CEON questionnaire, answered by members of civil society groups in Cuba, shows that, according to the activists' perceptions, although citizens fear possible consequences of transitions to democracy and to markets, people nevertheless want both transitions to take place. The fears cannot explain the low degree of popular participation in opposition activities. All groups in the study affirmed that people have fears about a political transition. The most common are that: (1) there will be violence and revenge; (2) exiles will take away their homes by claims to confiscated property; and (3) people will lose access to free education and health care. The CEON questionnaire also asked if activists perceive that there are fears in the population about a transition to a market economy. Fifty-seven percent of the groups in the study say that at least some people have fears about a transition to markets. For example, people fear a high degree of unemployment and losing a social safety net, such as retirement benefits. Despite fears of what could ensue from political and economic transitions, 86 percent of the groups in the CEON study maintain that citizens want transitions to democracy and to a market economy. The CEON data basically replicate the findings of the Roberts et al. survey regarding fears in the population about transitions.

Sixty-six percent of the groups in the CEON study do not think that fears associated with political and economic changes in the population are responsible for the low level of popular participation in opposition activities. The rest of the groups believe that these fears play a minor role in explaining the decisions of citizens to refrain from participating in acts of defiance.

Concerns in the Cuban population about losing homes, free education, and free health care, as well as fears about physical security during or after a political transition, are at odds with declarations made by many opposition groups. For example, the Agreement for Democracy is a document signed in 1998 by forty-six opposition groups in the United States and twenty-three groups in Cuba. In it, the groups acknowledge that: (1) the citizens have the right to public health and education, (2) people should be protected from arbitrary expulsion from their homes, and (3) people should be protected from arbitrary aggression. Even the Cuban American National Foundation (CANF), which

64   *Democracy Delayed*

has a strong neoliberal orientation, in one of its documents (dated May 1993) entitled "A Transition Program," declares that once the dictatorship falls, the eviction of people from where they live should be prohibited and that their right of possession should be recognized. Moreover, the document advocates that all citizens, regardless of their ability to pay, should have access to education and health care. CANF advocates the abolition of the death penalty and the provision of guarantees for the physical security of individuals.

The disjunction between fears of political change in Cuba and the declared commitments of opposition groups could be explained by deficient communication between the opposition groups and the general population. The paucity of samizdat literature in Cuba and the jamming of Radio and TV Martí by the Cuban government are fundamental obstacles to the ability of democratic activists, inside and outside Cuba, to communicate with the people in the island. Even under the assumption that if the opposition were able to communicate with the population in the island, people would not believe the promises of the opposition, the fact is that the available evidence shows that people now want transitions to democracy and to markets. Thus this desire is not contingent on people trusting the promises of the opposition.

A second alternative explanation for the low degree of participation by the population in opposition activities is that people have a negative perception of activists. The survey conducted by Roberts et al., however, shows that most people in Cuba sympathize with members of independent groups in the island. Only 14 percent of the respondents in the survey said that people have a negative opinion of activists, while 80 percent reported that people respect and/or help activists.[36] The CEON data are consistent with what Roberts et al. found. Eighty-three percent of the groups in the CEON study think the population is sympathetic toward independent groups. People provide activists with resources (e.g., transportation and food), greet activists in public places, and provide activists with information about government abuses. All responses in the study indicate that people perceive the efforts of at least some civil society groups as legitimate.

One group in the CEON study argues that people do not give more support to the opposition because people have little knowledge about what the opposition does. This idea is an additional indication of the importance of communication. Fifty-seven percent of the groups that answered the CEON questionnaire maintain that independent groups are not well known in the population, and 71 percent mention that citizens are uncertain about the aims of these

groups. It is reasonable to expect that the perception of these groups would improve with better communication. Seventy-one percent of the groups in the study think that, with some exceptions, people do not perceive leaders of independent groups as offering a democratic alternative to the Castro regime. Yet all the groups affirm that they want a democracy for Cuba. Another question asks whether activists perceive that people expect civil society leaders to try to meet the social, economic, and political aspirations of the citizens under a democratic regime. Again, 71 percent of the groups in the study report problems in people's perceptions of opposition leaders. The responses in this category are either that people do not know (because they do not have enough information) or think that only some leaders would try to fulfill the hopes of the citizens. However, responses to other questions show that all the groups want transitions to democracy and to a market economy. Three of the groups mention that they would like to preserve welfare policies of the Castro government, such as free education and health care. From the perspective of these activists, the aspirations of the population are the same as theirs.

Some in the United States criticize the material assistance that the U.S. government provides civil society groups in Cuba on the grounds that if opposition groups in Cuba are connected in any way with the U.S. government then the image of democratic activists in Cuba would be tarnished in the eyes of the population. Indeed, the Cuban government tries to damage the image of independent groups in Cuba by portraying them as agents of U.S. imperialism. Support groups in the United States have served as channels of resources from the USAID and the National Endowment for Democracy. The CEON data refute this claim. It is assumed that citizens would believe the claim of the Castro government that civil society groups are "agents of imperialism." Yet, with the exception of one case, none of the groups in the CEON study believes that the image of civil society activists in the eyes of the population would be harmed if people knew that they received assistance provided by the U.S. government. One group mentions that the aid from the United States is actually a source of legitimacy in the eyes of the population if the aid is used well and group leaders interact with the population in concrete projects.

Independent Communication and Political Efficacy

Knowledge of the fall of communism in Eastern Europe eventually spread in Cuba without producing a contagion effect. Perhaps Eastern Europe is not a frame of reference for Cubans and/or there is little knowledge about how

66   *Democracy Delayed*

those transitions took place. Huntington observes that contagion effects have been strongest among countries that were geographically proximate and culturally similar.[37] The apparent regional boundaries of diffusion effects is an interesting phenomenon that I do not address in this book. Yet, I discard the argument that "the Gorbachev factor" made Eastern European transitions unique and thus non-comparable to cases outside the region.

Karklins and Petersen argue that two factors that can foster mass demonstrations to demand democratization in communist dictatorships are: (1) increasing the consciousness among individuals that collective action will fail if the number of demonstrators is not large; that is, individuals should come to believe that their individual participation will be meaningful; and (2) making information about the time and place of demonstrations readily available to the population.[38] As in Eastern European countries, in Cuba the dissemination of knowledge about activities of civil society groups in their struggle for democratization as well as information about the spontaneous protests can cultivate a belief in political efficacy among the population.

According to Karklins and Petersen, in Eastern Europe informal social ties helped to spread information about the time and place of demonstrations. Individuals passed the directions by word of mouth in their workplaces, in social networks, and in transactions in the informal economy. While this micromobilization assisted in the dissemination of information, something else was available in Eastern Europe. Foreign radio broadcasts reached most of the population, and the production and distribution of samizdat literature was quite extensive. In Cuba, communication by word of mouth takes place, but does not disseminate enough information as widely as necessary to develop a sense of political efficacy in the population. Most people in Cuba do not know much about the activities and views of civil society groups.[39]

Differences between Cuba and Eastern Europe that are key variables in explaining the non-transition in Cuba are: (1) the dearth of belief in political efficacy among people in Cuba (this is the most crucial factor), and (2) the absence of channels of independent communication able to reach most of the people most of the time. The importance of independent communication for transitions can be evaluated by contrasting Eastern European cases with Cuba. To build a sense of political efficacy among the population, it is necessary for independent sources of news and information to reach a large percentage of the people on a regular basis. Independent communication of this nature is absent in Cuba.

Political Efficacy and Independent Communication   67

Opposition groups and other independent groups in Cuba have carried out a number of activities that can be considered successes of civil society. However, lack of independent channels of communication that could reach the population in Cuba prevent these activities from being widely known in Cuba. Successful activities have been: (1) labor strikes to defend workers' material interests from government abuses, (2) grassroots mobilization to demand resources from government authorities to alleviate shortages of basic necessities, (3) indoor activities by opposition groups, such as the forty-day fast in the summer of 1999, and (4) public protests under the protective cover of religion. Collective actions, such as protests, sit-ins, and strikes, to make socioeconomic demands on the government tend to be successful. In many cases the government has negotiated with the protesters and has sought to meet their demands, if only partially.[40]

Workers have engaged in collective action to ask for salary increases, to demand that fired workers be reinstated to their jobs, and to protest injustices committed against co-workers. For example, a strike took place in Santiago de Cuba on October 3, 1997. Two hundred and five independent truck drivers and truck owners went on strike to protest a 50 percent tax increase, and government officials sat down with the strikers to negotiate.[41] In March 1997, fishermen in Caibarién were fired by the government for keeping fish to feed their families. The crews of ten state-owned vessels went on strike to protest the firing of the fishermen. The strike ended when Communist Party authorities promised to reinstate the fired fishermen.[42] More recently, rail workers in a sugar mill in the province of Las Tunas carried out a successful strike on February 5, 2000, to demand back wages.[43] Small-scale strikes have spread throughout Cuba.[44] People in neighborhoods have joined together spontaneously to demand that government authorities provide them with food, water, medical supplies, or other essential needs.[45] On several occasions, government authorities have partially met these kinds of demands. The participation of citizens, who are not members of opposition groups, in spontaneous acts to make socioeconomic demands on the government suggests that people are willing to press demands on the government when they think that they have a chance of succeeding in attaining their demands. People are able to overcome their fear and go into the streets.

Despite the success that the Cuban government has had so far in controlling public spaces, opposition groups have managed to hold a few small, public demonstrations without being repressed on the spot. These public protests

68   *Democracy Delayed*

have been carried out in a religious context and labeled pilgrimages, even though what they have asked for is the release of political prisoners. On July 17, 1998, a pilgrimage of about thirty-four individuals went to the shrine of *El Cobre* in Santiago de Cuba. Participants loudly demanded freedom for political prisoners as they walked to the shrine.[46] The tactic was repeated on December 4, 1999, in Havana with similar success. After church services, about fifty activists marched silently from one church to another in Havana. The event was widely covered by the foreign press and by independent Cuban journalists. Marchers reported that the purpose of the activity was to demand the release of political prisoners and to denounce human right abuses by the government.[47]

The religious sphere in Cuba offers an example of the government's anxiety about the possibility of communication between opposition activists and the population. Ruling elites appear to be aware that such communication could lead to the development of mass protests. Since the current status of church-state relations calls for the government to allow some space for freedom of cult, the government faces the problem of having to tolerate ceremonies, such as street processions or important Masses in which large numbers of people gather. In this situation, the government has carried out preemptive arrests of opposition activists before the occurrence of important religious events or has prevented activists from traveling to the sites of the celebrations.[48]

The production of samizdat literature was much more developed in the GDR and in Czechoslovakia than in Cuba today. In the GDR, civil society groups received help from Protestant clergy to produce and distribute samizdat. For example, activists distributed hundreds of copies of samizdat literature at religious gatherings.[49] In January 1989, dissidents distributed leaflets in Leipzig urging citizens to strive for democracy, to be courageous in openly expressing their views, and to advocate freedoms of speech, of association, and of the press.[50] In Czechoslovakia, dissidents had the resources to produce a considerable amount of samizdat literature. The production of samizdat started in 1973 and grew after 1977, especially the political samizdat.[51] As of mid-1989, there were more than fifty independent periodicals.[52] With the aim of broadening activism, activists used the available channels of independent communication to encourage citizens to shed their fear of involvement in independent activities, even if the activities were non-political, such as advocacy of environmental protection.[53] In August 1988, an independent organization

Political Efficacy and Independent Communication 69

distributed leaflets asking the population to demonstrate, and about 10,000 participated in the demonstration.[54]

There is evidence that the spread of news and information through foreign radio and television broadcasts and via domestically produced samizdat literature played a fundamental role in Eastern European transitions. Radio Free Europe and Radio Liberty focused on coverage of internal affairs in the target countries. Samizdat works reached the population not only through its printed format but also via RFE/RL. These radio stations had "samizdat units" that collected samizdat works from the target countries to be used in their radio programs.[55] By 1988, Radio Free Europe was regularly featuring interviews with major figures of the opposition in its broadcasts to Poland and Czechoslovakia. RFE/RL also included interviews with dissidents in the programs broadcast to the Baltic states and Russia.[56]

Surveys done in 1979-80 with listeners of RFE from Czechoslovakia, Hungary, Poland, and Romania who had traveled to the West indicate that the majority of listeners considered RFE a unique station. Earlier studies of RFE listeners in three of these countries show that two reasons (jointly comprising 40 percent of the responses) for considering RFE unique were that: (1) our countrymen speak to us and give us moral support over RFE, and (2) RFE gives a truthful account of life, events, and problems in our country.[57] Interviews with large numbers of citizens in Czechoslovakia, Hungary, and Poland collected during 1974–75 and 1979–80 show that RFE influenced the opinion of the majority of its listeners. In addition, about half of the respondents thought that REF had considerable or great influence on general public opinion in their country concerning important internal political issues.[58] These data strongly suggest that RFE had the same impact on its audience and on public opinion in the late 1980s.

In Poland and Hungary, samizdat literature had an early and extensive development. Even under martial law, Solidarnosc issued hundreds of publications, such as the weekly newspaper *Solidarnosc*.[59] Jamming of foreign radio in Poland was intermittent.[60] In Poland, RFE provided an important means through which democratic activists communicated with the population. Solidarity used RFE to announce the times and places of meetings.[61] Jonathan Kwitny, a former investigative reporter for the *Wall Street Journal*, says that when he arrived in Poland in 1989 everybody told him that without Radio Free Europe, as an amplifier and conveyor belt for information, there would have been no Solidarity.[62] Jamming stopped in January 1988.[63] In Hungary,

70   Democracy Delayed

foreign radio broadcasts were not jammed, and in 1987, several dozen independent publications started.[64]

In the Soviet Union, the production and internal distribution of samizdat started well before Gorbachev became the leader. One estimate dates the beginning of samizdat publications to 1965.[65] But glasnost opened the space for a surge of samizdat publications as well as a significant reduction of censorship in the official press.[66] In 1987, several dozen independent publications started.[67] By early 1990, there were about 500 independent newspapers and journals in Russia alone and approximately 700 more in the other republics.[68] Jamming started to decrease in January 1987, when jamming of the BBC Russian language broadcasts ended. Jamming of most Voice of America (VOA) transmissions ended after May 1987. On November 29, 1988, jamming ended in the Soviet Union for Radio Liberty and for Deutsche Welle and in Estonia, Latvia, and Lithuania for Radio Free Europe. The same year, CNN could be seen on channel 24 in Moscow.[69] In explaining regime change in the Soviet Union, Karklins observes that glasnost fostered the transition by providing democrats with means of communication.[70] A demonstration took place on August 23, 1987, in Riga, the Latvian capital, and about 5,000 people participated. An organizer of that demonstration said in an interview published in the *New York Times* that, "without the western radio, we might have had 100 to 200."[71]

East Germans watched West German TV networks and listened to radio stations from West Germany. The communist regime could not block the electronic media from the West. A survey from 1985 indicates that 82 percent of East Germans watched West German television regularly and 17 percent often or occasionally. Saxonberg cites other survey data from 1988 showing that over 80 percent of East Germans watched West German TV and relied more on West German TV for information than on East German sources.[72] Western reporters and camera crews covered the opposition protests in the fall of 1989. For example, the attack on demonstrators by the East German police on October 7, 1989, was immediately broadcast back to East Germany by West German TV.[73] One example of the effect of coverage by foreign radio stations on demonstrations in 1989 is the broadcasts of the itinerary of the trains that Honecker ordered to transport refugees in the West German embassies in Warsaw and Prague across East Germany and into West Germany. The trains were scheduled to make a stop at Dresden, and several thousand people gathered there to try to get into the trains. When they could not, demonstrations broke out that lasted for eight days.[74]

Political Efficacy and Independent Communication   71

Dieter Buhl observes that West German television gave critical support to the opposition in East Germany in the 1989 democratic revolution. He argues that television served as a pulpit for dissidents. By showing mass demonstrations in East Germany, television conveyed the message to the people that the regime was losing power. Videos of protests recorded by amateur cameramen and verbal reports of the demonstrations on West German television were enough to incite more East Germans to participate in public protests.[75] By early summer of 1989, members of opposition groups in East Germany started appearing on West German television. From that time on, West German television increasingly became a stage for opponents of the East German regime. Dissidents could communicate to the population their criticism of the East German government and express their own political ideas. According to Buhl, these messages from dissidents helped to bring citizens into the streets in many East German cities.[76]

In Czechoslovakia, Radio Free Europe was difficult to hear in the cities due to jamming, but the BBC, Radio Free Europe, and other Western radio stations had better reception in rural areas.[77] A survey of Czechs and Slovaks conducted between June 1985 and February 1986 indicates that 77 percent of those interviewed listened to RFE or to some other Western broadcaster. Sixty-two percent of those who listened to Western stations other than RFE did not tune in to RFE for technical reasons (e.g., jamming).[78] RFE news programs had the largest audience among those who listened to the station.[79] Yet in Czechoslovakia, Western radio broadcasts ceased to be jammed before the surge of demonstrations in November 1989.[80] Jamming of RFE broadcasts came to an end in December 1988.[81] Also, glasnost in the Soviet Union contributed to the ability of Czechs to receive news and information that the Czechoslovak government would have considered subversive. Czechs could watch Soviet TV programs. On November 6, 1989, Soviet television broadcast an interview with Alexander Dubcek.[82] The BBC and RFE provided consistent and comprehensive coverage of dissident activities in Czechoslovakia. Members of Charter 77 and of the Committee for the Defense of the Unjustly Prosecuted (VONS) had their communiqués transmitted by RFE, giving millions in Czechoslovakia access to their criticism of the regime.[83] The day after the demonstration of November 17, 1989, the population in Czechoslovakia came to know what had happened through foreign radio and television stations.[84]

In Romania, foreign radio broadcasts were not jammed.[85] In the fall of 1989, Romanians had followed the fall of communism in Eastern Europe

72   *Democracy Delayed*

through foreign radio broadcasts and where possible on Hungarian television.[86] From the outset, foreign radio broadcasts played an important role in the events that led to the fall of Ceauşescu. Reverend Laszlo Toekes asked his parishioners on December 10, 1989, in Timisoara to help him resist the order to evict him from his church on December 15. A permanent vigil started in front of his church, and the news was broadcast by foreign radio. On December 15, when the authorities came to evict Toekes, a crowd of a thousand people had gathered outside the church. The clashes that took place then initiated the Romanian revolution.[87] The events in Timisoara on December 17 were reported by foreign radio stations. On December 18, the slogan "today in Timisoara, tomorrow in the whole country" was broadcast by RFE. News about what had happened in Timisoara sparked street protests in several cities throughout Romania and again were quickly reported by foreign radio.[88]

Hungarian television was seen across the border in Romania, and those who knew Hungarian translated for those who did not. Hungarian television tended to be watched by groups of twenty to thirty people crowded around a TV set. Four days before the uprising in Timisoara, a TV producer from Hungary went to Timisoara to film for a television program. He interviewed three Romanians who described what had happened in the uprising in Brasov in 1987. Then, when the uprising in Timisoara started on December 15, news reports and images were also broadcast on Hungarian TV.[89]

The Martís and Other Sources of Independent Communication in Cuba

In Cuba, almost every household has a radio and a TV. Roberts el al. found that of the recent Cuban arrivals to the United States surveyed in 1998 and 1999, 97 percent had a radio in their homes and 96 percent had a television.[90] One estimate is that about 74 percent of the televisions have the ability to receive UHF signals, the broadcast frequency of TV Martí.[91] Other surveys of Cubans coming to the United States as visitors or immigrants indicate that most people have medium-wave (AM) or short-wave radios. These data show access to short-wave radios in the range of 79 percent in 1990 to 90 percent in 1995. Likewise, the ownership of AM radios ranged from 91 percent in 1990 to 95 percent in 1995. Access to AM and short-wave radios is virtually the same among people who reside in Havana as among those who live outside Havana.[92]

The equivalent of Radio Free Europe/Radio Liberty in the case of Cuba is Radio Martí. It started to broadcast to Cuba in 1985. Its audience increased up

to 1990, when it peaked, and then started to decline due to increased jamming. Yet Radio Martí has had by far the largest audience of any foreign radio reaching Cuba. Radio Martí has been the main source of independent news and information for the population.

The Cuban government has not spared money or effort in jamming Radio and TV Martí. The jamming of TV Martí is practically total. All evidence shows that reception of the broadcasts among the general population is almost zero. For example, 96 percent of the people interviewed in the Roberts et al. survey could not receive the signal of TV Martí.[93] Yet if TV Martí could be seen, there would be a lot of interest in it, especially as a source of news and information. In a survey, 70 percent of respondents said that they had tried to tune in to TV Martí at some time; only 16 percent were able to do so, but only for 5 minutes or less.[94] The reception of other television broadcasts, independent from the control of the Cuban government, is practically nil.[95] One survey shows that only 1 percent to 2 percent of respondents watched Florida-based Spanish-language commercial TV stations.[96] In another survey, only 3 percent reported watching CNN regularly.[97]

People in Cuba have very little access to other sources of independent information such as foreign newspapers and magazines or to the Internet.[98] The government authorizes only some officials, scientists, and professors to have access to the Internet, a total of about 33,000 individuals.[99] The information coming in and out of the country via the Internet is censored and can be blocked. Public access is only provided at the National Capitol in Havana at the cost of $5/hour, in a country in which the average salary is about $10 a month. For foreigners, hotels offer e-mail services, and in one case the possibility of surfing the Internet. But, again, the Internet is not a source of independent information for the general population in Cuba. Few individuals have their own, private computer and even less have computers that are technically capable of having a connection to the Internet.[100] The Cuban case shows that the Internet is not necessarily a potent force for promoting transitions to democracy worldwide, as many believe.[101]

However, even in the Cuban case the Internet has helped spread information about the situation in Cuba. Opposition groups outside Cuba and other organizations have extensively used the Internet to publicize violation of human rights by the Castro government and other news and information about conditions in Cuba. One example is CubaNet, which places on its web site, among other information, articles written by independent journalists in

74   *Democracy Delayed*

Cuba. Such publicity on the Internet has promoted international pressures on the Cuban government to respect human rights and to adhere to other democratic norms. Such pressures provide civil society activists in Cuba with some protection from repression.

A series of surveys of recent Cuban arrivals to the United States shows the following pattern in the regular audience of Radio Martí: in 1986, it was 60 percent; in 1988, 80 percent; in 1990, 93 percent; in 1991, 78 percent; in 1995, 76 percent, and in 1999, 58 percent.[102] Self-administered questionnaires given to visa applicants at the U.S. Interests Section in Havana show that the regular audience was 54 percent in 1993, 26 percent in 1998, and 20 percent in 1999. Surveys done in Cuba among the population by research firms contracted by USIA also provide evidence of the decrease in audience. These latter data show that the regular audience of Radio Martí was 16 percent in 1994 and 9 percent in 1998. The size of the audience varies depending on the sample, but there is a clear pattern of decline over time. Since about 1998, numerous reports from independent journalists and democratic activists in Cuba maintain that government jamming makes it very difficult or impossible to hear Radio Martí. No quantitative data on the effectiveness of jamming have been collected, or made public, by USIA since 1995.

The decline in the audience of Radio Martí over time is paralleled by an increase in the effectiveness of jamming by the Cuban government. From the time Radio Martí started to broadcast in 1985, the Cuban government used low-power jamming. Then, an important point in the escalation of interference occurred in April 1990, when the Cuban government started high-power counter-broadcasting on Radio Martí's AM frequency, while continuing to use low-power jamming. Data to support the increasing effectiveness of government jamming from 1990 to 1995 are presented in table 2. Another turning point in the intensification of interference seems to have occurred in 1998, when the government installed a number of jamming antennas using Chinese technology.[103]

In surveys, people have reported that one of their reactions to increased interference of Radio Martí is listening to the station for shorter periods of time. For example, in a 1990 survey, 23 percent of respondents said that they were listening to Radio Martí less than in the past because of increased interference. The behavior of listening less as a reaction to greater jamming is supported by data showing that the average number of hours tuned in daily to Radio Martí

Political Efficacy and Independent Communication   75

Table 2. Increase in the Effectiveness of Jamming Radio Martí, 1990 to 1995

	Responses to Surveys about the Quality of Reception		
	Respondents reporting at least some interference	Respondents reporting little or occasional interference	Respondents reporting heavy or total interference
Early 1990	Within Havana AM: 23–30% SW: 19–27% Outside Havana AM: 9–20% SW: 10–23%		
Late 1990/ Early 1991	Within Havana AM: 48–54% SW: 34–43% Outside Havana AM: 45–61% SW: 35–52%	Within Havana AM: 41–46% SW: 30–31% Outside Havana AM: 41–42% SW: 33–34%	Within Havana AM: 2–13% SW: 3–13% Outside Havana AM: 2–17% SW: 2–18%
Late 1994/ Early 1995		Overall AM: 55–62% SW: 47–55%	Overall AM: 13–26% SW: 14–24%

Sources: Radio Marti Program Office of Audience Research, "Cuban Audience Survey: Radio Marti and its Competition," 19, 26–27; Office of Cuba Broadcasting, "1991 Cuban Audience Survey Report: A Survey of Media Habits of Cuban Arrivals," 3, 36–39; Office of Research and Media Reaction, "Radio Martí Audience Assessment: A Survey of Cuban Travelers in Miami, December 1994 thru February 1995," 24–25.

Note: Audience surveys ask about the quality of reception in the two radio frequencies, AM or SW (short wave), at different times of day. Data from Radio Martí studies are not very amenable to comparison across time because the questions asked and the information made available in reports tend to vary across studies.

by regular listeners was 5.8 in 1990 and 2.7 in 1991. Only 11 percent of the people interviewed stopped trying to tune in (for a time rather than permanently) because of greater difficulty in hearing the broadcasts.[104] The data for 1990 were collected before the Cuban government increased its interference of Radio Martí's AM frequency in April 1990.[105] Yet as interference increased after 1990, a greater percentage of listeners seems to have desisted from trying to hear the broadcasts. Survey data collected from late 1994 to early 1995 show that for 31 percent of the respondents the main reason for not listening to Radio Martí was inability to receive the signal.[106] More recent data, collected in 1998 and 1999, point to the erosion of the regular audience as a consequence of poor reception.[107] Greater interference seems not only to reduce the

76   *Democracy Delayed*

amount of time that regular listeners tune in, but also changes people from being regular to only occasional listeners (those who hear the station less than once a week).[108]

In Cuba, the domestic production and distribution of independent publications (samizdat) is practically nonexistent.[109] Since the end of the 1990s, some samizdat has been produced in very limited quantities, and the publications have been sporadic or discontinued.[110] The samizdat of opposition groups in Cuba urges the population to stand up for their rights and participate in the struggle for a peaceful transition to democracy.[111] These messages are on the right track from the perspective of fostering a transition from below. But unfortunately the amount of samizdat is meager. Insufficient resources are the main obstacle to the growth of samizdat publications. The distribution of flyers and other publications among the population is possible.[112] Some dissidents indicate that they would publish and distribute more samizdat literature if they had more resources to do so.[113]

The CEON study included a battery of questions on independent sources of communication in Cuba. All the groups in the study affirm that, with the exception of the publications of the Catholic Church, the amount of samizdat produced and distributed in Cuba is nil. Groups say that there are no publications or that some appeared but were discontinued or that there are few with very limited production; only one group mentioned this last alternative. One group says that it used to publish a bulletin that was very well received by the population. But this group had to discontinue production because they did not have the resources to continue.

Some in the United States argue that the production of samizdat in Cuba is impossible because of the high degree of government repression. The CEON study undermines this claim. Only one group argues that repression is the key reason for the absence of samizdat. Eighty-six percent of the groups say that the fundamental cause for the lack of samizdat in Cuba is that civil society groups do not have the resources (e.g., paper, printers, ink, and money) necessary for the production and distribution of samizdat. One group states that the production and distribution of samizdat in Cuba would be a powerful weapon in the hands of civil society. One view in the United States is that it would be futile to provide assistance to independent groups in Cuba to produce samizdat because the Cuban government aggressively tries to confiscate communication equipment, both at customs and in the hands of democratic activists.

Although the Cuban government can confiscate some of the equipment,

Political Efficacy and Independent Communication 77

it has been proven that equipment can be successfully smuggled into Cuba and used by democratic activists. Groups in Miami that provide assistance to the opposition in Cuba testify that whether the Cuban government succeeds in confiscating the equipment depends on how careful activists in Cuba are in concealing it.[114] Activists in the island have found ways to safeguard their material resources. The CEON data show that some groups maintain part of their membership anonymously to safeguard them from government surveillance and have them carry out opposition work in a clandestine manner, including keeping equipment in safe places. An interchange of ideas and experiences among nongovernment organizations (NGOs) in the United States that send material assistance to civil society groups in Cuba could increase the effectiveness of delivery channels. In a similar vein, groups in Cuba could learn from each other in trying to keep their resources from being confiscated.

CEON has demonstrated that there are ways to deliver materials successfully to independent groups in Cuba. For example, CEON has conducted a series of workshop interchanges with independent groups in Cuba by videotape. VCRs and video cameras were sent to independent groups. Workshops on various topics have been recorded in Miami and sent to groups in Cuba. In turn, these groups in Cuba record their workshops on the specified topics in response to those conducted in Miami, and the groups in Cuba send their videos to Miami. The history of samizdat in Czechoslovakia under communist rule and in the Soviet Union before glasnost are characterized by tales of how secretive the process was and how those involved in the production and distribution of samizdat risked being repressed.[115]

In the CEON study, answers to the question of what it would take for independent groups to disseminate their messages widely in the population synthesize some main points. All groups mention one or both of the following: (1) more material resources in the hands of civil society groups (e.g., equipment for writing and printing); and (2) foreign radio and TV broadcasts that actually reach most of the people and serve as surrogate stations for the opposition, both in Cuba and in exile, transmitting messages of democratic activists and news about their activities.

Although in the 1990s many independent journalists emerged in Cuba, their writings are published abroad.[116] The output of independent journalists is not directly distributed among the population in Cuba. Independent journalists reach people in Cuba indirectly. Some of their news reports are broad-

78   *Democracy Delayed*

cast by Radio Martí. Also, support groups in the United States reproduce some of their writings and send copies to Cuba for distribution. But these indirect means have considerable limitations in their reach.

Dr. Oscar Elías Biscet, a member of the board of directors of the Lawton Foundation of Human Rights in Cuba, understands the importance of communicating with the population. In an interview on January 20, 1999, in Havana, he maintained that "to develop civil society, it is necessary to reach the population. We need to inform more people, and not only us the activists but also the independent press has to reach the people. The independent press should publish abroad, but it has to publish for the Cuban people so that the people know what is happening in the island, not only through the [foreign] radio . . . but also directly giving to the people newspapers and documents."[117] In September 1999, an independent journalist observed that while the names of many opposition leaders and their organizations are well known outside Cuba, the majority of common folk in Cuba do not know who the activists are or the names of their groups.[118]

The CEON data, collected in 2000, provide further evidence of the effectiveness of the jamming of Radio and TV Martí broadcasts by the Cuban government. Every group says that TV Martí cannot be seen by the population. TV Martí programs can only be watched at the U.S. Interests Section in Havana. With respect to Radio Martí, all groups say that, in general, the reception is bad. It varies by geographical areas, by time of day, and by band. It is better on short-wave than on AM, but the SW frequencies are also jammed. Two groups mention that the AM frequency is completely jammed. Jamming is worse in the cities than in the countryside. It is reported that in Havana and in Santiago de Cuba (a large city in the eastern part of Cuba) jamming is particularly severe. Reception is better at night and during the early morning hours. It seems that the Cuban government makes greater efforts to interfere with Radio Martí broadcasts in areas and at times where the potential audience is larger. Despite intense jamming of RM programs, 83 percent of the groups estimate that the majority of the population tries to tune in to RM. This is indicative of the craving for news and information from independent sources among the people in Cuba.

Even though less people listen and those who do tune in do so for shorter periods of time, most people seem to keep trying to listen despite the poor quality of the reception. A survey conducted from December 1998 to April 1999 by Roberts et al. among Cuban refugees who had recently arrived in the

United States found that 58 percent of them listened daily to Radio Martí.[119] This sizable audience seems to be an indication of the intense desire in the population for news independent of the Cuban government rather than evidence of the success of Radio Martí broadcasts to penetrate jamming. The tenacity in trying to tune in despite high degrees of interference is reflected in most of the responses in an audience survey done in July 1998.[120]

The difficulty in hearing the broadcasts is also suggested by data from the survey done by Roberts et al. The individuals interviewed knew very little about opposition activists, their organizations, and their activities.[121] Moreover, many of those surveyed did not know about topics that must have been frequently mentioned on Radio Martí. For example, of the respondents only 29 percent were aware of the Cuban Council, 22 percent knew about the document "The Fatherland Belongs to All of Us," and 16 percent knew the document "Support for a Democratic Transition in Cuba."[122] So, the Roberts et al. study shows the apparently inconsistent findings of people reporting listening to Radio Martí but lacking knowledge about what is broadcast. This apparent puzzle is also reported in another survey done at the end of September 1999. When asked to name some of the programs they heard on the radio, many of the regular listeners recalled programs that had been off the air for a year or more and were unfamiliar with more recent programming.[123]

Consistently over the years, survey after survey shows that Radio Martí is considered by Cubans in the island to be a key source of news and information. Moreover, Radio Martí has by far the greatest audience of any media independent of the Cuban government. Other foreign radio or television stations, such as the VOA, the BBC, CNN, and Spanish-language radio and TV stations based in Miami have audiences in Cuba that are only a small fraction of the Radio Martí audience. Data from recent Cuban arrivals to the United States gathered from 1990 to 1999 indicate that audiences for the VOA have been from 1 percent to 8 percent, for the BBC from 1 percent to 6 percent, and for Miami-based radio stations 20 percent or less.[124]

News and information programs broadcast by Radio Martí have been popular among listeners over the years. This finding replicates the foremost interest of audiences in Eastern Europe in news programs transmitted by RFE. In 1990, Radio Martí's news and information programs had a much larger audience (ranging from 40 percent to 78 percent, depending on program and time/day of broadcast) than any foreign or domestic media.[125] Interview data from the end of 1994 and early 1995 show that 78 percent of respondents lis-

80   *Democracy Delayed*

tened to Radio Martí for news and information and that news reporting was a key element during the time periods when the audience for RM was the highest.[126] Data from 1998 and 1999 indicate the same high level of interest in RM news. In 1998, 71 percent of the respondents, and in 1999, 77 percent of those interviewed stated that they were interested in news on Cuba broadcast by RM.[127]

Evidence of the importance of RM as a source of news and information for the population in Cuba and data on the increasing effectiveness of the jamming of RM have now been available for years. It is technically feasible to improve substantially the ability of Radio and TV Martí to reach the Cuban population at only moderate financial costs.[128] For Radio Martí, it can be done, for example, by increasing the power of transmitters and broadcasting in more frequencies.[129] Yet the U.S. government during the Clinton years at the White House did practically nothing to counteract the intensification of jamming over time. During the administration of George Bush, jamming was a problem but not a major one. It is clear that the Clinton administration was not interested in improving the ability of the Cuban population to receive the broadcasts of Radio and TV Martí.[130] As I will argue in chapter 5, this attitude of the Clinton administration was part of a pattern of behavior that sought to maintain the status quo in Cuba. It now remains to be seen whether George W. Bush delivers on his promise, made in May 2001, to make the technical changes necessary to improve the reception of Radio and TV Martí in Cuba. On July 13, 2001, President Bush named Salvador Lew as director of the Office of Cuban Broadcasting (OCB). The OCB is in charge of Radio and TV Martí. In a White House press release announcing the appointment, Bush declared that "I have told Mr. Lew that my number one priority is to make sure that Radio and TV Martí are broadcast clearly to Cuba allowing every Cuban citizen access to accurate news and information. In order to do that, I have instructed him to use all available means to overcome the jamming of Radio and TV Martí. Once we open the flow of information, the demands for freedom will ring stronger than ever."[131]

In 1982, when the RM project was at the planning stage, the Presidential Commission on Broadcasting to Cuba argued that two AM transmitters were required for full coverage of Cuba with a strong signal: one located in Florida for western Cuba and another located in the Caribbean for eastern Cuba, since eastern Cuba cannot be reached effectively by AM broadcasts from Florida. The Commission also recommended using more than one AM frequency to

Political Efficacy and Independent Communication 81

make jamming of Radio Martí broadcasts more difficult.[132] In 1988, the Advisory Board for Radio Broadcasting to Cuba voted unanimously to recommend the purchase of a commercial radio station in Florida with the intention of upgrading it to have RM broadcast in a second AM frequency, as a measure to help overcome the jamming. The cost of purchasing and upgrading the station was estimated at $2.7 million for the 1990 fiscal year. But the Office of Management and Budget denied funds for the project.[133] In 1988, there were also plans to improve reception of Ratio Martí by using more powerful transmitters.[134] None of these plans were implemented.

Radio Martí currently (as of the end of 2001) broadcasts in one AM frequency and three short-wave frequencies. Until November 1999, Radio Martí AM broadcasts used two transmitters of 50-kilowatts each, and only at night was it allowed to combine the two AM transmitters to use 100-kilowatts. In November 1999, it was announced that the AM broadcasts of Radio Martí would start using a 100-kilowatt transmitter.[135] Despite the increase in the transmitter power for AM broadcasts, the jamming of Radio Martí still causes severe interference.[136] Radio Free Europe/Radio Liberty used a 150-kilowatt transmitter near Munich, West Germany, for AM broadcasts to Poland and Czechoslovakia.[137]

The permission by the executive branch to allow Radio Martí to use a 100-kilowatt transmitter came after a number of news articles in the Miami Herald and from independent journalists in Cuba reporting the problems of the reception of Radio Martí due to jamming. Yet the change in Radio Martí broadcasting was part of a pattern of cosmetic changes in Radio and TV Martí. In 1996, a response to the criticism that TV Martí signals were unable to penetrate the jamming was to switch broadcast frequencies from VHF to UHF channels. However, even before the change was implemented, it was anticipated that such a measure would not accomplish the goal of making a significant difference in the ability of TV signals to break through the wall of jamming.[138]

For short-wave broadcasts, Radio Martí uses 250-kilowatt transmitters. Since the 1980s, the international trend has been to use 500-kilowatt transmitters for short-wave frequencies.[139] In an initiative under the Reagan administration to improve the operational capabilities of RFE/RL, Congress authorized in the summer of 1985 the funds to install six 500-kilowatt transmitters.[140] Until then, RFE/RL did not have any 500-kilowatt transmitters.[141] RFE/RL started to use 500-kilowatt transmitters before 1989. Prior to the installation of 500-kilowatt transmitters, RFE/RL sometimes linked 250-kilowatt

82   *Democracy Delayed*

transmitters in pairs to increase the power of signals. The use of 500-kilowatt transmitters can achieve at least 50 percent channel effectiveness in a jammed environment, considered a reliable broadcast signal in such a situation.[142]

Besides utilizing more powerful transmissions, the number of frequencies used by RFE/RL to broadcast in key languages was much more than in the case of Radio Martí.[143] While Radio Martí uses three short-wave frequencies, RFE/RL used as many as thirty frequencies to broadcast in Russian during the evening and usually twelve frequencies at other times. For broadcasts in Polish and Czech, RFE/RL typically used eight frequencies for each language. The number of frequencies is more important for increasing channel effectiveness than whether the transmitters are 250 or 500 kilowatts.

As part of the technical improvements in RFE/RL started under the Nixon–Ford administrations and continued under the Reagan presidency, the number of short-wave transmitters was increased, making RFE/RL able to broadcast in more frequencies.[144] A transmitter modernization program begun in the Nixon–Ford years was completed in 1980, and RFE/RL acquired eleven new 250-kilowatt transmitters.[145] Then, from 1982 on, President Reagan launched a program to reinvigorate RFE and RL. These stations got $21.3 million for facility modernization and program enhancement and an increase in their annual appropriations. In 1987, a new 250-kilowatt short-wave transmitter was installed in Spain and eight 250-kilowatt transmitters in Portugal.[146]

Conclusions

In transitions by regime collapse, large and repeated protests to demand political change are necessary. These demonstrations do not take place unless there is a widespread belief among the population that individual participation in such acts of defiance is likely to be effective in achieving change, that is, there is a sense of political efficacy among the people. This feeling of efficacy spread in Eastern Europe at the end of the 1980s. It was scarce before that time. The belief in political efficacy is created under some conditions.

The transitions in Poland and Hungary, Gorbachev's decisions to implement glasnost in the Soviet Union, and his signals that the Soviets would not intervene militarily to save communist regimes in Eastern Europe supposedly generated a feeling of political efficacy among citizens in other Eastern European countries. But the development of a sense of efficacy in Eastern Europe was not entirely a matter of diffusion across countries. Domestic actors also

helped develop and spread this belief among their fellow citizens. What is important for the development of a sense of political efficacy are signals that change is possible, such as popular defiance and examples of partial successes against autocratic regimes.

In East Germany and Czechoslovakia, messages from democratic activists to the people urging them to shed their fear of involvement in acts of defiance and to strive for political freedoms, information about acts of opposition by dissidents, and news about the initial demonstrations must have been crucial in generating widespread feelings of political efficacy among citizens. In the GDR and Czechoslovakia, as in other Eastern European countries, dissidents communicated with the population via samizdat and through foreign radio broadcasts, especially RFE. West German television was also a channel of independent communication in East Germany. In Eastern Europe, foreign radio broadcasts reached most of the population, and the production and distribution of samizdat literature was quite extensive.

Two differences between Eastern European countries and Cuba that are fundamental to account for the non-transition in Cuba are that in Cuba: (1) most citizens do not think that their participation in protests to demand political changes will be effective; people feel impotent to bring about change; this is key to the explanation for the absence of repeated, large-scale protests to demand democratization; and (2) there are no channels of independent communication able to reach most of the people most of the time. The importance of a widespread belief in political efficacy and independent communication in accounting for the Eastern European transitions can be evaluated by comparing those transition cases to the non-transition in Cuba.

In Cuba civil society groups could, with greater resources and the ability to communicate with the population, cultivate a belief of political efficacy among the people. The dissemination of knowledge about spontaneous protests and other acts of collective action by citizens to confront the Castro regime would also help to foster a sense of political efficacy in the population. But means of independent communication in Cuba are either absent or severely obstructed by the Cuban government. News and information that can undermine the dictatorship must reach the people systematically. But the ability of independent sources of communication to reach most of the Cuban population regularly is a missing ingredient in the mixture of conditions that can promote a transition under the current autocracy. As the regime weakened in the 1990s due to numerous problems, like poor economic performance and

84   *Democracy Delayed*

greater discontent, and as the opposition movement has grown, the effectiveness of independent communication has declined.

It is technically feasible to improve substantially the ability of Radio and TV Martí to reach the Cuban population at only moderate financial costs. And civil society groups in Cuba could publish samizdat if they had the resources to do so. These are central obstacles to a transition in Cuba that could be removed by the U.S. government. The Clinton administration did not want to do so, as will be discussed in chapter 5. George W. Bush has promised to do what it takes to overcome the jamming of Radio and TV Martí and to significantly increase material assistance to the internal opposition. Let us see if he delivers on those promises.

CHAPTER 4

Assistance to Civil Society

Civil society activists can help develop a widespread sense of political efficacy in a population by conveying messages and information to that population. Citizens can be encouraged to participate in acts of defiance against a regime. Also, activists can inform people about outrageous acts committed by the authorities, and wrath can move people to engage in public protests. Activists can inform citizens about spontaneous protests, about labor strikes, and about socioeconomic demands on the government by grassroots collective action. Civil society activists can also organize their own demonstrations and inform citizens about them. In short, civil society can play a catalytic role in promoting the repeated mass demonstrations that can bring about transitions. These large demonstrations are particularly necessary in transitions from hardline regimes like those in Cuba today and in East Germany, Czechoslovakia, and Romania in 1989.

For civil society activists to induce a belief in the population that individual participation in protest can bring about change, independent sources of communication are necessary. In addition to foreign radio and television broadcasts as surrogate stations for opposition groups under communist rule,

86   *Democracy Delayed*

the production and distribution of samizdat, written by civil society activists living under the dictatorship, is also a means of communication among these activists and between them and citizens at large. But for samizdat to be produced and distributed in significant quantities in communist regimes, material assistance to civil society activists from abroad is essential. Material assistance from foreign sources is also important in other ways. It can increase the organizational capacity of independent groups. For example, in Cuba public transportation is in a disastrous condition. And other than high-ranking government officials, few people have cars. For independent groups to coordinate acts of defiance across the island and to distribute resources and samizdat, paying for private transportation makes doing these things a lot easier, as well as more surreptitious. The more coordination among opposition groups in carrying out acts of defiance, the more people participate in those activities and the more effective those activities can be in fostering a sense of efficacy in the population, if people find out about them.

In Cuba, humanitarian assistance to civil society activists out of prison and to political prisoners and their families can increase the membership and effectiveness of independent groups. One of the most powerful means of repression used by the Cuban government is economic strangulation of civil society activists and their families. In contrast to the situation of dissidents in Czechoslovakia and East Germany, the Castro regime has a policy of trying to suffocate economically civil society activists by denying them all legal means of earning a living. These individuals are denied jobs in public enterprises, as well as foreign establishments, and are unable to obtain licenses to work as independent entrepreneurs. To sustain themselves and their families is a daily preoccupation that saps their attention and energies from the struggle for democratization. Activists either engage in illegal economic activities, giving the government an additional reason to prosecute them, or they come to depend on the charity of friends and assistance from abroad. Activists frequently claim that if assistance from abroad were enough to guarantee a modest level of subsistence, a lot more people would become members of civil society groups. Larger membership could result in bigger protests, even if only activists participate. Consequently, there would be a greater positive impact on the sense of efficacy in the population.

Churches, the only legally recognized independent institutions under hardline communist regimes, can help civil society groups endure, obtain material resources, and communicate with the population. By doing these things,

churches can play an important role in fostering political transitions, even if the clergy does not have that as a final goal. Opposition activists can meet in churches and participate in religious activities with a higher degree of protection from government repression. Under this shield, activists can communicate their messages to those attending religious services and churches can serve as channels of material assistance to civil society groups. Churches can help bring about political change, but they are not essential for political transitions to occur. In Hungary, the role of the church in the transition was insignificant; in Czechoslovakia, the Catholic Church was very passive before 1988.[1]

In East Germany at least some clergy of the Protestant Church contributed in important, although indirect ways, to the development of mass protests. Besides holding the peace prayers in Leipzig, priests helped foster communication among dissidents and between dissidents and the population by providing groups in civil society with resources and opportunities for communication.[2] For example, dissidents were allowed to use church rooms, bulletin boards, and even printing facilities to publish samizdat literature.[3]

Opp, Voss, and Gern consider that the peace prayers in Leipzig were a necessary prerequisite for the emergence of spontaneous mass protests. The peace prayers provided a forum for discussion and served as a coordination mechanism for the initial mass demonstrations in Leipzig. During 1989, peace prayers became increasingly politicized and statements on current political events increased. Many people went to church only to receive current political information and opinions.[4] As I will show, top authorities of the Catholic Church in Cuba have prevented the Church from playing a similar role.

In Poland, the Catholic Church was conducive to the 1980 Solidarity uprising.[5] The Church provided forums for the dissemination of ideas and values different from those of the communist regime. For example, the Church established and maintained an independent university, the Catholic University of Lublin. Sometimes, the Church publicly criticized the regime. After the 1976 workers' revolt was suppressed, the Church assisted the Committee in Defense of the Workers (KOR) in its attempt to end the prosecution of workers. KOR was the group that first succeeded in bringing workers and intellectuals together to struggle against the regime, leading to the formation of Solidarity in 1980. In 1976, the Church gave aid, and organized communities for this purpose, to people and their families who had lost their jobs or who were imprisoned as a consequence of the uprising. Some view the visit of the pope

88   *Democracy Delayed*

to Poland in 1979 as a model of independent organization of society and as a sign to the people that the regime did not have a monopoly on mobilizing citizens. The pope gave the Polish people moral support and encouragement in their struggle for democratization. After martial law was imposed in Poland in 1981, the Church provided support and refuge for persecuted Solidarity activists. Even if the Church in Poland until 1989 sought to play the role of mediator between the government and the opposition, it helped in important ways to achieve a political transition.

The Catholic Church in Cuba

Upon his return to Rome after his visit to Cuba in January 1998, Pope John Paul II stated that he hoped his visit would bear the same fruits as his trip to Poland in 1979.[6] However, this hope has not materialized. In an apparent contradiction of the pope's wishes, the Church hierarchy in Cuba has refused to help strengthen civil society. Cardinal Jaime Ortega, the leader of the Church in Cuba, and other members of the Catholic hierarchy have adopted a conciliatory attitude toward the government. In the words of the auxiliary bishop of Havana, Alfredo Petit Vergel, the mission of the Catholic Church in Cuba is not to topple Castro; consequently, the Church has not engaged in political opposition.[7] From the perspective of the cardinal and those in his faction, the mission of the Church is strictly spiritual. The Church seeks to distance itself from democratic activists.[8] It is not even willing to serve as a channel to send medicines to political prisoners.[9] The hierarchy of the Catholic Church in Cuba does not want to risk a confrontation with the government by helping democratic activists. The Church has printing facilities to produce large quantities of copies, but it does not provide democratic activists access to those facilities.[10] Nor is the Church willing to hold large Masses connected to some political issue, such as asking for the release of political prisoners. This behavior is different from that of the Catholic Church in Poland or the Protestant Church in East Germany.

The Catholic Church in Cuba, despite having gained a somewhat greater space for worship after the pope's visit, is much more constrained by the regime than the Protestant Church in East Germany was under communist rule.[11] Catholic schools are prohibited. The government has denied the Church access to the mass media, except on a few occasions. Permission for religious processions is often denied.[12] The government does not allow the construction of new churches. And of the 120 Catholic churches confiscated in

the first years of the Castro government, only five have been returned to the Church.[13]

The accommodating position of the Church hierarchy toward the government seems motivated by a long-term view in which the Church seeks to avoid a crackdown on the limited freedom of cult that has been allowed in order for the Church to continue to evangelize while waiting passively for the demise of the dictatorship. The Church hierarchy might also hope that by assuming a meek position vis-à-vis the government the latter may grant the Church further concessions. The Church keeps demanding access to the mass media, the right to operate Catholic schools, freer admission of missionaries to Cuba, and more autonomy for Caritas (the Church's humanitarian relief agency) to distribute humanitarian assistance to the population.

However, the conciliatory position of the Church toward the government has not moved the Castro regime to grant it greater freedoms to carry out evangelization and services to society. Thus, there is always the possibility that the Church hierarchy in Cuba might reassess its strategic behavior toward the government and the opposition and take steps to help the latter, even if doing so increases the level of confrontation with the government.

By mid-2001, the Castro government seemed poised to launch a campaign to hinder Church activities, especially in Havana. A list of measures to be implemented with this purpose was given to the Administrative Council of the City of Havana by the Provincial Bureau of the Communist Party in June 2001. A confidential document of the Communist Party of Cuba, which the *Miami Herald* made public in June 2001, describes the concerns of the Cuban government about religious and social activities of the Catholic Church.[14] The document is entitled "Political Analysis of the Religious Phenomenon in the Capital." In it, the government complains that the Church has increased its activities to evangelize, like going door to door. Another area of concern is that churches may increase the number of followers by providing humanitarian assistance and social services to the population, filling in voids left by the failure of the government to meet basic social needs. A third point of concern is the increasing number of Church publications.

Despite the political position of members of the Catholic hierarchy in Cuba, activists have used churches as places to meet and carry out symbolic political events. For example, during February 24–28, 1998, members from seven different dissident organizations in Cuba and other individuals went on a hunger strike to commemorate the second anniversary of Concilio Cubano

90   *Democracy Delayed*

and to pay tribute to the pilots of Brothers to the Rescue who were killed by the Cuban air force on February 24, 1996. The objective of the hunger strike was to promote respect for civil and political rights. Those in the hunger strike met at two Masses on behalf of political prisoners.[15] Some priests have been willing to accept requests from democratic activists to hold an occasional Mass in honor of victims of the dictatorship. But when the gatherings of dissidents at churches become frequent and the numbers of participants start to grow, the Church hierarchy moves to put an end to such events.

Sixty-six percent of the groups in the CEON study think that churches can serve as spaces where democratic activists can communicate with each other and with the population. These activists argue that there are opportunities for conducting symbolic acts of protests in churches, such as Masses on behalf of political prisoners, but such opportunities are very limited. Doing so depends on the moment, or on the priest in charge of the local church, or on the position toward democratic activists held by the bishop in the area. The groups in the study are evenly divided on whether they should use opportunities in the Church and religious activities to promote political opposition among the population.

The accommodating stance of the Church in its relationship with the state has led the Church hierarchy to halt opportunities for energizing civil society under the mantle of religion. One example is the case of Masses to pray for political prisoners held at the Santa Bárbara Church in Havana. Members of the opposition, other civil society activists, and independent journalists had gathered at the church to pray for political prisoners on previous occasions. But on March 1, 2000, the gatherings became a weekly affair, meeting every Wednesday. The number of activists participating grew. In November 1999, twenty activists attended a Mass.[16] On March 15, 2000, more than fifty activists were at the Mass, and the expectation was that the numbers would continue to grow.[17] Members of the general population attending the services showed solidarity with the activists.[18] Although the political police were present inside and outside the church during these Masses, they did not move on any occasion to disrupt the services nor to arrest democratic activists. The case seems to have been the initiation of a phenomenon similar to the weekly peace prayers at the Nikolai Church in Leipzig, East Germany.

From the outset of the Masses, the main priest of the Santa Bárbara Church, Oscar Pérez, had collaborated with democratic activists at the church. He read during the services the names of some of the political prisoners and asked all

Assistance to Civil Society 91

individuals at the Mass to pray for the prisoners.[19] Then, on March 22, 2000, the government reacted to what it perceived was a growing challenge at the Santa Bárbara Church and threatened to arrest all civil society activists who dared to promote Masses in favor of political prisoners at that church.[20] At the Mass held on March 22, Father Pérez told the fifty-eight civil society activists at the church that he could no longer allow Masses on behalf of political prisoners at his church and that dissidents could not gather there either. He explained that the government had complained to the Catholic hierarchy in Cuba about the Masses.[21]

The democratic activists chose another church in which to continue with the weekly Masses. On March 30, 2000, thirty-three dissidents gathered at the Los Pasionistas Church to pray for political prisoners. Members of the independent press in Cuba covered the event.[22] By the end of April, a priest at the church asked opposition activists attending Masses to stop using the church as a gathering place because the Catholic hierarchy had lodged a protest with the priests at the Los Pasionistas Church for allowing the activists to meet there. Yet the dissidents decided to continue gathering at the church. By May 11, the head priest at the Los Pasionistas Church, Carlos Elizarde, apparently in desperation, insulted and threw out of the church over fifty dissidents who had gathered there for the weekly Mass. Elizarde told the activists, "If you come back next Wednesday, I will call the police to have them evict you from the church."[23]

The position of the top Catholic leadership with respect to the government is not shared by some priests, bishops, and members of the laity. This faction criticizes the government for violating human rights and favors solidarity with democratic activists. A foremost exponent of the anti-hierarchy position is Pedro Maurice, the archbishop of Santiago de Cuba. He delivered the most explicit attack on the Castro regime in a public speech during the pope's visit to Cuba. His archdiocese is in Santiago de Cuba, in the eastern part of Cuba. Interestingly, members of the clergy in this region have been characterized by their advocacy of human rights and political freedoms.[24] In July 1999, the dioceses of Santiago de Cuba, Holguín, Bayamo-Manzanillo, and Guantanamo published a document entitled "Cuba, Its People and Its Church Facing the Beginning of the Third Millennium." It strongly critiques communism as a totalitarian or post-totalitarian regime, encourages people to struggle against it, and censures the Church hierarchy for not supporting opposition activists and for taking a passive position toward the government.[25] Public statements of

92   *Democracy Delayed*

the Vatican are in tune with clergy in Cuba who diverge from the conciliatory position toward the government adopted by the Cuban Catholic hierarchy.[26]

Eighty-three percent of the groups in the CEON study perceive that there are divisions in the Cuban Catholic Church about helping the opposition movement. Sixty-six percent of the groups perceive that the Church hierarchy in Cuba is against allowing civil society groups to use the spaces of churches and religion to convey their messages to the population. Groups mention that the Church hierarchy does not want to get the Church involved in politics and thereby get in trouble with the government.

Also, eighty-three percent of the groups in the CEON study think that it is not possible to channel material assistance to civil society groups through the Catholic Church. All the groups affirm that the Church has provided very little or no assistance to civil society groups. There is no evidence of systematic assistance to civil society groups by sympathetic clergy and laity. But in some isolated cases priests have promoted the struggle for democratization. For example, in May 2000, Dagoberto Valdés, the director of the Center for Civic-Religious Training (Centro de Formación Cívico-Religiosa), Zbigniew Romaszewski, a Polish senator who presides over the Commission of Human Rights and Legalities of the Polish Senate, and a member of the Polish Embassy in Cuba set up an exhibition about Solidarity and its struggle against the Polish dictatorship.[27] The exhibit was shown at the San Juan de Letrán Church in Pinar del Rio. The Polish senator met with the bishop of Pinar del Rio and a number of democratic activists.

International Material Assistance to Civil Society in Eastern Europe

Material assistance from abroad to independent groups in Eastern Europe focused to a large extent on developing means of communication such as the production and distribution of samizdat and on providing humanitarian assistance to dissidents and their families. This is an important difference, to the detriment of the prospects for a transition in Cuba, between the assistance that civil society groups in Cuba receive and those in Eastern Europe did. Neither USAID nor NED has spent much of its Cuba budget in financing two of the most effective types of assistance that civil society activists in Cuba can receive: resources for the production of samizdat and humanitarian aid.

Assistance to civil society groups in Eastern Europe before the fall of communism came mostly from the National Endowment for Democracy. Yet there

Assistance to Civil Society 93

were also other sources of funding to send money and other types of assistance, such as printing equipment, to civil society groups. Having various sources of funding not only increases the amount of resources but also increases the flexibility in the expenditure of the funds. In the case of Cuba, almost all the funding to provide aid to civil society groups has come from NED and USAID, mostly from the latter. The expenditures of the USAID Cuba Program have been subject to the Cuba policies of the U.S. executive, which as I will show, wanted to avoid a transition in Cuba during the Clinton years at the White House. The Clinton policy toward the USAID Cuba Program was to minimize the effectiveness of the program by misdirecting and in other ways undermining the effectiveness of the aid.

Before the creation of NED in 1984, Solidarity received between $300,000 and $500,000 a year from various sources in the West, mainly from trade unions.[28] Jan Hus organizations in several countries raised private funds to finance independent academic seminars, research, and samizdat publications in Czechoslovakia. In the 1980s, Jan Hus organizations in Europe and North America financed the production of samizdat literature in Czechoslovakia. Activists in Czechoslovakia acquired typewriters with memory, computers with printers, photocopy machines, and binding equipment for the production and reproduction of samizdat.[29]

The Jan Hus Foundation in the United Kingdom raised £7,524 between 1979 and 1982 for academic activities. From 1983 to 1989, George Soros's Open Society Fund gave matching grants to the Jan Hus Foundation. And from 1987 on, the National Endowment for Democracy also gave annual grants to the Jan Hus Foundation. In 1981, the Association Jan Hus was registered in France. It raised funds for the same purpose as its British counterpart. The Jan Hus Fund was established in Canada and the Jan Hus Educational and Cultural Fund in the United States. The U.S. Jan Hus raised $10,000 in its first year, but by 1984 ended its operation. The Canadian organization had very little money before 1985, but in 1985 raised enough money to distribute $10,000 in grants. Part of the funding for the Canadian Jan Hus in 1985 came from grants from the Open Society Institute and the Ford Foundation.[30]

In 1986, The Central and East European Publishing Project was created with money from a number of foundations, including the Rockefeller Foundation, the Ford Foundation, and the John D. and Catherine T. MacArthur Foundation. The Central and East European Publishing Project supported samizdat and exiled publications. For example, it provided money and equipment to

94   *Democracy Delayed*

publishers of samizdat in Czechoslovakia.[31] None of these foundations have granted any funds to help civil society groups or to facilitate the production of samizdat in Cuba.

The National Endowment for Democracy, from its creation in 1984, provided money to Solidarity. Substantial amounts of money were used to finance samizdat and humanitarian assistance. In 1984, NED made two grants for a total of $181,825 to support civil society groups in Poland, provide humanitarian assistance to political prisoners and their families, and finance the production and distribution of samizdat literature.[32]

In 1985, NED grants to help groups in Poland increased to $600,000. Most of the money was channeled through the Committee in Support of Solidarity and the office of Solidarity in Brussels. The latter assisted the Solidarity movement mainly with communication activities, such as the publication and distribution of underground periodicals. NED also supported many small independent publishing houses in Poland.[33]

From 1986 to 1989, NED funding for Poland amounted to $7,862,034. The grants were essentially for aid to Solidarity and to support other projects that sought to disseminate independent communication in Poland and/or provided humanitarian assistance to political prisoners and their families. Assistance to independent communication included the distribution of films and samizdat or other literatures sent to Poland from abroad. For example, NED gave the Institute for Democracy in Eastern Europe $116, 000 in 1987 to provide assistance, such as equipment and supplies, to independent publishing houses in Poland.[34] In 1987 and in 1989, the International Rescue Committee served as a channel for $1 million to Solidarity. These moneys were for Solidarity's social fund to provide health care and other social services to workers and their families.[35]

In 1986, NED started to finance activities in the Soviet Union. As in other cases of NED funding to Eastern Europe, the grants were made for the most part to projects with activities geared to the dissemination of independent communication inside the Soviet Union and/or to provide humanitarian assistance to political prisoners and their families.[36] Support for independent communication included the production and distribution of samizdat or the dissemination of literature or videos sent from abroad. For example, in 1986, NED made the following grants: (1) $175,000 to the Center for Democracy to provide material assistance to political prisoners and their families and $25,000 for distribution inside the Soviet Union of literature and videos pro-

duced in the West; (2) $38,550 to the CREMONA Foundation to conduct interviews with Soviet émigré authors (the interviews were videotaped and distributed in the Soviet Union); and (3) $25,000 to the Time and We publishing house in the United States to produce a greater number of copies of a bimonthly Russian-language periodical for distribution in the Soviet Union. Another example was the grant of $125,000 to the Center for Democracy in 1988. Its main activity was to provide assistance to independent publishers in the Soviet Union in the form of computers, printers, and manuals and software developed by the Center. For fiscal year 1987-89, NED granted $1,432,439 for projects on the Soviet Union.[37]

NED gave grants to activities in Hungary from 1986 on. For example, NED gave Freedom House $55,000 in 1986 and $71,000 in 1988 to help the Hungarian Cultural Centre in London. The Centre provided funds for distribution of books by Hungarian émigrés, samizdat, posters, tape recordings, and video cassettes inside Hugary.[38] In fiscal year 1988–89, NED funding for Hungary increased to $468,095. All of it, except for $74,615, went to programs that had among their activities the spread of independent communication in Hungary, such as literature or television commercials.[39] Between 1987 and 1989, NED gave $105,000 to the Foreign Policy Research Institute to publish a new Romanian-language quarterly for distribution in that country; the journal used samizdat writings from Romania.[40]

NED also provided funds for projects on Czechoslovakia. The first grant, for $30,000, was made in 1985 for the publication of the journal *Pravo Lidu* in West Germany for distribution in Czechoslovakia. The journal was published by exiled Czechoslovak democratic and union leaders. Funding for Czechoslovakia increased afterward. Between 1986 and 1989, NED granted $801,612 for projects on Czechoslovakia. For the most part, the assistance went to projects that diffused in Czechoslovakia independent literature and promoted independent cultural and scholarly activities. Grants were made to the Jan Hus Educational Foundation, the Jan Palach Information Research Trust, and the Institute for Democracy in Eastern Europe, all of which helped produce samizdat literature in Czechoslovakia.[41]

International Material Assistance to Civil Society in Cuba

Comparing the available data on international assistance to civil society groups in Eastern Europe and in Cuba, one can observe that the important difference is not in the amounts budgeted but in the types of activities financed

96   *Democracy Delayed*

and the actual amounts of aid delivered, which differ from the amounts budgeted for assistance. The vast majority of NED grants to Eastern European countries were to projects that sought to help in the production of samizdat literature and/or to provide humanitarian assistance to democratic activists and their families. Solidarity received a large part of the assistance for Poland, but Solidarity produced and distributed a number of samizdat publications. In the case of Czechoslovakia, the Jan Hus and the Jan Palach organizations also assisted in the production of samizdat literature. Activists in Eastern Europe got computers, printers, fax machines, photocopiers, supplies, and money to write, print, reproduce, and distribute samizdat publications. In the Cuban case, not even a single grant has been made with the intent of financing the production and distribution of samizdat publications inside Cuba.

In Poland, Hungary, and the Soviet Union the political liberalization that took place at the end of the 1980s facilitated the production of samizdat, and thus the assistance that was provided by NED found a more propitious environment for that activity than in Cuba today. But the contrast does not hold when Cuba and Czechoslovakia are compared. Their regime types and the level of repression were similar. As in Cuba today, no political liberalization occurred in Czechoslovakia. Yet the production of samizdat in Czechoslovakia was quite developed.

Another important difference between outside assistance to civil society in Cuba and in Eastern European countries is that activists in Cuba need more humanitarian assistance than in the Eastern European cases. The amounts of humanitarian assistance that activists in Cuba are getting is small. In contrast with Eastern Europe, one of the typical tactics of repression in Cuba is economic deprivation. Activists are fired from their jobs and are denied any alternative employment, including licenses to work as independent entrepreneurs. This situation contrasts with what occurred in Czechoslovakia. In the latter, if democratic activists were fired from their jobs, they could find jobs of lesser pay and status, in which they could still make a living. A professor might have ended up washing windows, but he could eat. Such is not the case in Cuba. Humanitarian assistance to activists and their families is important to increasing the strength of civil society groups. The majority of opposition activists are unemployed and have an especially hard time obtaining food. Oswaldo Paya Sardiñas, the leader of the Christian Movement of Liberation (Movimiento Cristiano de Liberación), portrays many democratic activists as barely able to find sustenance, experiencing hunger and not receiving assistance from abroad.[42] This is a point that is commonly made by activists in

Cuba. The inadequacy of humanitarian assistance not only erodes the existing democratic movement but also hinders its expansion. When activists can barely find sustenance, they are more likely to abandon their opposition activities. Consequently, the perception in the population is that joining the democracy movement is a road to a greater degree of economic deprivation than is typical for Cuban citizens; people are less likely to join.

Giving humanitarian assistance to members of civil society groups has political implications beyond helping their members. When civil society groups distribute part of the things they get from abroad, such as medicines and shoes, among the population, they foster solidarity. In some cases, neighbors have come out to defend dissidents against repressive forces after the opposition activists have distributed medicines in the neighborhood.[43] Even when activists do not distribute assistance in the population, when people see that dissidents receive assistance, the activists are more admired and respected. Sometimes, resentment among citizens toward the Cuban government increases because the government is not providing similar assistance to them. The Cuban government is aware of the political implications of humanitarian assistance to civil society groups and is worried about it.

To give some examples, at the end of 1999, two campaigns were organized in Miami to distribute toys to children in Cuba for the Three Wise Men Day, January 6. One effort was organized by the Corpus Christy Church. The toys were sent in the name of children from Miami schools to children's homes in Cuba via Wilson International Service. Of the 881 toys sent, the Cuban government sent 781 back to Miami and confiscated 99; only one toy was delivered.[44] In a similar effort, money was sent from Miami to an independent journalist in Cuba who bought toys in a free shop there to distribute among poor children. The government arrested the journalist and sentenced him to six months in prison for "hoarding toys." In another case, a member of the political police in Cuba informed an independent journalist that he was very worried about the humanitarian assistance that members of an independent farmers' cooperative had received. The assistance consisted of work clothes and shoes. Other farmers in the area, who worked for government cooperatives, were furious because they were working in appalling conditions without work clothes or shoes. Farmers working for the government were inquiring how they could join the independent cooperatives.[45]

The Cuban government has prevented the independent distribution of humanitarian aid by foreign institutions. Besides the political reason for cur-

tailing the distribution of assistance by independent entities, the Cuban government confiscates some of the foreign humanitarian assistance for commercial purposes or to distribute among government cadres. For example, the humanitarian aid that goes to Cuba through Caritas, the relief agency of the Catholic Church, is partially controlled by the Cuban government. The government has refused to allow Caritas to have autonomy in the distribution of the aid.[46] Government officials in Cuba have gone as far as to prohibit doctors from writing prescriptions for patients to obtain the medications in Caritas's offices in Cuba, even when the medicines are not available in government pharmacies. Caritas distributes the medications for free but requires prescriptions to certify that the patients need the medicines.[47] The Spanish chapter of Doctors Without Frontiers suspended its humanitarian activities in Cuba due to the desire of the Cuban government to control its operations.[48]

The distribution of humanitarian aid by some Cuban American groups is more successful in getting the goods directly to civil society activists because the aid is sent via numerous small deliveries, such as individuals traveling to Cuba and taking 20 pounds to 30 pounds of goods each. Yet the Cuban government has at times confiscated some of this aid. Sending cash assistance to democratic activists in Cuba is cheaper to deliver and more successful in circumventing the control of the Cuban government than sending commodity humanitarian aid. But Cuban American groups that want to send cash have little money, and the USAID Cuba Program prohibits using its funds to send cash assistance to civil society groups in Cuba.

This limitation is not based on any legal constraint regarding aid to independent groups in Cuba. Section 109 of the Helms–Burton Act has no limitation on the form of assistance that can be sent to civil society activists in the island. This USAID constraint on assistance to democratic activists in Cuba differs from NED assistance to democratic activists in Eastern Europe. The Jan Hus Foundation and other organizations that received grants from NED sent cash to Eastern European dissidents. USAID may not be the proper agency to send material assistance to democratic activists in Cuba. Its bureaucratic procedure in the disbursement of aid is geared to environments in which the recipients are governments or legal NGOs. In such environments, USAID can safely apply its requirements of documenting the delivery of the aid.

The prohibition against providing cash assistance to dissident groups in Cuba might be due to a bureaucratic accounting requirement. Also, USAID has

the practice of calling democratic activists in Cuba to check whether the aid that was channeled through NGOs in the United States was actually delivered. Personnel of the USAID Cuba Program or officials of the U.S. Interests Section in Havana visit democratic activists in Cuba to monitor delivery of assistance. Such direct and open contacts between USAID personnel and dissidents in Cuba can be risky to activists in the island. Civil society groups in Cuba are considered illegal by the Castro government. By providing the Castro government with information about who is receiving aid, USAID can assist the Cuban government in charging dissidents with illegal activities.

Some are skeptical about providing more material assistance to civil society groups in Cuba and doubt that U.S. government officials will be able to identify groups in Cuba that will use the aid effectively. Neither the USAID Cuba Program nor NED gives material assistance to civil society groups in Cuba directly. The aid is channeled through support groups in the United States, almost all of which are directed by Cuban Americans. The support groups work closely with civil society activists in Cuba. Over time, these groups have acquired extensive knowledge about individual activists, their groups in Cuba, and how well they operate. They know who is effective and responsible and who is not. The decisions about what kind of assistance, who should receive it, and how best to deliver it to democratic activists in Cuba do not have to depend solely on civil servants in Washington who might lack detailed information about civil society in the island. Those who insist on belittling civil society in Cuba and argue that it is wasteful to give substantial aid also object that civil society groups in the island are penetrated by government informants. These critics lack comparative perspective and knowledge about communist rule in Eastern Europe. Government penetration of dissident groups was standard practice in Eastern Europe.[49]

Material assistance to civil society groups in Cuba has been financed by grants from the National Endowment for Democracy and the USAID Cuba Program. Except for a grant that the Open Society Institute gave CubaNet (an NGO based in Miami), no foundation has provided material assistance to the opposition in Cuba. CubaNet provides some assistance to independent journalists in Cuba, but its key activity is to post on the Internet news about Cuba, including articles written by independent journalists in Cuba. What CubaNet produces is for consumption outside Cuba, since in Cuba the general population does not have access to the Internet. Other than the U.S. government, there is no evidence that foreign governments have provided material assis-

100   *Democracy Delayed*

tance to civil society groups in Cuba. If any has been given, the amounts have been insignificant.

From 1984 to 1991, NED gave a total of $780,000 in grants to the Cuban American National Foundation. These grants were to publicize internationally the violations of human rights in Cuba.[50] From 1990 to 1999, excluding the grants to CANF, NED gave a total of $5,269,452 in grants for projects related to Cuba. Of that amount, $2,091,365 (40 percent) went to projects that had among their activities sending literature to Cuba and/or providing humanitarian assistance to democratic activists. Humanitarian aid has been a very minor item in NED assistance to Cuba. Almost all the literature sent to the island has been written abroad in spite of the fact that samizdat produced by democratic activists in Cuba is more in tune and up-to-date with the realities in the island and the perceptions of the population. A samizdat bulletin about activities of civil society groups in Cuba, for example, should be more effective in fostering a sense of political efficacy among the people than a book such as *Animal Farm*. Between 1990 and 1999, only $153,750 of NED money was granted to projects that included the production and dissemination in Cuba of publications that had some articles written by individuals inside the island. NED has not funded any project whose primary purpose has been to help produce and disseminate samizdat in Cuba.

By contrast, of the assistance that NED gave to Eastern European countries, 65 percent or more (depending on country and year) was granted to projects that included in their activities one or more of the following: (1) the distribution inside Eastern European countries of literatures produced in the West, (2) sending humanitarian assistance to activists and to political prisoners and their families, and (3) helping the production and distribution of samizdat or other means of independent communication inside the respective countries. In the Eastern European cases, NED showed that it considered support for the publication of samizdat an important endeavor.

The grant-making policy of the USAID Cuba Program during the Clinton years was heavily influenced by the Cuba policies of this presidency.[51] The administration, especially after 1995 when it reached immigration accords with the Castro government, sought to maintain the status quo in Cuba.

Section 1705(g) of the Cuba Democracy Act of 1992 and section 109a of the Cuba Libertad Act of 1996 (Helms–Burton) called for appropriations to support efforts to bring about a transition to democracy. The U.S. government funds to help civil society groups in Cuba have been administered by the

Assistance to Civil Society 101

USAID Cuba Program. The USAID Cuba Program originated in October 1995 and made its first grant in 1996. In 1995, before the implementation of section 109a of the Cuba Libertad Act, the Clinton administration announced a token grant of $500,000 to Freedom House for its work on Cuba. According to a former government official involved in U.S. policies toward Cuba, it was an effort to counteract the Helms–Burton bill, versions of which had passed both houses of Congress.[52] From 1996 on, the budget allocation to provide assistance to democracy-building efforts in Cuba has been about $2 million a year.[53] Up to April 2000, the USAID Cuba Program had granted $6,419,275.

The literature that USAID-funded projects have sent to Cuba has been literature produced abroad, such as books, bulletins, and copies of the Universal Declaration of Human Rights. No project funded by USAID stated in its description the intention of helping the production and distribution of samizdat literature in Cuba. Although some office equipment has been sent, the amounts allocated for doing so appear to be very little. For example, an evaluation report of the USAID Cuba Program released on July 21, 2000, shows that the Center for a Free Cuba, which had received $900,000 up to that time, had sent 40 fax machines to Cuba.[54] In a similar vein, humanitarian assistance has not been a priority. For example, the largest program to send humanitarian assistance to civil society groups in Cuba, under the direction of the Support Group to the Dissidence (GAD), received, up to January 2000, only $370,000 from USAID.[55]

From the perspective of promoting a transition in Cuba, the USAID Cuba Program has had a serious flaw, that of wasting a considerable amount of its funds. During the Clinton years, activists in Cuba received as material assistance only a fraction of the USAID funds. Substantial amounts were spent on projects that were irrelevant or of little utility in helping the development of civil society in Cuba and promoting a political transition. A question that arises is whether this outcome was intentional. Was the ineffective expenditure of funds in the USAID Cuba Program a well-conceived plan to help avoid the possibility of undermining the Cuban dictatorship? A positive answer to this question would coincide with the policy orientation of the Clinton administration toward Cuba. Two key decision makers in the allocation of funding to projects under the USAID Cuba Program were the head of the Cuba Desk at the State Department and the official in charge of Cuban affairs in the National Security Council (NSC).[56] These policy makers followed the Cuba policy orientation of the Clinton administration. In one case, the NSC officer op-

102   *Democracy Delayed*

posed a project to provide food, literature, and office equipment to independent groups in Cuba because he said it was "subversive."[57]

The document, "USAID Program Mandate for Cuba," available on the USAID Cuba Program web page, states that the U.S. government intends to support activities that offer "favorable prospects for serving a catalytic or leveraging role in promoting a peaceful transition."[58] However, the Cuba Program has given large grants to projects that are practically useless for fostering a transition. For example, the International Foundation for Election Systems received a $136,000 grant to study what electoral arrangements should be established in Cuba after a transition to democracy. The U.S.-Cuba Business Council has gotten $567,000 in grants. In the USAID project description, the grant is to prepare for the post-transition period by surveying private-sector resources and making plans to help in the reconstruction of the Cuban economy. On its web page, the Council claims to assist U.S. corporations in donating humanitarian assistance to Cuba under U.S. government regulations.[59] Such regulations specify that humanitarian assistance must be made to individuals or independent groups in Cuba. U.S. corporations are not making donations to those recipients. They have donated food and medicine, but it has gone to the Cuban government, not to civil society groups in Cuba. I wrote a letter to the president of the U.S. Business Council asking for information on what humanitarian assistance the Council had helped deliver to Cuba and who the recipients had been. The letter remains unanswered. The Pan American Development Foundation received $236,700 from the USAID Cuba Program to show Cuban NGOs how NGOs function under democratic regimes in protecting the natural environment. Not only was it a frivolous project from the perspective of fostering a transition to democracy, but as of February 2000 the Pan American Development Foundation had done nothing with the money.[60] Also, USAID gave the American Center for International Labor Solidarity $168,575 and the National Policy Association $225,000 to try to persuade foreign capitalists investing in Cuba to respect the rights of Cuban workers and to promote democracy. All these examples suggest either that the official purpose of the USAID Cuba Program is not taken seriously by those who made the grant decisions or that there was a conscious intent to divert funds from more effective efforts.

Moreover, the amount of funding for the USAID Cuba Program pales in comparison to the funds budgeted for the USAID Democracy and Governance Program and in comparison to other cases of U.S. support for efforts to bring

Assistance to Civil Society 103

about transitions to democracy. The USAID Democracy and Governance Program had a budget of $507.8 million in 1998 and $664 million in 1999.[61] In the case of South Africa under apartheid, the "Comprehensive Anti-Apartheid Act of 1986" (Public Law 99-440; October 1986) set, among other policies toward the regime in South Africa, financial assistance from the U.S. government to help the civil society in South Africa in the struggle against apartheid. This law allocated $1.5 million (Title II, Sec. 202) for 1986 and years thereafter for a "human rights fund." This fund was intended to provide assistance to political prisoners and their families, as well as to help other activities on behalf of human rights. In addition, the Act provided $40 million for 1987 and years thereafter to finance activities to end the apartheid system (Title V, Sec. 511). Another example is the case of Iraq. Between May and September 1998, the U.S. government appropriated $15 million for Iraqi opposition groups.[62] These funds were allocated for such activities as organization, communication and dissemination of information, and development of agreements among opposition groups. Then, in October 1998, Congress passed the "Iraq Liberation Act" in which an additional $97 million in military assistance was authorized for Iraqi opposition groups. Moreover, it is reported that the CIA spent about $100 million from 1991 to 2000 in support of various groups in northern and southern Iraq.[63] Yet there is no indication that opposition groups in Iraq and in exile are stronger or more united than the Cuban opposition.[64]

An important question is why no bill had been introduced in the U.S. Congress to provide substantial funding to the opposition in Cuba, as in the case of South Africa with the Comprehensive Anti-Apartheid Act of 1986, until May 2001. Senators Jessie Helms (R-N.C.) and Joseph Lieberman (D-Conn.) introduced a bill in the Senate to provide $100 million over four years to civil society groups in Cuba. At the outset, it enjoyed bipartisan support, with ten other senators supporting the bill. Several days after the bill was introduced in the Senate, President George W. Bush declared his support for the proposed legislation.[65] The bill is known as the "Cuba Solidarity Act" of 2001. It specifies sending money, food, medicines, photocopiers, fax machines, and other equipment to civil society groups, political prisoners, and their families following the model of aid to dissidents in Eastern Europe under communist rule. The bill also instructs the president to strengthen the signals of Radio and TV Martí to overcome the jamming by the Castro government.[66] In a meeting with Cuban Americans at the White House on May 18, 2001, to celebrate the anniversary of Cuban independence, President Bush, directing his words to

104   *Democracy Delayed*

Castro for his jamming of Radio and TV Martí, said, "We will look for ways to use new technology, from new locations, to counter your silencing of the voices of liberty." In a sign of anxiety about the Cuba Solidarity Act, the Castro government immediately started to criticize the bill as soon as it was introduced in the Senate.[67] Yet the bill (S.894) seems to have experienced oblivion. It has lingered (as of January 2002) since May 16, 2001.

The major Cuban American political forces in Washington, the Cuban American National Foundation and the three Cuban American members of the House of Representatives, expressed support for the Cuba Solidarity Act of 2001.[68] Jorge Mas Santos, the head of CANF, in reference to the Cuba Solidarity Act, stated that "we now will actively support the brave individuals, the men and women who dare to speak out, that seek to promote democracy and human rights on the island."[69] It remains to be seen if CANF is really willing to push for a major increase in assistance to civil society activists in the island.

The Cuban-American Community and Assistance to Civil Society

The exiled community has provided little financial assistance to the pro-democracy movement in Cuba. To account adequately for this behavior would require survey research. However, various pieces of evidence point to a multi-faceted explanation.[70]

First, most exiles have never done much, if anything, to help topple the Castro government. They have been detached from Cuban politics. This is an interesting topic for research. Yet many others have contributed over the past forty years to numerous attempts to bring about the demise of the dictatorship. However, attempts to get Castro out of power have been met with a series of failures. Sometimes funds have been misappropriated. Consequently, it is understandable that some exiles are reluctant to finance further ventures.

Although fewer exiles today may be willing to contribute, recent fund-raising attempts among exiles in Miami to finance concrete political projects have been fairly successful. On August 16, 1999, Radio Mambí in Miami conducted a "radio marathon" to raise funds for the legal defense of seven Cuban exiles who were accused of planning to assassinate Fidel Castro in Venezuela. In eighteen hours, $57,000 was raised.[71] On another occasion, during the weekend of March 11–12, 2000, the directors of two radio stations in Miami led a group of seven radio stations in another radio marathon to solicit donations for the legal defense of Elián González. Over the weekend, more than

Assistance to Civil Society 105

$220,000 was pledged for the Elián González Defense Trust Fund.[72] No such effort has been made to raise funds to help democratic activists in Cuba.

Whatever the reasons for the lack of enthusiasm among some Cuban American leaders to give substantial material aid to the internal opposition, some strategic blunders by opposition leaders in Cuba and in exile may very well have contributed to the reluctance of the exile community to contribute financially. These strategic mistakes have slowed the advance on the road toward a political transition. Some dissidents in Cuba have adopted positions shared by the Cuban government, such as opposition to the embargo and petitioning for the return of Elián González to Cuba.[73] These behaviors on the part of some activists in Cuba must have damaged their image in the eyes of many exiles.[74] The majority of Cuban exiles have strong feelings in favor of the embargo and were ardent supporters of Elián González staying in America. The adverse perception among exiles of some activists in Cuba is reinforced by the fact that the international media tends to focus their attention on activists in Cuba who oppose the embargo, such as Elizardo Sánchez Santacruz, and/or who advocate negotiations with the Castro government as a way to bring about a transition to democracy. The idea of trying to get the Castro government to accept political liberalization, in addition to being perceived by exiles as a waste of time, is considered morally repugnant. Elizardo Sánchez Santacruz pushes his anti-embargo position at every opportunity and tries to portray other activists as also being strongly against the embargo.[75] He is an advocate of negotiating with Castro as the best way to achieve a political transition. He is probably the dissident in Cuba who is most interviewed by the international news media.

A number of exile leaders in Miami have been against U.S. government funding to opposition groups, either inside or outside Cuba. Among such persons is José Basulto, the leader of Brothers to the Rescue, and Armando Pérez Roura, a radio personality and member of Unidad Cubana.[76] Some, like Basulto, strongly resent the U.S. government, the behavior of the United States in the Bay of Pigs invasion being one of the reasons. Others criticize groups getting funding from USAID and NED because of jealousy. Unidad Cubana applied to the USAID Cuba Program for a grant and did not get it. Now Unidad Cubana denounces those who have gotten USAID funding. Opposition to funding from USAID and NED on the part of some exile leaders serves to undermine the fund-raising efforts in the community of support groups that do receive funding. Exile leaders who criticize the groups that work with USAID

106   *Democracy Delayed*

and NED claim that the groups are at the service of the U.S. government and lack the autonomy to determine their plan of action in struggling against the Castro government. Moreover, the critical position on the part of some exile leaders in Miami reduces the political pressure on Cuban American members of Congress to push for increases in the budget of the USAID Cuba Program.

The Cuban American National Foundation is the only exile organization that has succeeded in raising large amounts of private funds. This organization has been able to attract the contributions of wealthy Cuban Americans, spearheaded by the fact that the founder, Jorge Mas Casnosa, and his family are millionaires. CANF, despite all the economic resources it has available, had not provided sizable material assistance to opposition groups in Cuba until 2002. One reason seems to have been an aversion to many of those groups.[77] This may be due to the image problem mentioned above. It might have been a political calculation by CANF, not wanting to strengthen potential political rivals in a post-transition period. If this is so, it can also be seen as a strategic error. As long as the dictatorship in Cuba endures, there will not be a post-transition period. CANF may aspire to be the predominant group after the transition. In personal conversations with activists in Miami from different organizations, the common story is that CANF has provided assistance to some groups in Cuba, but only on the condition that the recipients follow the directives of CANF. This is a condition that most groups in Cuba refuse to accept. The scant aid that CANF had provided opposition groups in Cuba contrasted with public statements by the organization. On March 24, 1999, Jorge Mas, the chairman of CANF and son of the CANF founder, spoke before the House International Relations Subcommittee on Western Hemisphere Affairs. One of the demands made was for the U.S. government to start without delay a program of material support for the opposition in Cuba, similar to what was provided to Solidarity in Poland after the implementation of martial law in 1981. But CANF does not seem to have used its considerable lobbying power in Washington to push for such a program. At least, there was no visible sign. In May 2001, when the Cuba Solidarity bill was introduced in the U.S. Senate, CANF voiced strong support for the bill. Will CANF seriously push for this bill?

On May 24, 2000, Congressman Lincoln Díaz-Balart (R-Fla.) introduced in the House the "Cuban Internal Opposition Assistance Act of 2000." The purpose of the bill was to provide assistance (e.g., communications equipment and humanitarian aid) to independent NGOs in Cuba and to the victims of the most extreme political repression, such as families of political prisoners

Assistance to Civil Society 107

and opposition activists. No amount of assistance was specified, just as in section 109(a) of the Cuban Liberty and Democratic Solidarity Act of 1996. Actually, the Cuban Internal Opposition Assistance Act of 2000 did not call for any funds in addition to those made available under section 109(a) of the Cuban Liberty and Democratic Solidarity Act of 1996. The bill that Lincoln Díaz-Balart introduced did not seem to be a real attempt to provide substantial assistance to the internal opposition. One indication is the timing of the measure. It has been obvious for years that the assistance reaching the internal opposition is meager. Yet none of the Cuban American representatives had introduced a bill to increase the assistance until May 2000. Why then? Because in the spring of 2000, the most successful push to weaken the U.S. economic embargo came to fruition in the U.S. Congress. The real intention of the Díaz-Balart bill appeared to have been to help derail the anti-embargo campaign. An anonymous congressional source stated that the Díaz-Balart bill added a new ingredient to the congressional discussions about the lifting of the embargo on food and medicines.[78] This strategy is not new. In 1997, Senator Christopher Dodd and Representative Esteban Torres introduced a bill in Congress to lift the embargo on food and medicines. In February 1998, the Cuban American National Foundation reacted to the Dodd–Torres bill by promoting an initiative, introduced by Senator Jesse Helms, for the U.S. government to provide humanitarian assistance to the population in Cuba through the Red Cross and the Catholic Church. Ninoska Pérez-Castellón, a spokesperson for CANF, in a newspaper interview disclosed that the main purpose of CANF humanitarian assistance initiative was to defeat the Dodd–Torres bill.[79]

Yet the attitude among the exile community in Miami, including the Cuban American National Foundation, regarding assistance to the internal opposition in Cuba is changing. As indicated above, CANF has voiced strong support for the Cuba Solidarity Act of 2001. Something that has been going on for some time, and might explain at least in part this change in attitude, is an international campaign to publicize the courageous activities of civil society activists in Cuba and show that their goals are to achieve transitions to democracy and to markets.

The Cuban Revolutionary Directorate (Directorio Revolucionario Democratico Cubano) has been one of the Cuban American NGOs conducting this campaign. The publicity has been particularly strong in Miami. For example, videos have been taped in Cuba with images and messages depicting the ideas and activities of opposition groups in the island. Recognition of the merit and

the need to help these activists in Cuba has started to sink into the consciousness of the Cuban American community in Miami. The idea of helping civil
society activists in Cuba is gaining popularity. The negative perceptions of
civil society groups in Cuba that may have existed in the past seem to be dis-
sipating. To cite an example, the Cuban Revolutionary Democratic Directorate
held in Miami on September 9, 2000, the "Conference for a Free Cuba: Coming Together for a Common Strategy." The purpose of the conference was to
discuss ways in which the exiled community could provide political and material assistance to democratic activists in Cuba. About 200 individuals, including members of some Cuban American organizations, attended. The idea
of helping the internal opposition and coordinating the struggle for democracy among groups in exile and civil society groups in Cuba was enthusiasti-
cally received by the audience.[80]

Conclusions

The Cuban Catholic Church has not helped civil society groups endure, obtain material resources, and communicate with the population as the Catholic
Church did in Poland or the Protestant Church did in East Germany. Those
who have controlled the Cuban Catholic Church, mainly Cardinal Jaime Ortega, have followed accommodation with the government in an apparent attempt to maintain and expand its ability to carry out evangelization and services to society. Hence, the Church hierarchy in Cuba has distanced itself from
democratic activists and their work and has avoided the risk of a confrontation with the government by refusing to help the opposition. The conciliatory
position of the Church toward the government thus far has not been very successful in increasing its freedom of action. The Catholic clergy in Cuba is divided with respect to its political role. Some prominent members criticize the
government for violating human rights and favor solidarity with democratic
activists. But largely the conciliatory position has dominated the behavior of
the Church.

Greater material assistance to civil society groups in Cuba would increase
their ability to develop a sense of efficacy in the population. The membership
of these groups would grow, they would be better able to coordinate their activities and be more effective, and activists could publish and distribute samizdat literature to the population. In Cuba, humanitarian assistance to civil society activists and their families is particularly important due to the severe
economic repression. And, given the crucial role of communication in transi-

tions, the production and distribution of samizdat in Cuba would be quite valuable. But, in contrast to the material assistance that was given to opposition groups in Eastern Europe, the aid sent from abroad to civil society in Cuba has included very little humanitarian assistance and practically no means with which to produce samizdat. The nature of the assistance to the opposition in Cuba has reduced the effectiveness of the budgeted aid in promoting democratization. Also, the amounts of aid budgeted for Cuba have been meager in comparison to the assistance provided to democratic activists in South Africa under apartheid and to activists in other countries struggling for democracy.

The amounts budgeted by the U.S. government for assistance to the opposition in Cuba have not been much different from the amounts allocated to the Eastern European dissidents. But funds of the USAID Cuba Program have been wasted in projects that have been of little or no use to the internal opposition in its struggle for democratization. Both the form and amounts of the assistance provided USAID have been subject to the Cuba policies of the U.S. executive, and as I will discuss in the following chapter, the Clinton administration sought to maintain the status quo in Cuba while Fidel Castro ruled. Thus, the problems with the type and amounts of the aid sent to Cuba were in tune with a key goal of the Clinton Cuba policies. It remains to be seen whether President George W. Bush provides greater assistance to democratic activists in Cuba.

The apparent reluctance of major political actors and of many individuals in the Cuban American community to provide material assistance to opposition groups in Cuba may, at least in part, be explained by strategic mistakes on the part of opposition leaders in Cuba and in exile. Some dissidents in Cuba have antagonized the exile community, and some exile leaders, including those of CANF, were shortsighted about the importance of providing as much assistance as possible to the internal opposition. However, there are indications that a learning process has taken place as knowledge about democratic activists in Cuba has increased in the exile community. Members of this community now appear more willing to help the internal opposition.

CHAPTER 5

U.S. Policies toward Cuba

The centerpiece of U.S. policy toward Cuba in the 1990s has been the endeavor to oust the Castro government.   JORGE I. DOMÍNGUEZ

Our primary concern regarding Cuba is stability. Economic failure, political discord or civil disorder in Cuba produces potentially hundreds of thousands of migrants in the Florida straits in a very short period of time.

MICHAEL KOSAK, CHIEF OFFICER OF THE U.S. INTERESTS
SECTION IN HAVANA IN THE 1990S

Overview of the 1959–1993 Period

Before discussing the policies toward Cuba during the presidency of Bill Clinton, I want to provide an overview of the Cuba policies of previous American administrations since 1959. Doing so will identify the policy goals over time and whether anything changed in the Clinton years. An analysis of U.S. policies through time is also useful to address the common misperception that a key goal of the United States has been to topple the Castro government. I do not aim to provide a detailed account of the 1959–93 period. My contribution to the literature on U.S. policies toward Cuba is limited to the Clinton years. I focus on the Clinton presidency because that period is of fundamental importance in explaining the non-transition in the island.

U.S. policy toward Cuba in the early years of the Castro government was marked by confusion and uncertainty. This was due to two factors: (1) the United States did not take Cuba seriously, and (2) there were sharp disagreements in the Eisenhower administration about Castro. Some thought that Castro was not a Communist and that he would end up leading a democratic

regime. Others were of the opinion that he was a Communist. The first view predominated at least up to 1960. The result was a series of ad hoc reactions to Castro's initiatives. At the outset, the United States tried to establish good relations with Castro by ignoring his more provocative actions. Patience and understanding, however, failed to stop Castro from radicalizing the revolution. Major attacks on U.S. interests were met with some retaliatory actions. By the end of 1959, the U.S. government was hoping that internal political pressures would bring about the demise of the Castro government. Yet by March 1960, the Eisenhower administration decided to topple the Castro government. The plan included the creation of a unified political opposition, a propaganda offensive, support for covert activities in Cuba, and the development of a guerrilla force outside Cuba for future actions in the island. The CIA was put in charge of implementing the various aspects of the plan. On August 18, 1960, Eisenhower authorized $13 million for the anti-Castro program.[1] The intention at the time was for the guerrilla force to introduce exiles into Cuba covertly in order to carry out actions to help overthrow the government. But by the end of the Eisenhower administration, in November 1960, the CIA presented a plan to increase the number of Cuban exiles in training for an amphibious assault on Cuba.[2] As it turned out, the Eisenhower administration was the only one that really sought to overthrow the Castro dictatorship.

Kennedy thought, as he was campaigning for the presidency, that the United States could not get rid of Castro and could only attempt to contain the spread of communism in Latin America.[3] During the transition period between the Eisenhower and the Kennedy administrations, the CIA changed the plan from one of only infiltrating a guerrilla force to an outright invasion in order to increase the probability of dislodging Castro from power.[4] When Kennedy first heard about the new plan, he consented to its continuation, but was not committed to its eventual implementation. He just wanted to have the option of deploying the exiles, a contingency plan.[5]

Even as plans for the Bay of Pigs invasion were being developed, the Kennedy administration was equivocal about trying to terminate the Castro government.[6] A number of key men influencing U.S. foreign policy, including Senator J. William Fulbright, then chairman of the Senate Foreign Relations Committee, Chester Bowles, undersecretary of state, and Arthur M. Schlesinger Jr., assistant to the president, opposed the invasion. Those opposed to the invasion were concerned with a negative impact on public opinion toward the

112   *Democracy Delayed*

administration and the United States. Hesitancy about the goal of ending Castro's rule militarily and concern about public awareness that the United States was behind the venture led to changes in the plans that critically weakened the military effectiveness of the invasion. The most important change was the decision to drastically reduce air support for the invasion, which would basically leave the exiles at the mercy of the Cuban air force. Even if the chances of toppling the Castro government at the time were slim, the Bay of Pigs invasion was not a serious attempt by the Kennedy administration to eliminate the dictatorship.[7] According to Arthur Schlesinger Jr., Kennedy inherited the operation plan from the Eisenhower administration and perceived the 1,200 Cubans who had been trained in Guatemala for the invasion as a "disposal problem." Kennedy and some of his advisers thought that canceling the invasion and disbanding the expeditionary force would be politically costly, both domestically and in Latin America. They believed that the exiles would go around saying what they had been doing; the Republicans would call Kennedy chicken; Latin Americans would perceive lack of resolve on the part of the United States in fighting communism. There was also the potential problem that the exiles in Guatemala might resist being disarmed. Thus, Kennedy's decision was to send the exiles where they wanted to go—to Cuba, but as quietly as possible.[8] After the invasion failed, Kennedy visited Eisenhower to ask his advice on what to do next. Eisenhower asked why the necessary air support was withheld. Kennedy answered, "My advice was that we must try to keep our hands from showing up in the affair." Perceptively, Eisenhower responded, "How could you expect the world to believe we had nothing to do with it?"[9]

The Kennedy administration made two decisions that, before anyone even landed on Cuba, eliminated any chance of success that the invasion might have had.[10] One concerned the landing site. Originally, the expeditionary force was to land near the city of Trinidad, close to the Escambray Mountains, where a guerrilla force of about 1,000 men were already fighting the Castro government. The plan called for the invading force to link up with the guerrillas, seek support from the town's residents, and fly in a provisional government as soon as a beachhead was secured. If the exile forces could keep Castro's armed forces at bay for ten days or so, the provisional government was to call for U.S. aid. But Kennedy imposed a "low noise" constraint on the invasion with the objective of enabling the United States to deny its involvement in the enterprise. Kennedy considered the Trinidad plan to be "too spectacular." Consequently, the landing site was changed to the Bay of Pigs area, a

U.S. Policies toward Cuba   113

swamp far from the Escambray Mountains. Also, the plan called for the destruction of Castro's air force before the invasion by flying forty-eight sorties from Nicaragua. The first pre-invasion air strike of eight sorties wrecked five of the approximately thirty planes in Castro's air force. It was made to appear that the strike had been carried out by defectors from Cuba's air force. However, almost immediately after the strike, the suspicion that the United States was involved in the event gained publicity. Adlai Stevenson, then U.S. ambassador to the UN, was preparing to address the General Assembly on Cuba's charge that the United States had aggressive intentions toward Cuba. When Stevenson learned the true story behind the air strike, he threatened to resign as ambassador if further air strikes were authorized. Dean Rusk supported Stevenson's position, believing that the association of the United States with attacks on Cuba would be politically costly in the international arena. Kennedy ordered the suspension of additional pre-invasion air strikes. What remained of Castro's air force was left unchallenged, and it inflicted decisive military damage on the invading force at the outset.[11]

After the Bay of Pigs disaster, an act of war against Cuba had no support. Cuba was not seen as a direct military threat, to either the United States or Latin America.[12] Moreover, as part of the agreements reached by Kennedy and Khrushchev to end the Cuban missile crisis, the United States promised that it would not invade Cuba.[13] Since the Castro government could only be overthrown militarily, Americans came to accept the permanence of the Castro regime. The basic U.S. policy became one of containment. The economic embargo was maintained to reduce the resources available to the Castro government to promote guerrillas in Latin America and to advance communism elsewhere. But the embargo by itself was seen as insufficient to bring down the Cuban government. The United States considered negotiations with Cuba as another means of containing the international behavior of the Cuban government, not its domestic policies. Prerequisites for negotiations or normalization of relations with Cuba consisted of demands to change some of Cuba's foreign policies, such as ceasing to support guerrillas in Latin America and ending Cuba's dependence on the Soviet Union.[14] Yet despite the continuity of the policy of containment across U.S. administrations, the degree of animosity toward the Castro regime varied over time, with periods of colder or warmer relations.

By 1971, a clamor arose in the American press, supported by some in academia and in Congress, for the United States to end the embargo and reestablish diplomatic relations with Cuba. Some former supporters of the embargo changed

114   *Democracy Delayed*

their minds and added their voices to demands for normalization of relations. By 1974, pressures to lift the embargo intensified, and a resolution pushed by Jacob Javits and Claiborne Pell to review U.S. policy toward Cuba passed the Senate.[15]

During the Ford administration, the State Department reviewed U.S. policies toward Cuba and concluded that Cuba did not represent a security threat to the United States and that relations with Cuba should be normalized. In 1975, Secretary of State Henry Kissinger held secret meetings with Cuban government officials to negotiate the normalization of relations. Contacts with Cuban officials to explore the possibility of normalization started in 1974, at the end of the Nixon administration. Publicly, Ford eased the economic embargo by allowing U.S. multinational corporations to conduct business with Cuba from their subsidiaries in Latin America. In 1975, the United States voted in favor of an Organization of American States resolution to lift its economic sanctions on Cuba. But in late 1975, Castro sent 30,000 troops to Angola, putting an end to U.S. efforts to normalize relations.[16]

By 1976, tensions between the United States and Cuba had diminished. Cuba announced that it would begin to withdraw some troops from Angola, and that Castro would only give moral support to the Puerto Rican independence movement, in contrast to the possibility of providing material support. The Carter administration was encouraged enough by Cuba's announcements to seek a dialogue with the Cuban government. Carter's intention was to normalize relations. In April 1977, Terence Todman went to Cuba to sign a fishing and maritime border agreement. Afterward, the United States and Cuba established Interests Sections in each other's capitals. The Carter government also facilitated tourism from the United States to Cuba by easing restrictions on the expenditure of dollars in Cuba and allowing charter flights. The United States was moving toward normalization when the Cuban government sent 20,000 troops to Ethiopia in 1978. The same year, Katangese exiles entered the Shaba province of Zaire from Angola to try to capture land, and it was suspected that Cuba was assisting the Katangese. As in the Ford administration, Cuban military involvement in Africa brought U.S. attempts to normalize relations to a halt. Then in 1980, tensions between Cuba and the United States increased when the Castro government unleashed a mass exodus from the Cuban port of Mariel. The Cuban government announced that exiles could go to pick up relatives in Cuba, and a flotilla of boats sailed from Florida to Mariel. About 120,000 Cubans came to the United States. Once Cuban exiles were in Mariel to pick up relatives, the Cuban government forced them to take addi-

tional human cargo. Patients from mental institutions and criminals serving time in prison were sent along with the exiles' relatives.[17]

Despite the tough rhetoric of the Reagan administration against the Cuban government, Reagan basically continued the containment policy that had been the hallmark of U.S. policy toward Cuba since the Kennedy presidency.[18] During the first year of the Reagan administration, Alexander Haig, then secretary of state, raised the issue of blockading Cuba and possibly moving to overthrow the Castro government. The main motivation was to end arms supplies to the guerrillas in El Salvador. Haig wanted to "go to the source." Officials in the Reagan administration believed that taking such actions against the Cuban government would require substantial military efforts and that there was not enough support among the American people for such actions. In addition, Secretary of Defense Caspar Weinberger feared that the Soviet Union might intervene militarily in another part of the world in response to a U.S. invasion of Cuba.[19] The primary concern of the Reagan administration regarding Cuba was the international behavior of the Castro government, and the U.S. response was to increase the economic and diplomatic costs to Cuba by maintaining the economic embargo and not reestablishing diplomatic relations with the island.[20] Reagan also sought negotiations with the Cuban government to get Cuba to take back those from Mariel who were mentally ill or had committed serious crimes. After that was accomplished, Reagan sought to reach an agreement to establish normal migration from Cuba.[21]

Under Reagan, the relations between the United States and Cuba were colder than under the presidencies of Ford and Carter. The Reagan administration's steadfast support for Radio Martí as a surrogate radio station focusing on news about Cuba was crucial to the establishment of the station. Some senators and the National Association of Broadcasters strongly opposed the project. Antagonists to Radio Martí almost succeeded in preventing RM from being a surrogate station. Opponents to RM wanted the station to be a branch of the Voice of America without a Cuba focus. Reagan did not intend to topple Castro with the establishment of Radio Martí. At the time, bringing about the demise of the Cuban dictatorship was not considered possible without a U.S. military invasion. Radio Martí was a measure to break the dictatorship's monopoly on information in Cuba. Another way in which the United States pounded the Castro government was by tightening economic sanctions. The restrictions on travel from the United States to Cuba that Carter had relaxed were reimposed, and a legal challenge in U.S. courts to end all travel restrictions to Cuba was defeated by the administration.[22]

116   *Democracy Delayed*

George Bush adopted a passive position with respect to Cuba, neither increasing nor decreasing tensions, apparently due to the belief that after the end of communist rule in the Soviet Union the Castro government would fall on its own.[23] From 1989 to 1991, Bush opposed a bill proposed by Connie March (R-Fla.) to prohibit subsidiaries of U.S. firms in third world countries from trading with Cuba. In 1992, Bush also opposed the Cuban Democracy Act (CDA), a bill introduced by Robert Torricelli (D-N.J.) and Senator Bob Graham (D-Fla.). The CDA had two tracks. One was to strengthen the embargo by prohibiting U.S. subsidiaries from doing business with Cuba. The other (track-II) was to increase contact with Cubans in the island, including providing assistance to independent groups in Cuba. It was not until Bill Clinton, as a presidential candidate, endorsed the bill that Bush decided to support it and signed the bill into law two weeks before the presidential election. Clinton decided to back the CDA in exchange for financial contributions from Cuban Americans and to force Bush to spend time and money in Florida to compete for the Cuban American vote.[24]

Policies during the Clinton Administrations

During the last two years of the Bush administration, the serious troubles faced by the Cuban government in the 1990s were just starting to become evident. It was not until Bill Clinton became president that the extent of the deterioration of the Cuban economic, social, and political circumstances became obvious. The cracks in the dictatorship widened and became more visible. Opposition and other independent groups started to grow in 1995, coalescing into Concilio Cubano in 1996. For the first time since 1959, a political transition in Cuba pushed by civil society groups and the population in a nonviolent manner became possible. Sending the Marines or arming Cuban exiles was no longer necessary to topple the dictatorship.

The long-standing policy since the Kennedy administration of containment as the guiding principle of U.S. policy toward Cuba was no longer justifiable. With the loss of its Soviet patron and the transitions to democracy in Eastern Europe, Castro was too weak to pose a threat to other countries or to engage in international ventures to help spread communism.[25] The discourse of the U.S. executive about prerequisites for the normalization of relations with Cuba could no longer focus on Cuba's international behavior.

During the Clinton administration, the spotlight was placed on the domestic policies of the Cuban government.[26] The issues of democratization

and respect for human rights came to the forefront. The rhetoric of the U.S. executive about Cuba was full of references to the desirability of a transition to democracy in Cuba. Many scholars took these pronouncements at face value and asserted that the public statements of the Clinton administration showed that the aim of the U.S. executive was to topple Castro. Indeed, the received view is that Clinton wanted to bring about the demise of the dictatorship.[27] Scholars who make this assumption argue that since Cuba no longer represents a security threat to the United States, the failure of the United States to normalize relations with Cuba can only be understood as the desire of the United States to bring about a political transition in Cuba. The asserted aim to overthrow the Castro government is seen as contrary to balance of power precepts and thus in need of an explanation. Jorge Domínguez explains U.S. policy by claiming that it is motivated by ideology.[28]

U.S. policies toward Cuba underwent a fundamental change under the Clinton administration. Containment was no longer the main motivation for the Cuba policies of the executive.[29] But Clinton did not want to bring about the demise of the Castro government either. Although it may sound unbelievable, given four decades of contentious relations between Cuba and the United States, the main purpose of the Clinton administration was to maintain the status quo in Cuba despite the opportunity to bring about a political transition in the island. The Clinton administration sought to avoid doing anything that might have jeopardized the Castro government. Ideology did not play a role. Quite to the contrary, the Clinton administration subordinated the ideal of establishing democracy in Cuba to other considerations. Concerning the Castro government, Clinton basically stood Eisenhower on his head.

From Clinton's inauguration until the 1994 wave of Cuban rafters, the Cuba policies of the Clinton administration exhibited ambivalence.[30] U.S. officials used strong words to criticize the Cuban government and maintained the economic pressure incorporated in the Cuban Democracy Act.[31] At the same time, the U.S. executive showed signs of being conciliatory toward the Castro government.[32] But following the wave of rafters from Cuba in 1994, the Clinton administration settled into a pattern of trying to ease tensions with the Cuban regime and abstaining from measures that could subvert it.

In 1994, the Castro government, once again, unleashed a migration wave by telling the population in Cuba that people would not be stopped if they wanted to leave the country by sea. This occurred at a time when there was a

118   *Democracy Delayed*

deep anti-immigration mood in the United States. As the migration flow to Florida increased, White House aides told one another, "no new Mariel."[33]

Eventually, the Clinton administration effectively ended the decades-long policy of welcoming Cuban refugees into the United States and ordered the Coast Guard to intercept rafters at sea and take them to the U.S. naval base at Guantanamo, Cuba. The Cuban government kept letting rafters go, and the wave of migration continued, undeterred by the prospect of spending time in Guantanamo. When the number of Cubans detained at Guantanamo grew, the Clinton administration sought negotiations with the Castro government. Clinton ordered Peter Tarnoff, undersecretary of political affairs at the State Department, and other officials to seek an agreement with the Cuban government to end the outflow of migrants to the United States.[34]

In September 1994, the United States and Cuba reached a migration agreement and declared that they had a mutual interest in preventing rafters from coming to the United States. The Cuban government committed itself to preventing another wave of rafters. In turn, the U.S. administration agreed to accept at least 20,000 Cubans a year into the United States. In a subsequent deal with the Clinton government in May 1995, Castro consented to taking back future rafters apprehended by the U.S. Coast Guard before touching U.S. soil.[35]

In 1994, congressmen observed that Clinton was not interested in promoting the end of the Castro dictatorship. From 1994 on, the U.S. executive signaled on various occasions that it wanted to lift or loosen the economic embargo on Cuba, including a National Security Council paper suggesting that the embargo be terminated.[36] In December 1994, as part of the effort to smooth ties with the Castro government, Clinton ordered U.S. intelligence personnel to stop active recruitment of new agents in Cuba and to cease activities in the island aimed at destabilizing the Cuban government.[37] Then, Clinton opposed the Helms–Burton bill, designed to strengthen the U.S. embargo, while its supporters sought to obtain congressional approval in 1995. The administration enlisted corporate executives in opposing the bill.[38] The effort to involve U.S. businessmen in campaigns against the embargo was later escalated with the help of the Cuban government. In October 1995, the Clinton administration relaxed travel and other restrictions on Cuba. In an interview with journalists in June 2000, Clinton stated that he was moving toward normalization of relations with Cuba when Castro shot down the Brothers to

the Rescue planes.[39] In the view of Elliot Abrams, former assistant secretary of state, individuals in the administration such as Samuel Berger, Peter Tarnoff, and Morton Halperin perceived the embargo as a fossil of the cold war and advocated normalization of relations with the Cuban government.[40] Even after the planes were destroyed, Clinton retained the ban on covert operations by the CIA in Cuba.[41]

On February 24, 1996, the Cuban air force shot down two small, unarmed U.S. civilian aircraft in international air space, killing the four men who piloted the planes. Clinton had no choice but to sign the Helms–Burton bill into law. He did so on March 12, 1996. The support in Congress for the bill was such that a Clinton veto would have been overridden. Yet Clinton was able to negotiate a deal with the main congressional backers of the legislative proposal to include a waiver for Title III of the bill,[42] which allowed Clinton to suspend the implementation of the title for periods of six months at a time. Title III of the Helms–Burton Act has never been implemented, and Title IV hardly. Titles III and IV aim at hindering foreign investment in properties confiscated from Americans or Cubans by the Castro government.

The Clinton administration was sympathetic toward efforts spearheaded by members of the anti-embargo movement to weaken the embargo and improve relations between the United States and the Cuban government. For example, when Illinois Governor George Ryan went to Cuba in October 1999 to promote lifting the U.S. economic embargo, Charles Shapiro, then director of the Office of Cuban Affairs at the U.S. State Department, sent a message to Ryan saying that the State Department was "very pleased" with the governor's visit. Fulton Armstrong, the Cuba man at the National Security Council, called Ryan to tell him that President Clinton was "delighted" with Ryan's visit to Cuba.[43] The administration facilitated and encouraged trips to Cuba by U.S. businessmen.[44] And in July 1999, the State Department gave two Cuban officials visas to come to a reception in the U.S. Capitol to meet with agricultural leaders, part of the anti-embargo campaign in the United States.[45] In July 2000, after sales of food and medicines to the Cuban government were approved in the House and the Senate, Clinton declared his support for the sales.[46] In October 2000, President Clinton criticized the deal worked out in Congress to sell Cuba food and medicines for not going far enough in weakening the embargo and for its restriction on U.S. tourism to Cuba. He wanted to provide financing for the sales and was in favor of allowing U.S. tourists to

120   *Democracy Delayed*

visit Cuba.[47] Despite Clinton's encouragement to weaken or dismantle the embargo, he was restrained by the fact that the Helms–Burton transferred control over this foreign policy from the executive to Congress. Yet the president had room to maneuver in determining relations with Cuba, and he promoted a policy of "people-to-people" contacts between the United States and Cuba.[48]

In March 1998, the Clinton administration announced permission for direct passenger and cargo flights to Cuba and for cash remittances by Cuban Americans to their families. The charter flights were banned when the Brothers to the Rescue planes were shot down in February 1996, and the remittances had been suspended in August 1994. Also as part of the relaxation of restrictions in 1998, the sale of medical equipment and supplies to Cuba by U.S. firms was permitted. This venue for commerce in medical goods later led to authorization for U.S. firms to hold trade shows in Havana and for a subsidiary of a U.S. multinational to commercialize internationally a vaccine developed by Cuba.[49] On January 5, 1999, the Clinton administration announced a number of measures to relax restrictions on relations with Cuba even further. Clinton presented them as an expansion of the measures his administration had set forth in March 1998. The new measures included greater leeway to send money to people in Cuba, expansion of people-to-people contacts by streamlining visa and license procedures for travel between Cuba and the United States, and authorization of charter flights to cities other than Havana and from cities other than Miami.

President Clinton and officials of his administration justified the steps taken to reduce restrictions on transactions with Cuba and to promote people-to-people contacts in terms of helping the population in Cuba, developing civil society, and promoting a transition to democracy.[50] However, when one takes a close look at the Cuba policies of the Clinton administration, one notices that there was not a serious effort to develop civil society and foster a political transition in Cuba. The people-to-people policy of the Clinton administration can be better explained as an attempt to promote engagement with the Castro government, including weakening the embargo, rather than an effort to bring it down.

Clinton's people-to-people efforts were subject to manipulation by the Cuban government. An example is the authorization by the U.S. government for the baseball games between the Baltimore Orioles and a Cuban team. When the Orioles went to Cuba, admission to the stadium was not open to the public. The Cuban government decided who could get seats in the stadium.

For the game in Baltimore, Castro sent at least two security agents for each player. The players were kept under tight surveillance; they were not allowed to go sightseeing or to have contact with the public or with Orioles players. Despite the tight control by the Cuban guards, one player managed to defect. At least 2,000 tickets for the Baltimore game were distributed among opponents of the U.S. embargo, such as the Maryland Coalition to End the Embargo of Cuba. And on the giant television screen at the stadium, videos promoting tourism in Cuba were shown. Taking banners into the stadium was prohibited as a measure to prevent Cuban Americans from expressing their opposition to the Cuban government.[51]

The Cuban government also used U.S. visitors for its own ends. A key component of the anti-embargo movement has been to have U.S. entrepreneurs go to Cuba to meet with government officials to persuade them that they are missing very profitable business opportunities because of the U.S. embargo. As part of the anti-embargo efforts, groups of U.S. students traveling to Cuba have been shown indications of physical decay, and are told that the embargo is the cause. For example, in 1999, a group of college students from St. Joseph University went to Cuba. They said that they saw the effects of the embargo everywhere, and most decided that it should be lifted.[52] With a monopoly over the news media, the Cuban government has also told the population that foreign visitors have traveled to Cuba to show their support for the Cuban government. Such manipulation could be counteracted if independent sources of information were able to reach most of the people in Cuba. But the Clinton administration was not willing to make that possible.

Radio and TV Martí are under the control of the U.S. government and thus are part of U.S. foreign policy toward Cuba. As I mentioned in chapter 3, TV Martí broadcasts are completely jammed by the Cuban government, and the reception of Radio Martí has progressively deteriorated since 1991. Despite the availability of technical means to improve significantly the ability of these sources of news to reach the Cuban population, the Clinton administration did nothing to make it possible. Given the importance of independent communication for the development of a sense of political efficacy in the population, the failure of the Clinton administration to do what it takes to substantially improve the reception of Radio and TV Martí is an indicator of how far the public rhetoric about the desire to foster a political transition was from the actual behavior of the administration.

122 *Democracy Delayed*

The Cuba Democracy Act of 1992 and the Helms–Burton law of 1996 called for material assistance to civil society groups in Cuba. According to Peter Orr, former director of the USAID Cuba Program, Clinton's support for independent groups in Cuba was window dressing from the start.[53] Despite Clinton's endorsement of the Cuba Democracy Act as a presidential candidate in 1992, he did not grant any funds for material assistance to civil society groups in Cuba until the fall of 1995. That year, various versions of the Helms–Burton bill had passed the House and the Senate, and Clinton announced in October a grant of $500,000 to the Cuba program of Freedom House as a way to help derail support for Helms–Burton in Congress. The administration wanted to give the impression that it had a proactive Cuba policy.

The Freedom House grant was not awarded until July 1996, following prompting by members of Congress. One more year passed before the administration acted on grant applications that had been submitted in response to section 109 of Helms–Burton authorizing funds for assistance to independent groups in Cuba. The administration was spending the money budgeted for that assistance on activities in other countries. Not until members of Congress pressured the administration did it move to provide other grants to help groups in Cuba.[54] And as I mentioned in chapter 4, substantial amounts of the funds budgeted for assistance to civil society in Cuba were wasted on irrelevant projects.

I base my conclusion that the real intention of the Clinton administration was to maintain stability in Cuba on various indicators: (1) actual behaviors of the administration, in contrast to its public proclamations of the desirability for a speedy transition to democracy in Cuba, (2) personal conversations with Washington insiders, and (3) statements of officials in the executive branch who were involved in Cuba policies. The web page of the U.S. Interests Section in Havana has a document entitled "U.S. Policy Toward Cuba," which states that the United States remains committed to preventing mass migration from Cuba to the United States.[55] Administration officials often repeated that a "chaotic" transition in Cuba was undesirable.[56] The Clinton administration concluded that a political transition while Fidel Castro was alive would be chaotic and would result in a wave of mass migration to Florida. Hence, a transition while he was in power was something to be avoided. Statements by Clinton officials point to the administration's goal of preventing the collapse of the dictatorship. This aim was couched in terms of the desire to maintain stability in Cuba. Actually,

it is not unprecedented that U.S. governments have preferred stability over democracy in some Latin American countries.[57] On September 28, 1998, Michael Kosak, the principal officer at the U.S. Interests Section in Havana at the time, referring to U.S. policy toward Cuba, declared, "Today, however, our primary concern is the one that did not exist twenty years ago. That is the issue of stability. If there is instability in Cuba, United States interests are directly implicated. The geography of the two countries is such that economic failure, political discord or civil disorder in Cuba produces potentially hundreds of thousands of migrants in the Florida straits in a very short period of time."[58] In his remarks, Kosak stated that chaos can be avoided only if there is negotiation between political reformers in the regime and members of the opposition. But there are no political reformers in the regime. Thus, it is assumed that a push by civil society and the population for a transition to democracy, as it occurred in East Germany and Czechoslovakia, would be chaotic in Cuba and hence should not be promoted by the U.S. government. Kozak, in an interview with the *Miami Herald* on March 6, 2000, reaffirmed that the most worrisome aspect of a political transition in Cuba would be a wave of rafters coming to Florida.[59] Similarly, Michael Ranneberger, the head of the Cuba desk at the State Department until July 1999, stated in a speech given at Tulane University on November 9, 1998, that an unstable and chaotic transition in Cuba would be against the interests of the United States.[60] In previous remarks, Ranneberger expressed a preference for a "smooth landing" in Cuba and mentioned that members of the ruling elite in Cuba have a common interest with the United States in that type of transition.[61]

Those who determined the Clinton administration's policies toward Cuba wanted to avoid the collapse of the Castro government out of fear of a migration wave to Florida and possibly for other reasons as well, such as indolence toward the suffering of the people in Cuba, as Irving Horowitz suggests.[62] Apparently, the intention of U.S. policy makers in the State Department and in the National Security Council was to maintain stability in Cuba while Castro was alive and wait until his natural death to see if the regime type changed to make a transition from above possible, maybe along the Nicaraguan path. Stuart Eizenstat, undersecretary of state in the Clinton administration, stated in 1999 that a transition to democracy in Cuba would not occur until the death of Fidel Castro.[63] An apparent purpose of the relaxation of restrictions in dealings with Cuba and the people-to-people measures of the Clinton administra-

124   *Democracy Delayed*

tion was to build links with and confidence among members of the ruling elite in Cuba. Clinton officials perhaps hoped that members of the elite might turn out to be softliners (something very hard to determine since no latent softliner dares to make his views known) and play a role in a negotiated transition once Fidel Castro dies.[64] But what might happen after the death of Fidel Castro is highly uncertain.

CHAPTER 6

The Economic Embargo

Whether the United States should maintain its economic embargo on the Castro government has been a controversial issue for a long time, but since the Cuban Liberty and Democratic Solidarity (Libertad) Act of 1996, commonly known as the Helms–Burton Act, was enacted in March 1996, the degree of contention has reached an unprecedented degree of intensity.[1] Does the unilateral U.S. embargo on the Cuban government "work"? At a general theoretical level, scholars and political critics of the U.S. embargo argue that unilateral sanctions are ineffective.[2] They maintain that it imposes unjustified costs on U.S. firms in terms of forfeited business opportunities with Cuba and that engagement would be more effective in accomplishing political liberalization and democratization.

The question of whether economic sanctions work cannot be answered without considering their objectives, that is, the foreign policy goals that the sanctioner expects to achieve by imposing sanctions. Although a sanctioner may have more than one objective in a given case, the purpose of economic sanctions can be classified according to the main foreign policy goal sought.[3] For example, in their study Gary Hufbauer, Jeffrey Schott, and Kimberly Elliott

126   *Democracy Delayed*

classify the goals of sanctions using five categories: (1) to change the target-country policies in a relatively modest way, (2) to change the target-country policies in a major way, (3) to destabilize the target government, (4) to disrupt a minor military venture, and (5) to impair the military potential of the target country.[4] Additional objectives of economic sanctions noted by Lawrence Brady include: (1) to signal a target country that there is resolve to resist its aggression, and (2) to signal the target country that its conduct is considered unacceptable by some and to raise the possibility that others will condemn it as well.[5]

Currently, the most salient foreign policy objectives in the discussion of the U.S. economic sanctions on the Castro government are: (1) to change the policies of the Cuban government, (2) to signal disapproval of violation of human rights and other reprehensible behavior, and (3) to destabilize the Cuban government and bring about a transition to democracy. In this chapter I consider whether the embargo is working from the perspectives of these three goals. The objective of impairing the military potential of the Cuban government is important, but I will not include it in my discussion.[6]

Critics and supporters of the U.S. embargo on Cuba have barely, if at all, addressed the relevant scholarly literature. Such literature has important theoretical insights and empirical findings that are germane to answering whether the U.S. embargo should be maintained. Bringing the scholarly literature into the discussion can provide stronger grounds on which to base an answer to this question.

While the international relations literature about economic sanctions in general can help assess the utility of the U.S. embargo against Cuba, the Cuban case in turn provides data to help evaluate whether unilateral economic sanctions can work.[7] Another benefit of the analysis is that it can link two previously isolated bodies of literature. The literature on sanctions identifies one of its possible objectives as fostering a change in political regimes (from dictatorships to democracies). Yet scholars writing on economic sanctions disregard the extensive theoretical and empirical works on transitions to democracy. Nor have arguments in favor or against Helms–Burton paid attention to theoretical works or evidence on transitions to democracy, despite the fact that those in favor of the law claim that it helps bring about the end of the Cuban dictatorship.

Sanctions to Change Targets' Policies

Changing targets' policies or behaviors as a goal of economic sanctions is important in the discussion on the U.S. embargo because this goal is implicit

The Economic Embargo   127

in one of the main critiques of the embargo. For example, when USA Engage argues that unilateral economic sanctions are ineffective, referring to results from the work of Hufbauer, Schott, and Elliott, the ineffectiveness is evaluated in terms of the utility of economic sanctions in changing targets' policies.[8]

Hufbauer, Schott, and Elliott, however, do not say that economic sanctions tend to be ineffective regardless of the objective pursued. As the authors indicate, the purpose of sanctions must be identified to assess their effectiveness. Their evaluation of the effectiveness of sanctions is from the perspective of changes in targets' policies as the main goal of sanctions. They conclude that sanctions often do not succeed in achieving this objective but can be considered successful if evaluated in terms of another purpose.[9]

Keeping in mind the conclusion of Hufbauer, Schott, and Elliott regarding the effectiveness of sanctions for changing targets' policies, one can understand the frequent claim in the literature that economic sanctions, particularly unilateral ones, are ineffective. The literature on sanctions commonly assumes that the purpose of economic sanctions is to change targets' policies or behaviors in accordance with the desires of the sanctioner(s).[10] When the goal of sanctions is taken to be policy or behavioral changes in the target, unilateral sanctions are seen as particularly ineffective because the hope for success is placed on inflicting high economic costs on the target. Such costs would not be likely in situations of unilateral sanctions because other countries could substitute for the sanctioner in trading with the target and/or in providing loans.[11]

It is unfounded to criticize the U.S. embargo in terms of the usual ineffectiveness of unilateral economic sanctions in changing targets' policies or behaviors. If the U.S. embargo had such an objective in the past, it no longer does. It is unreasonable to believe that the embargo will change Fidel Castro from a hardliner to a softliner and move him to take steps toward political liberalization. In chapter 1, we saw that it is unreasonable to expect that the type of regime under Castro would implement political liberalization, even in the face of serious economic difficulties. The term *standpat* applies to the Cuban regime and connotes its refusal to accept fundamental changes, such as respect for human rights. Supporters of the embargo in the U.S. legislature and in the executive branch have stated that the foremost aim of the embargo is to help bring about a regime change, that is, to foster a transition to democracy, by weakening the Castro government. Congressional supporters of Helms–Burton have reiterated this goal.[12] Helms–Burton is supposed to contribute to

a transition mainly by tightening the economic embargo and further reducing the hard currency available to the Castro government.

Consistent with previous findings on the successes of economic sanctions in destabilizing target governments, the U.S. embargo, at this juncture in Cuban history, weakens the Castro government by reducing its access to financial resources such as those that could come from U.S. tourism to Cuba. The Cuban government is in a precarious financial situation, having trouble paying even its short-term commercial debts. As I have indicated in previous chapters, there is evidence that in Cuba poor economic performance is associated with greater discontent and acts of opposition against the Cuban government. This empirical connection supports theoretical arguments in the literature on the political economy of transitions which claim that dictatorships tend to fall when they face economic hard times.

It is also unreasonable to believe that engagement, the establishment of diplomatic and economic relations with the Cuban government, will lead to political liberalization. The hypothesis in the engagement thesis—that economic development generates democracy—is refuted by strong evidence, and the assumption that foreign enterprises would promote political change in the host country is untenable.

Before discussing Helms–Burton, I will provide a brief overview of the components of this law. The Helms–Burton law has four titles. Title I seeks to strengthen international sanctions against the Castro government. Among the clauses of Title I is the instruction to U.S. executive directors of international financial institutions to oppose loans to Cuba and Cuban membership in those institutions until a transition to democracy occurs in the island. Title II mandates the preparation of a plan for U.S. assistance to transitional and democratically elected governments in Cuba.

Title III enables U.S. nationals to sue in U.S. courts those who "traffic" in properties that were confiscated by the Castro government from U.S. citizens or businesses. Trafficking is understood as buying, selling, leasing, marketing, or otherwise benefiting from expropriated assets.[13] President Clinton allowed Title III to become law, but under a provision of the Libertad Act, the president has the authority to waive enforcement of Title III for periods of six months. Title III has never been enforced. The president has always deferred enforcement. Title IV, which also targets firms that traffic in properties confiscated from U.S. nationals, denies entry into the United States to these firms' corporate officers and main shareholders, and their spouses and children under

eighteen years of age. Foreign firms that traffic in confiscated properties can avoid the sanctions by divesting themselves of such properties. Thus far, this aspect of the law has only been applied to two large foreign investors in Cuba: Grupo Domos (from Mexico) and Sherritt International (from Canada).[14] Warning letters were sent to a number of other firms.[15]

Titles III and IV engendered widespread, strident criticism of Helms–Burton, especially from Mexico, Canada, and Western European countries, claiming that Helms–Burton violates trade accords and is an infringement on the sovereignty of other countries by its "extraterritorial" attempt to apply U.S. laws to foreign enterprises.[16] The Libertad Act has been condemned in assemblies at the United Nations, at the Organization of American States (OAS), and in other international forums. Countries of the European Union (EU) were about to sue the United States at the World Trade Organization (WTO) over the Helms–Burton law, but an agreement was reached between the EU and the United States to have the case withdrawn from the WTO.[17] The United States has not applied Title IV to any European firm.

The claim that Helms–Burton is conducive to a transition to democracy in Cuba has been reproached by prestigious academics, government officials, Cuban dissidents, and other personalities. According to Jimmy Carter, Helms–Burton is an obstacle to a transition to democracy in Cuba.[18] Carl-Johan Groth, the former special investigator for Cuba of the UN Human Rights Commission, in his 1996 report to the commission, concluded that outside pressure like the U.S. embargo only worsened the human rights situation in Cuba.[19] Eloy Gutierrez-Menoyo, a Cuban exile who heads a dissident group called Cambio Cubano (Cuban Change), agrees with Groth.[20] Elizardo Sánchez Santacruz, a dissident living in Cuba, thinks that the United States should discard Helms–Burton and follow the European Union's policy of promoting investment in Cuba while pressuring for political changes.[21] Mesa-Lago believes that the U.S. embargo is counterproductive for a democratic transition in Cuba.[22] It is interesting that popular views in Cuba about the embargo are more perceptive than these negative opinions of the embargo. The survey of Roberts et al. among recent arrivals from Cuba shows that only 7 percent thought that lifting the embargo is necessary for significant changes to occur in Cuba.[23]

Engagement to Change Regimes

Even if one accepts that a key criterion for judging the utility of the U.S. embargo is its contribution to destabilization of the Cuban dictatorship and pro-

130   *Democracy Delayed*

motion of a political transition, critics of the embargo insist that engagement would be a more effective policy for achieving the same end.[24] In their dispute with the United States over Helms–Burton, officials from Western European countries have repeatedly argued that the way to achieve political reform in Cuba is to increase trade with the Castro government.[25] Several scholars advocate the same position. For example, Carmelo Mesa-Lago and Horst Fabian suggest that internal democratization could be encouraged by a policy of dialogue, bargaining, and openings in trade. They argue that the hostile U.S. approach has failed to change Cuba for more than three decades.[26] Hence, we should consider whether the engagement thesis bears examination.

Engagement advocates also contend that regime elites would be willing to allow some political liberalization for the sake of maintaining economic relations with foreign countries. It should be kept in mind that the U.S. economic embargo is not a blockade. Practically every country in the world has diplomatic and commercial relations with Cuba. The fact that the U.S. embargo has been in place since 1962 and the Cuban dictatorship has endured is used by critics of the embargo as an indication that the economic sanctions have been ineffective in achieving a change of regime, and thus that engagement should be given a chance to bring about a political transformation. Those who make this argument disregard the fact that, for a long time, Cuba has had diplomatic and commercial relations with most countries. Whether one takes a long-term perspective (the 1960s to the present) or views the results of engagement in the post–cold war period, the engagement has failed to bring about political change in Cuba.

Many democratic countries (e.g., Canada, Mexico, and countries in Western Europe) never broke diplomatic relations with Cuba after Castro took over power. So, for over forty years, officials of the Castro government have had diplomatic relations, commerce, and personal contacts with citizens of democratic countries. Before the collapse of the Soviet Union and the end of the large subsidies that Cuba received from that country, the Castro government was economically quite independent from the capitalist world. Hence, one may argue that before 1990, engagement with democracies could not have its alleged positive effect on political liberalization in Cuba. But, after 1990, the Castro government has had more contacts than ever with democracies while Cuba has become highly dependent on business relations with these democracies. Yet no political liberalization has taken place.

The nature of the Cuban regime is such that it is unjustified to think that

The Economic Embargo   131

engagement can induce the Castro government to implement political liberalization.[27] Not only have Latin American and European countries engaged the Cuban government in diplomatic and trade relations, but some leaders from these countries have repeatedly tried to persuade Castro to take steps toward political liberalization such as granting amnesty to political prisoners.[28] Over the years, officials from various countries and international organizations have asked the ruling elite in Cuba to respect human rights and move the country toward democracy. Felipe González (former prime minister of Spain) had a close and supportive bilateral relationship with the Castro government, but his attempts to convince Castro to introduce democratic reforms were unsuccessful.[29] The list of foreign dignitaries who have attempted to get the Cuban government to respect human rights and/or to carry out political reforms is long and includes Jakob Kellenberger (Switzerland), José María Aznar (Spain), Carlos Menem (Argentina), Vaclav Havel (the Czech Republic), and Lech Walesa (Poland).[30] None of these dignitaries succeeded in their attempts to get Castro to change his policies regarding political liberalization and respect for human rights.

Fidel Castro joined twenty-two other heads of state of Latin American nations plus Spain and Portugal at the sixth Ibero-American Summit held at Viña del Mar, Chile, November 10–11, 1996. The focus of the conference was democratic governability. At the Summit, the heads of state, including Castro, signed a final document, the "Declaration of Viña del Mar," which has three parts. The first reaffirms a commitment to democracy, maintaining that democracy has to be representative. The signatories pledged to support political pluralism; freedom of speech and freedom of association; free, regular, and transparent elections; and respect for human rights.[31] However, after returning to Cuba from Chile, in a speech to the Havana leadership of the Communist Party, Castro derided what he called "recipes" for democracy and maintained that in Cuba the Communist Party is enough.[32] Harassment, beatings, and imprisonment of peaceful dissidents and independent journalists by Cuban authorities continue to this day.[33] In a more recent example of Castro's intransigent position with respect to calls for democratization, heads of state once again asked him to implement a democratic opening at the ninth Ibero-American Summit in November 1999, and once again he flatly refused.[34]

The visit of Pope John Paul II to Cuba in 1998, visits of government officials from many countries, and other signs that "the world was opening up to Cuba" (as the pope advocated) have also failed to achieve political liberaliza-

132   *Democracy Delayed*

tion. For example, in March 1999, the Cuban government established a law to impose up to twenty years in prison and other punishments on people who dare exercise their rights of free speech.[35] The same month, the Cuban government carried out a closed-door trial and sentenced four dissidents to prison terms ranging from three and a half to five years. These four individuals had been imprisoned since July 1997 because they wrote a document, "The Homeland Belongs to All of Us," criticizing the Castro government.[36]

The Cuban government has not responded to positive reinforcements from engaged countries. Despite the precarious situation of Cuba's economy, the Castro government has been unwilling to exchange internal measures of political liberalization for external economic assistance. The European Union made Cuba such an offer in 1996, and the Cuban government turned it down. In December 1996, the European Union officially made respect for human rights and indications by the Castro regime of political liberalization prior conditions for the establishment of an economic cooperation accord. The EU policy is binding on its fifteen members. Since 1994, EU officials had been telling Cuban authorities that reaching an economic cooperation agreement with Cuba was contingent on respect for human rights and political reforms.[37] A cooperation agreement with the EU would facilitate trade, investments, and aid.[38] In a more recent example of the refusal of the Cuban government to move toward political liberalization as a quid pro quo for economic assistance, Cuba withdrew its candidacy to membership in the group of African, Caribbean, and Pacific countries that have an economic cooperation agreement with the European Union because the European Union made political changes in Cuba a precondition for membership.[39] At the sixth Ibero-American Summit, José María Aznar offered Fidel Castro improvement in the EU's relations with Cuba if Castro took some steps toward democracy, but Castro rejected Aznar's offer.[40] Both Fidel Castro and his brother Raúl, the second in command in the ruling elite, have reiterated that their government will never negotiate better relations with the United States based on conditions for changes in Cuba's domestic policies.[41]

There are some who advocate engagement because of the alleged positive impact personal contacts can have in fostering political change. Advocates of this line of thinking assume that engagement would allow foreigners to travel to Cuba, exercise freedom of speech, make contacts with dissidents, and strengthen the opposition, eventually pushing the Castro government toward political liberalization. Another related line of thinking holds that exposure of

The Economic Embargo   133

the Cuban elite to countries with democracy and/or capitalism would weaken the loyalty of these persons toward the Castro regime, and hence would help bring about a transition.

Some scholars claim that in Eastern Europe contacts between political elites in the East and the West over time eroded the legitimacy of communist system among its own elites. Thus, personal contacts were important in accounting for the fall of communism in Europe. There are various problems in using this thesis as an argument against the U.S. embargo of the Castro government. First, the legitimacy of the Cuban regime among its own elites is already in doubt, as I have indicated in previous chapters. Second, if personal contacts with individuals from democratic countries have any impact in subverting the belief in communism among elites in Cuba, there are already plenty of contacts with people from "Western" countries, including Canada, Mexico, and Western Europe. Foreigners have traveled to Cuba and members of the Cuban elite have traveled to these countries. Moreover, personal contact is not the only possible reason for elites to doubt the legitimacy of communism systems. Dismal economic performance, especially the failure to improve the living standards of the population, shatters the ideological legitimacy of a system that claims to be superior to capitalism and promises prosperity to its citizens. Castro's unfulfilled promises of good economic times are as old as his regime. The economic failure of the Castro government affects the mind-set of the common citizens and of regime elites.

Moreover, the U.S. economic embargo has not precluded contacts between people in the United States and those in Cuba. Over the years, thousands of Cuban exiles have visited their relatives in Cuba; there have also been visits and contacts between scholars in the United States and academics in Cuba. The Cuban Democracy Act (1992) officially intended to push for a "track II" policy of fostering personal contacts between the two countries and seeking to help NGOs in Cuba. Raúl Castro denounced the track II U.S. policy as a "rotten carrot" and exhorted Cubans to resist it. Referring to the track II policy, he said, "We are not [sitting] with our arms crossed, we are ready and prepared to reply in this politico-ideological area, to confront it in every dimension."[42]

Foreign journalists who have been critical of the regime have been denied visas to visit Cuba or have been expelled from the island.[43] In January 2001, Fidel Castro threatened foreign journalists in Cuba with expulsion and cancellation of their agencies' licenses to operate in Cuba if they continued spreading "lies and insults" against the revolution.[44] Foreigners who have met

134   *Democracy Delayed*

with alleged dissidents have been expelled from Cuba, and the Cubans contacted have been repressed.[45] For example, a Belgian tourist was arrested in
Cuba on May 31, 2000, by the political police after he visited a number of
independent libraries in the island and met with members of civil society
groups. Members of the Department of State Security, one of the branches of
the political police, threatened him with charges of "collaborating with the
enemy," and told him that tourists were only allowed in Cuba for recreation,
although they were free to meet with government organizations. The notes
and videos he had taken were confiscated.[46] In August 2000, three Swedish
journalists were arrested by members of the Cuban Ministry of Interior after
the journalists met with Cuban independent journalists. On August 17, 2000,
the same thing happened to a French journalist.[47] In January 2001, the Cuban
government arrested Ivan Pilip, a member of the Czech Republic's Chamber of
Deputies, and Jan Bubenik, a student leader during the 1989 revolution in
Czechoslovakia, for meeting with members of civil society groups in Cuba.
They were accused of "subversive contacts" as agents of the U.S. government.[48]

This reaction of the Cuban government to personal contacts taking place
without official control between foreigners and common citizens is similar to
the policy of "setting limits" (Abgrenzung) implemented by the East German
government in response to the policy of Ostpolitik. The latter was a policy of
détente with the East German government that Chancellor Willy Brandt of
the German Federal Republic introduced in the 1970s. The case of Ostpolitik
is another example of the failure of engagement to induce political liberalization in hardline regimes. Actually, the government of Eric Honecker responded to Ostpolitik by increasing the size of the political police (the Stasi)
as well as the degree of repression against dissidents.[49] The East German government paid special attention to the "Western contacts" of its citizens in
order to prevent precisely the positive effects the West Germans were hoping
for in facilitating contacts.

Attempts by international actors to have the Cuban government respect
human rights and take steps toward democratization are not limited to efforts
by government executives. Numerous NGOs and international institutions
throughout the world have become advocates of the cause of human rights
and democracy in Cuba. A transnational network has emerged to push for respect of human rights and a transition to democracy in Cuba. Human rights
violations by the Castro government have been regularly denounced by
Amnesty International, the Interamerican Commission of Human Rights of

the Organization of American States, Human Rights Watch, the Interamerican Press Society, Reporters Without Frontiers, the United Nations Commission of Human Rights, and the International Society of Human Rights. Various other entities and ad hoc groups have joined the campaign for the cause of freedom in Cuba. To give some examples, forty-five distinguished former members of opposition groups in Eastern Europe under communist rule signed a document expressing their solidarity with the Cuban opposition. The Foundation Andrei Sakharov works with the Cuban Committee Pro Human Rights. NGOs in Guatemala, Nicaragua, and Mexico have also become involved in the effort to defend human rights in Cuba. Forty-seven civic organizations in Mexico, under the umbrella International Promoter of Human Rights, as well as the European Parliament and government parties in Poland, Hungary, Estonia, Romania, Slovenia, Lithuania, Israel, Costa Rica, Nicaragua, and El Salvador have expressed their solidarity with the Cuban opposition and called for political liberalization in Cuba. The Dutch branch of Pax Christi launched in 2000 the European Platform for Human Rights in Cuba, and twenty European human rights groups joined. The project seeks to coordinate programs and exchange information among groups to help Cubans obtain basic civic rights. Chinese, Vietnamese, and Cuban human rights organizations have networked to coordinate activities.[50]

Daniel Thomas has addressed the question of how important the Helsinki Accords of 1975 were in the transitions to democracy in Eastern Europe.[51] He views the Accords as a very important determinant. Democratic activists in Eastern Europe and international actors in the West took advantage of the Accords to pressure Eastern European governments to abide by the document and respect human rights. Non-state actors in the West got Western governments to take up the human rights issue and exert diplomatic pressure on Eastern European governments concerning respect for human rights. Thomas argues that because Eastern European governments wanted economic benefits, such as access to technology and credits, from the West, they were vulnerable to pressures to respect human rights. The more economically vulnerable, the more susceptible they were to pressures on the human rights issue. The effect of the campaigns in favor of human rights was to reduce the repression against democratic activists in Eastern Europe.

The case of Cuba supports this latter conclusion. The international campaigns in favor of human rights and democracy in Cuba have given some protection from government repression to democratic activists in Cuba. There are

136   *Democracy Delayed*

numerous cases in which activists have been released from prison after international efforts on their behalf. One example is the case of the four prominent activists who were imprisoned for writing the document "The Homeland Belongs to All of Us." After they were nominated for the Nobel Peace Prize, three of the four were released. Activists in Cuba maintain that international attention to their activities and to them as individuals shields them somewhat from repression. Democratic activists frequently mention that international pressure on the Cuban government in solidarity with activists helps to counter the repression. This does not mean that international pressures have succeeded in preventing the Castro government from systematically and routinely violating human rights. The government is not willing to bargain spaces of freedom for something else. Citizens have no guarantees that they will not be harassed, beaten, imprisoned, or otherwise repressed for criticizing the government, meeting with dissidents, or exercising other human rights. The government might release a political prisoner or refrain somewhat from repressing dissidents to reduce international condemnation. But if the government feels it should repress, it does. If it does not want to release a political prisoner, it does not. For example, international campaigns for the release of Dr. Oscar Elías Biscet and Vladimiro Roca, two prominent dissidents, have been unsuccessful.

The case of Cuba suggests that the importance of international norms, such as those promoted by the Helsinki Accords, are not as decisive for transitions as Thomas implies. Even though international pressures in favor of human rights reduce repression, dictatorships can endure despite strong demands by international actors to abide by democratic norms. The Castro government signed a document similar to the Helsinki Accords, the Declaration of Viña del Mar, at the sixth Ibero-American Summit in Chile in 1996. The Cuban government committed itself to respect human rights, to grant all sorts of political freedoms, and to establish a representative democracy. European governments have incorporated the issue of human rights in their diplomatic relations with Cuba. Thomas's view that the more economically vulnerable the country is the more sensitive it will be to international pressures to respect human rights should be particularly relevant to Cuba since the Cuban economy is in dire straits and quite dependent on trade, investment, bilateral credits, and tourism from democracies in Europe, Latin America, and Canada. However, a transition has not taken place in Cuba, the government has not taken steps toward political liberalization, and the regime continues to violate human rights systematically.

Economic Development and Democracy

The engagement thesis has a macro dimension, that of the expected effect of economic development on the emergence of democracy. As countries reach higher levels of economic development, democracies are established. The hypothesis comes from the work of Seymour Martin Lipset in the 1950s.[52] This old hypothesis has now been adopted by advocates of engagement to criticize the embargo. Yet there is solid empirical evidence contradicting this hypothesis.[53] Countries under dictatorial regimes are not necessarily more likely to experience a transition to democracy as they reach higher levels of economic development.[54] Nevertheless, the idea that development generates democracy continues to be presented as if it were true.

Huntington has also argued that economic development produces democracy.[55] However, the intervening mechanism between development and democracy in Huntington's reasoning does not hold in the Cuban case. He thinks that economic development leads to democracy because economic development creates new sources of wealth and power outside the state. But if increased wealth just accrues to the state, then Huntington acknowledges that the additional revenue merely increases the power of the state, and there is no contribution to democratization.[56] The latter scenario is the only one that applies to the case of Cuba. The growth of civil society in Cuba is not due to the enclave capitalism that the government has implemented. Members of independent groups in Cuba are routinely fired from their jobs in state institutions or enterprises, cannot obtain employment in joint ventures with foreign capitalists, and are denied licenses to operate as individual entrepreneurs. Activists have to rely on the generosity of family members, friends, and/or supporters from abroad.

Foreign investment in Cuba is through joint ventures with state enterprises, which are the majority shareholders (with rare exceptions). Foreign joint ventures employ only 1.3 percent of the working-age population. The Cuban workers in these joint ventures are subjected to super exploitation by the state. One of the most important, if not the largest, source of revenue to the Cuban state from foreign investment comes from wage confiscation. Foreign firms cannot hire workers directly. The state provides the workforce through special government employment agencies; the main one is Agencia de Contratación a Representaciones Comerciales, SA (ACOREC). On average, the state receives from foreign investors $450 a month per worker while the government pays

138   *Democracy Delayed*

workers in Cuban pesos the equivalent of approximately $10 a month, an amount that hardly suffices to cover basic living expenses.[57] Wage confiscation nets the state approximately $361 million a year. The Cuban government also markets its labor force abroad following the same exploitative practices. The government places its subjects, from doctors to cooks, in positions outside the country, collects their salaries in hard currency from the employers, and in turn pays the workers a tiny fraction of the income they earn.[58]

Workers strive to get jobs in joint ventures not to get better wages but to have access to dollar tips, informal gifts from tourists, and *javitas*, small care-packages containing basic necessities such as toothpaste and soap that employers may provide their workers as a bonus. Hence, foreign investment is not a mechanism for the generation of wealth and power among the population. Rather, it is an important source of hard currency for the state. The slight impact of joint ventures on the well-being of the population is reflected in a survey by Roberts et al. of recent arrivals to the United States. Answering questions about the importance of different economic reforms in Cuba, very few respondents considered the establishment of joint ventures as an important reform. Five percent thought that the mixed enterprises were the most important reform, 10 percent that they were the second most important reform, and 16 percent that they were the third most important reform. By contrast, government permission for the operation of free farmers' markets was considered the most important reform by 49 percent of the respondents.[59]

The capitalism that Castro has been forced to accept because of the demise of Soviet subsidies, in order for the government to muddle through economically, is fundamentally contained in joint-venture enclaves in which the key actors and beneficiaries are foreign capitalists and the Cuban state. The very limited space that the government allowed after 1993 for Cuban citizens to engage in private entrepreneurship has been subjected from 1996 on to substantial stifling measures.[60] A drive to crack down on Cuban private businesses has driven thousands of these enterprises to close and intensified the difficulties for those who still manage to continue operating.[61] Despite the U.S. embargo, the Cuban government could very well allow more market reforms such as a greater space for independent entrepreneurship among farmers. The U.S. embargo does not prevent the Cuban government from doing so. The government's refusal is its own decision. Lifting the U.S. embargo would not lead to a significant expansion of market reforms in the domestic economy.[62]

The end of the embargo would mean more income for the state with little diffusion of wealth among citizens at large. Interview data from recent Cuban arrivals to the United States, surveys conducted in Cuba by an entity of the Catholic Church, and reports from independent journalists in Cuba show that the vast majority of the population realizes that the key culprit for the poor economic conditions in Cuba is the Castro government and not the economic embargo.[63] These popular views are contrary to the claim by some anti-embargo advocates that the embargo is responsible for hunger and the deterioration of health care in Cuba. These data also indicate that the attempt by the Cuban government to blame Cuba's economic troubles on the embargo is hardly believed by the people.

Despite measures that have strengthened the embargo since 1992, the United States has been the largest source of humanitarian aid to Cuba.[64] The European Union sends Cuba about $20 million a year in humanitarian aid.[65] From 1992 to 1997, the Clinton administration authorized the delivery of more than $1 billion in humanitarian aid to Cuba, including food, medicine, and medical equipment.[66]

Foreign Capitalists as Promoters of Democracy

Besides the diplomatic and economic relationships among states and the connection between economic development and democracy, there is a third facet of the engagement thesis: foreign enterprises promote political change in the host country. But, as William Hawkins argues, foreign companies investing in countries ruled by dictatorships come to defend the dictatorships as a way of protecting their business interests.[67] This would be even more likely in countries such as Cuba, in which foreign investment takes the form of joint ventures with the government.

Foreign investors in Cuba seem to receive substantial concessions from the government, such as 100 percent repatriation of profits. Foreign firms operate under a labor system of gross exploitation of Cuban workers, and some foreign investors have used property confiscated by the government from Americans and Cubans. Moreover, joint ventures are violating laws that protect the natural environment, with government consent. Thus, one likely result of the end of the dictatorship and the advent of a democratic government would be that foreign investors will have their business agreements with the dictatorship changed or nullified. It is also possible that large fines will be imposed on foreign investors to clean up the environment and to compensate workers for their past wage confiscation. In addition, in cases of utilization of confiscated

140   *Democracy Delayed*

property, Americans and Cubans will confront such investors with property claims.[68] Finally, foreign investors in Cuba will face, after a political transition, a political backlash.[69]

Many Cubans, both in exile and in the island, consider foreign investors to be collaborators of the dictatorship who help lengthen the life of the Castro government and thus are partially responsible for prolonging the suffering of the Cuban people. One example indicating the resentment among people in Cuba against foreign investors is a pamphlet (dated March 1999) addressed to all foreign enterprises and circulated by a pro-democracy group in Cuba. Among the points made in the flier are that: (1) the businesses in which you are involved are illegal and perpetuate the communist regime in power; (2) when the change toward democracy occurs, you will be taken to court because of your illegal actions in alliance with Castro's regime; (3) do not assume that the Cuban communist regime can offer you any kind of security; none of the documents signed by the present regime, their entities, or third authorized parties will be of any value after we have a democracy; and (4) you will be taken to court to clarify the legality of your businesses; afterward you will be free to conduct business in Cuba under a democratic legal system.

In June 1999, Cuban American lawyers filed a class action suit in Florida against foreign investors in Cuba for violating international labor laws.[70] In a similar vein, in July 1998, representatives of various independent groups in Cuba warned foreign investors about possible demands for wage compensation that they could face under a future democratic government since foreign investors were violating international labor laws by their participation in the wage-confiscation scheme.[71] Jorge Mas Canosa, the founder of the Cuban American National Foundation, in a speech to The Society of International Business Fellows at the Biltmore Hotel in Miami on January 29, 1996, referred to foreign investments in Cuba as "blood deals" and stated that these deals will not be forgotten when democracy is established in Cuba. He argued that when that time comes, foreign investors will be placed in two categories: those with ties to the Cuban dictatorship and those who refused to provide economic support to the dictatorship.

Foreign entrepreneurs in Cuba seem to have tied the fate of their businesses to the survival of the dictatorship. Thus, they are bound to be defenders of the dictatorship rather than promoters of political change. Jesús Zúñiga observes that each foreign investor in Cuba ends up being a lobbyist for the Cuban government abroad.[72] Moreover, in Cuba, foreign enterprises are not breeding

The Economic Embargo   141

grounds for democracy. Data from 1,023 interviews of recent exiles show that 75 percent of them think that workers in foreign enterprises are subjected to more control by the political police than is usual for Cubans.[73]

Sanctions to Change Targets' Governments

Economic sanctions can seek to destabilize foreign governments, often involving a superpower (the sanctioner) and a smaller country (the target). Hufbauer, Schott, and Elliott conclude that economic sanctions, accompanied by other policies, are quite successful in undermining governments. In over half of the cases that they considered, the sanctions were successful. Yet they emphasize that economic sanctions unassisted by complementary measures seldom succeed in this objective.[74] These authors observe that international cooperation is not important in determining the success of sanctions in destabilizing target governments.[75] Hence, the unilateral nature of U.S. sanctions against the Cuban government would not preclude the ability of the sanctions to undermine the Castro regime. The authors argue that political variables can influence the success of sanctions. Among these variables are the presence of international assistance to the target, the political and economic health of the target, and policies implemented by the sanctioner to supplement the economic sanctions.[76]

The view in the international relations literature that economic sanctions can serve to destabilize target governments by having a negative impact on the target's economy has a corresponding observation in the literature on transitions to democracy. Major works on transitions to democracy indicate that dictatorships tend to fall when faced with crises, including economic ones.[77] A cross-national statistical study involving 139 countries from 1950 to 1990 concluded that dictatorships are more likely to survive when their economies grow and are more likely to be destabilized when they face economic crises.[78] Another study found that in a data set of twenty-seven dictatorships, twenty-one experienced economic decline prior to transitions to democracy. All communist dictatorships in that data set (Poland, Nicaragua, Romania, Hungary, and Czechoslovakia) experienced economic deterioration or stagnant, low rates of growth in the years before the demise of the dictatorships.[79]

A widespread observation among scholars of Eastern European politics is that a key factor underlying the pressures leading to the fall of communism in Eastern Europe was economic deterioration. A declining standard of living decreased people's tolerance for the regimes. As their situations grew worse, the

142   *Democracy Delayed*

populations became increasingly aware of the failure of their own regimes to provide an acceptable level of prosperity.[80] The connection between deterioration of economic performance and transitions to democracy is also observed in Latin America, where economic decline and drops in standards of living preceded the wave of democratization in the region during the 1980s.[81]

Two ways in which poor economic performance seems to contribute to the demise of dictatorships are: (1) by fostering latent or active opposition to the regime among citizens and groups in civil society; people blame the government for their increased poverty and withdraw support or acquiescence; and (2) by reducing benefits to active supporters and coalition allies.[82] Even in cases where economic crises are not the main source of factional conflicts within the ruling elite, deterioration of economic performance tends to widen cleavages among the rulers.[83] In Cuba in the 1990s, economic deterioration was accompanied by the development of civil society, spontaneous popular protests triggered by economic grievances, and greater discontent among government cadres fueled by decreases in material resources.[84]

The Effect of the U.S. Embargo on Cuba's Economy

Before the end of Soviet subsidies to Cuba, the economic pressure on the Castro government as a consequence of the embargo was not a major challenge to the stability of the regime.[85] But since the end of non-market economic relations between Cuba and Eastern European countries, the embargo has significantly reduced the amount of resources available to the Castro government. Thus, the embargo has come to have a destabilizing effect on the dictatorship. Hufbauer, Schott, and Elliott point to the logical observation that governments in distress are more easily destabilized. They also make the point that the extent to which the target country's economy is hurt by the sanctions is relative to the gross national product (GNP) of the target; the lower the GNP, the greater the economic impact.[86] According to these arguments, the embargo should be particularly harmful to the Castro government. The Cuban GNP is very low, and the economy is in a dire state. Mesa-Lago estimates that in 1985, Cuba's gross domestic product (GDP) per capita was $334, similar to that of Haiti; in 1996, the Cuban GDP per capita had dropped to $61.[87]

The Cuba Libertad Act (Helms–Burton) has significantly curtailed hard-currency income to the Cuban government in at least the following ways: (1) decreasing new investment in Cuba by non-U.S. firms, (2) getting some firms that had investments in Cuba to divest, and (3) solidifying the maintenance

of the embargo (since lifting it now requires congressional approval), thus decreasing the possibility that U.S. investors and tourists will spend their money in Cuba.

Data on the economic costs of the embargo to the Cuban government since 1990 indicate that the costs are significant. Juan Triana Cordoví, the director of the Center for Studies of the Cuban Economy in Havana, says that the direct costs of the embargo on the Cuban economy for 1998 was $700 million (which was larger than the net revenues to the government from the tourist sector at the time).[88] According to a study by a European Union think tank, during its first year, the Cuba Democracy Act of 1992 cost Cuba about $1 billion.[89]

Revenues from U.S. tourism might be the largest source of income to the Cuban government the embargo is blocking. In 1996, it was estimated that an end to the embargo would quickly double the number of tourists traveling to Cuba.[90] When President Clinton seemed to be considering lifting or weakening the embargo, there were plans in the shipping sector to dock four cruise ships simultaneously in Havana. Under the embargo, ships calling on Cuba have to wait six months before making a port stop in the United States, reducing the number of cruise ships that stop in Cuba.[91] In 2000, a high-ranking official in the Cuban tourist industry estimated that the end of the ban on U.S. tourism to Cuba would represent an increase of 5 million tourists going to Cuba by 2010.[92] In the short term, allowing tourism from the United States would represent about 1.4 million new tourists going to Cuba, estimated to bring approximately $950 million in revenue to the Cuban treasury.[93]

Carlos Lage, the Cuban economy minister, acknowledges that Helms–Burton has slowed down foreign investment in Cuba.[94] According to Canada's ambassador to Cuba, Mark Entwistle, Helms–Burton has had a "chilling effect" on investment decisions in Cuba by Canadian businessmen.[95] Part of this chill has been due to the unwillingness of Canadian banks to provide loans for Canadian business ventures in Cuba. The underlying motive has been the desire among banks to avoid conflicts with the United States due to the Helms–Burton Act.[96] Foreign firms have canceled, frozen, or quietly deferred plans for investment in Cuba.

Two firms that ended their business in Cuba after the signing of the Libertad Act are the Spanish firms Occidental Hotels and Paradores Nacionales.[97] Cemex, a Mexican company, also left Cuba just days before its top executive was to receive a U.S. State Department letter warning him that he might be vi-

144   *Democracy Delayed*

olating provisions of Helms–Burton.[98] Cemex has four cement production plants and eight distribution sites in the United States, and its CEO wanted to avoid losing his ability to come into the United States. According to Archibald Ritter, professor of economics at Carleton University in Canada, Irving Corporation pulled out of Cuba in August 1995 largely because of concerns over its liability in the United States presented by the Helms–Burton bill, which was then being considered in the U.S. Congress. Irving Corporation owns property in the United States.[99] Other companies that have reportedly abandoned Cuba since the passage of the Helms–Burton law include the Canadian sugar-trading house Redpath, the South African mining company Gencor, and Mexican companies PEMEX and Grupo Vitro.[100] The Mexican firm Grupo Domos, the largest foreign investor in Cuba at the time, decided to divest from its share in the Cuba's telephone firm Empresa de Telecomunicaciones de Cuba, SA (ETESCA). Domos had been singled out by the U.S. government for application of Title IV of the Helms–Burton law; Domos executives and their families were barred from entry into the United States. Moreover, Domos was short $300 million to complete the original deal with the Cuban government, and apparently Domos could not find a partner willing to invest in ETECSA because potential investors were afraid of being subject to similar sanctions.[101]

Despite the problems that Cuba continues to have in attracting foreign investment due to political and economic problems unrelated to the U.S. embargo, it is to be expected that if the United States were to lift its embargo, there would be a number of U.S. firms willing to invest in Cuba.[102] Before the Cuban air force shot down the civilian planes on February 24, 1996, killing three U.S. citizens and one U.S. resident, the Clinton administration gave the impression that it wanted to ease relations with the Cuban government. There was the expectation that the U.S. economic embargo was going to be lifted or at least weakened. This perception prompted a surge of U.S. entrepreneurs traveling to Cuba to scout business deals. Between 1994 and 1996, about 1,500 representatives of U.S. firms went to Cuba, and according to an official of the Cuban government, more than one hundred U.S. companies signed non-binding letters of intent with state enterprises to do business in case the U.S. embargo ended.[103]

Even if one were to assume that a negotiated political transition is possible in Cuba after Fidel Castro dies or becomes physically or mentally incapable of ruling, a reduction in the resources available to the ruling elite would help increase the probability of a transition by fostering the emergence of softliners

The Economic Embargo   145

able and willing to negotiate. As the literature on transitions to democracy from authoritarian rule has emphasized, crises, including economic ones, tend to motivate softliners to implement political liberalization and also strengthen them in confronting hardliners.[104] The U.S. economic embargo reduces the amount of resources available to the dictatorship for sustaining acquiescence in the population and for distributing benefits among regime supporters. Thus, the argument by embargo critics that lifting the embargo would help achieve a negotiated transition in Cuba is self-contradictory. For a negotiated transition, viable softliners are necessary, and it is when authoritarian or mature post-totalitarian regimes face serious difficulties that these softliners tend to appear.

Sanctions to Signal Commitment to Norms

I want to consider one final goal of economic sanctions, that of signaling commitment to international norms. A frequent goal of economic sanctions is to demonstrate resolve against unacceptable behavior. This objective contributes to the maintenance of internationally accepted standards of conduct. The United States has often used sanctions to assert its leadership in the world by dramatizing its opposition to reprehensible behavior on the part of foreign governments, even if it is unlikely that targets would change their behavior. Sanctions add teeth to diplomacy. They are a middle ground between words or diplomatic acts of disapproval and war. This signaling purpose can be achieved by unilateral or multilateral sanctions, and success can be seen in terms of the reaffirmation of the norms of acceptable behavior. Even though the moral and psychological impact of imposing sanctions to signal commitment is hard to measure, it should not be underestimated.[105]

The signals of commitment to norms are directed to international actors, such as the allies of the sanctioning country, as well as to domestic actors. In the case of the U.S. embargo against the Castro dictatorship, one audience is the Cuban people in exile and in the island. The symbolic aspect of the embargo is articulated by supporters of the embargo when they say that lifting the embargo would give Fidel Castro a moral and political victory. Indications of solidarity with the cause of democracy in Cuba are morally and psychologically quite important for Cuban activists because there is a strong tendency toward double standards with respect to the struggle for democracy in Cuba among individuals or groups with liberal/left positions in the United States, Europe, and Latin America. This double standard is shown in various forms,

146   *Democracy Delayed*

from refusing to publicly criticize the Castro government to being an acolyte of the Cuban regime.

One example of the double standard is the contrast between the position that some actors had in the case of South Africa under the apartheid system and their position toward the Castro government. To cite one case, TransAfrica advocated sanctions and divestment in the case of South Africa. U.S. corporations in South Africa were seen as providing support for white minority rule and as detrimental to the process of political reforms. One TransAfrica activist argued that "Americans are getting rich from the semi-slave labor of black South Africans and our government is encouraging them to continue doing that."[106] How apropos for the current Cuban situation! Anti-apartheid activists maintained that it was a duty to act against South Africa because of ideals of democracy and justice.[107] Yet in February 1999, Randall Robinson, the president of TransAfrica, visited Fidel Castro and denounced the U.S. embargo.[108] TransAfrica is very active in efforts to end the embargo on the Cuban dictatorship.

The Inadequacy of Complementary Measures

The U.S. embargo weakens the Cuban dictatorship. But the embargo is not sufficient to bring about a political transition. The embargo has to be supplemented by other measures. The argument that the embargo has to be accompanied by other policies concurs with the point made by Hufbauer, Schott, and Elliot that the success of economic sanctions in destabilizing targets' governments depends on complementary measures, specifically, covert actions, quasi-military activities, and regular military activity.[109] This list is too limited. There are other measures that the sanctioner can pursue to reinforce the effects of economic sanctions in promoting political transitions from autocratic rule. Two other possibilities are: (1) providing enough material assistance to "fertilize" the growth of civil society and (2) giving most of the population access to independent channels of news and information. The Clinton administration did neither. In other chapters, I have shown the importance of material assistance to civil society groups and of independent sources of communication to promote a political transition in Cuba. I have also indicated the paucity of complementary measures to the embargo. Such measures were not implemented by Clinton because his administration sought to avoid a political transition in Cuba pushed by groups in civil society and the population.

The Anti-embargo Movement

In an article published in 1998, Horowitz analyzed what he calls the "Cuba lobby."[110] This is a set of actors who concur in their opposition to the U.S. embargo on Cuba, although some differ sharply on other issues. The anti-embargo camp is made up of strange bedfellows. As Horowitz indicates, it is uncertain to what extent they coordinate their efforts to push for the end of the embargo. But there is evidence of collaboration among some, and it is reasonable to assume, given the extent and success of the anti-embargo push, that others coordinate their activities, at least some of the time. Thus, they comprise an anti-embargo movement. Horowitz's list of actors includes (1) intellectual-academic organizations, (2) business associations, (3) policy-oriented think tanks, (4) foundations and other grant-making agencies, and (5) political or social organizations, such as a few groups of Cuban exiles representing a minority opinion within that community.

The composition of the anti-embargo movement in the United States is indeed impressive. The number of organizations behind this effort is large. It includes leftist groups that are highly pro-Castro, like Pastors for Peace, and such bastions of capitalism as the U.S. Chamber of Commerce and the National Association of Manufacturers. There are religious organizations such as the World Council of Churches and groups of Cuban Americans like Cambio Cubano and the Cuban Committee for Democracy. The Americans For Humanitarian Trade with Cuba is a coalition of business, religious, political, labor, and medical leaders formed for the sole purpose of ending the embargo on the Cuban government. It boasts of having chapters in twenty-five states, and its list of advisory board members includes corporate executives such as Dwayne Andreas, CEO of Archer Daniels Midland, celebrities like Francis Ford Coppola, and highly regarded former government officials such as Paul A. Volcker, former chair of the Federal Reserve Board. One finds the Arca Foundation, highly partisan in its support of the Cuban government, and prestigious foundations like the Ford Foundation and the John D. and Catherine T. MacArthur Foundation. In Congress, Democrats like Senator Christopher Dodd (Conn.) and Republicans like Senator John Warner (Va.) have led the task of gathering votes to weaken the embargo. One of the most effective actors in the fight against the embargo has been the farm lobby. The success in Congress of the effort to allow the sale of food and medicines to the Castro government has been due to a large extent to the efforts of a large number of

148   *Democracy Delayed*

agricultural associations. In the summer of 2000, more than thirty-eight farm groups were involved in pushing for the end of sanctions on food sales. The list of entities and individuals involved in the anti-embargo movement goes on and on. Besides the farm groups, there are at least twenty-one other well-known organizations I have not mentioned.

For a long time, since at least the 1970s, some congressmen and business-men have expressed their opposition to the U.S. embargo. Horowitz traces the Cuba lobby to 1978. But it was in the 1990s that the anti-embargo campaigns intensified. These efforts came to fruition in 2000, when the most successful challenge to the embargo materialized in the Senate and in the House with votes in favor of partially lifting the embargo. It is not by coincidence that the intensification of the anti-embargo efforts occurred in the 1990s. When Cuba lost its Soviet subsidies at the beginning of the decade, the U.S. embargo be-came a real problem for the Cuban economy, and as I have argued, a political problem for the goal of the Castro dictatorship to maintain itself in power. Hence, the Cuban government has been an active member of the anti-em-bargo movement.

On the pro-embargo side, the NGOs that have confronted the anti-embargo movement have been organizations of Cuban Americans, mainly the Cuban American National Foundation, which represents the majority opinion in the Cuban American community concerning the embargo. As the anti-embargo forces gained strength at the end of the 1990s, Jorge Mas Canosa, the founder of the Cuban American National Foundation, died of cancer. His death left a leadership void at the Foundation that after a period of disarray was partially filled by naming Mas Canosa's son as the head of the organization. The imag-ination and energy of the organization declined. These Cuban American or-ganizations have failed to build coalitions in favor of the embargo. Not until the summer of 2000, when the momentum of the forces against the embargo was leading to victories in Congress, did a non-Cuban American organization, the American Israel Public Affairs Committee, join the effort in favor of the embargo. The 2000 legislation to lift the embargo on the sale of food and med-icines to Cuba also contained provisions to soften sanctions on North Korea, Sudan, Libya and Iran.

The political clout of Cuban Americans based on their electoral strength in south Florida and north New Jersey and their lobbying efforts in Washington, D.C., no longer guarantees their ability to defeat anti-embargo forces. Cuban American organizations opposed to the embargo have not conveyed their

The Economic Embargo   149

messages to individuals and organizations in communities all across the United States, as anti-embargo forces have extensively done. Roiled by the successes of the anti-embargo movement in the summer of 2000, the Cuban American National Foundation started to realize the importance of appealing to the American people, in contrast to the Foundation's traditional strategy of lobbying politicians in Washington directly. In the fall of 2000, CANF showed television commercials in favor of maintaining the embargo in the congressional districts of two members of the House who had played a major role in pushing for the weakening of the sanctions.[111]

The arguments made by anti-embargo advocates are mainly those I have mentioned before. They include claims that trade fosters democracy and/or greater economic reforms, that the embargo has not toppled Castro while it has cost U.S. capitalists potential profits, and that the embargo hurts the common people in Cuba and not the Cuban government.

Anti-embargo groups have been well financed. U.S. foundations alone have provided substantial sums of money to groups that oppose the embargo. Business groups, individual firms, and wealthy business executives have also contributed money for anti-embargo activities. Foundations have financed legislative efforts in Congress and seminars in academic, business, and news media contexts about the negative impact of the embargo. Foundations have also given grants for public campaigns in favor of lifting the embargo, studies on the harmful effects of the embargo on U.S. businesses, and trips to Cuba by Americans who would criticize the embargo upon their return to the United States. The Arca Foundation, from 1994 to 1997, provided about $2.6 million to organizations favoring the normalization of relations between the United States and Cuba. In 1999, Arca gave $359,700 to groups working in the anti-embargo movement. Between 1995 and 1997, the General Services Foundation granted $384,000 to anti-embargo groups. In the same period, the Ford Foundation gave $370,000 to organizations with the clear purpose of lifting the embargo and $1,251,042 to other projects on Cuba whose assistance to the anti-embargo cause is unclear.

Some of the groups promoting normalization of relations between the United States and Cuba that received grants during 1995-97 are: (1) the Cuban Committee for Democracy, received $88,500 from Arca and $130,000 from Ford; (2) the World Policy Institute, received $330,000 from Arca to educate the U.S. business community about the negative consequences of the embargo; one of the activities of the World Policy Institute was to finance a study concluding

150   *Democracy Delayed*

that annual food and medicine sales to Cuba from the United States would be as high as $400 million; (3) the Center for International Policy, received $304,000 from Arca and $240,000 from Ford; the Center promotes the end of the embargo among members of Congress; (4) the American Association for World Health got a grant of $124,000 from Arca, $10,000 from the General Services Foundation, and other grants from the Christopher Reynolds Foundation and the John D. and Catherine T. MacArthur Foundation to write a report on the impact of the embargo on the health of the people in Cuba; the report concluded that the embargo has placed the nutrition and health care of the Cuban population at great risk, particularly after the tightening of the embargo in 1992.[112] The report has been extensively used by anti-embargo advocates even though it is highly flawed empirically and methodologically.[113]

The Cuban government has been a team player, mainly in conjunction with the business lobby, in the campaigns conducted in the United States against the embargo. Those who argue that the Cuban government really does not want the embargo to end because it is useful as a scapegoat for Cuban's economic problems should look at all the effort exerted by Cuban officials to end the embargo. It makes no sense to argue that the Castro government does not want the embargo lifted. A key message of the Cuban government to U.S. businessmen is that they are missing very good opportunities to make money because of the embargo. Cuban officials have met with entrepreneurs and U.S. politicians in Cuba, in the United States, and in Cancún, Mexico. Representatives of business associations, groups of individual entrepreneurs, and U.S. politicians have been traveling to Cuba for years, but with particular intensity in 1999 and 2000, as the campaign to lift bans on the sale of food and medicines to Cuba gained strength. The vice president of the U.S. Chamber of Commerce, Craig Johnstone, declared to the press upon his return from Cuba on May 30, 2000, that the foremost priority of the Chamber was to fight to end the U.S. embargo on Cuba. The Chamber mounted an intense lobbying effort in favor of lifting sanctions on the sale of food and medicine in the summer of 2000.[114]

The Cuban government and business groups in the United States have organized four "business summits" since 1997 in Cancún, where Cubans have gotten together with representatives of such firms and groups as Pepsi Cola, United Airlines, Caterpillar, and the U.S. Rice Producers Association. At the fourth summit, held in June 2000, Raúl de la Nuez, Cuba's minister of foreign commerce at the time, told the participants that the embargo was holding

them back from business opportunities and that Cuba was willing to buy everything if the U.S. embargo was lifted. At the meeting, Donald Riegle Jr., deputy chairman of Shandwick International, said, "We have to find a way to end this embargo."[115]

Cuban officials have also come to the United States or traveled around the country from the Cuban Interests Section in Washington, often with the purpose of speaking at a university, to meet with entrepreneurs and entice them to do business with Cuba. For example, in June 1998, a high-level Cuban diplomat, visiting Minnesota for a university engagement, stopped at Radisson headquarters to meet with T. Peter Blyth, the president of Radisson Hotels Worldwide Development. The Cuban official told Blyth that three sites were still available for hotel development in Cuba and urged Radisson to develop them. After the meeting, Blyth said, "There is a huge pent-up demand for Cuba. When restrictions are lifted, there would be a huge influx [of tourists]."[116] In July 1999, Maria de la Luz B'Hammel, the Cuban director of trade policy for North America, was a guest speaker at the U.S. Grains Council's annual meeting. She said that removing the ban on agricultural sales to Cuba would open up significant opportunities for U.S. farmers. At the meeting, Susan Keith, public policy director for the National Corn Growers Association, mentioned that farmers must make their voices heard if they want the embargo lifted. De la Luz B'Hammel went on to Washington and Iowa to take the same message to other farmers.[117] Farmers have really come to believe that if the embargo is lifted they will be able to make large profits by selling to Cuba. Hence, farm groups, like the American Farm Bureau Federation, the Illinois Farm Bureau, and the American Soybean Association, have come to exert pressure on U.S. senators and congressmen to act against the embargo.[118] U.S. congressmen and senators have even gone to Cuba with members of farm groups and other representatives of the agricultural sector to meet with government officials.[119]

Anti-embargo activists have also enlisted state-level politicians in the movement. A case in point was the trip to Cuba in October 1999 by George Ryan, then governor of Illinois. In this case one can observe the coordination of efforts between activists and Cuban government officials. José Serrano, the head of the Illinois chapter of the Americans for Humanitarian Trade with Cuba, the umbrella organization formed to push for the end of the embargo, was a key figure in orchestrating Ryan's trip to Cuba and the grassroots effort to convince Illinois farmers to lobby in favor of the anti-embargo cause. Ser-

152   *Democracy Delayed*

rano contacted Fernando Ramirez de Estenoz, the chief at the Cuban Interests Section in Washington, and arranged for repeated visits of Cuban officials to Illinois to meet with businessmen and farmer groups. De Estenoz told entrepreneurs in Illinois that Cuba and Illinois would be natural trading partners if the United States would lift the embargo, that Cuba imported $1 billion in food (a false statement), which would increase to $2 billion in five years, and that Cuba would import almost all its food from the United States, especially from the Midwest. By May the Illinois Soybean Association (ISA) was telling its members to mail 3,000 postcards to the White House asking for an end to the embargo and had plans to lobby the U.S. Congress. Tom Wallace, ISA president, mentioned that "what is most exciting is that we are the nearest market for Cuba. If we could ship to them for lower costs than their existing suppliers, we could sell more product."[120] The Illinois farmers had bought the sales pitch of Cuban officials.

Serrano worked in Ryan's electoral campaign, and when Ryan was elected, de Estenoz's second in command at the Interests Section, Johana Tablada, was at Ryan's inauguration party. Serrano and his old friend and ally of Ryan, former State Representative Edgar López, set out to convince Ryan that he should go to Cuba and speak out against the embargo. Ryan must also have been prodded by farmers' groups and big businesses based in Illinois, such as Caterpillar and Archer Daniels Midland, two business concerns that have been very active in the anti-embargo efforts. According to Ryan, there were lots of opportunities for Illinois businesses in Cuba, and he was going to Cuba to be in line and ready to do business as soon as the embargo is lifted. Ryan became a strong advocate against the embargo.[121]

These efforts to build grassroots support for ending the embargo eventually paid off in moving a lot of U.S. congressmen and senators from farm-states to push hard for the partial lifting of the embargo. The incorporation of individual entrepreneurs and business and farm associations in the anti-embargo movement has made the difference between success and failure for the Cuba lobby. The traditional individuals and groups that had battled the embargo had gotten nowhere until corporate America and the farmers got on board.

The anti-embargo lobby had its first taste of success on August 4, 1999, when the U.S. Senate voted 78 to 28 to end sanctions on the sale of food and medicines to the Cuban government. The measure was introduced as an amendment, written by Senator John Ashcroft (R-Mo.), to the Agriculture Appropriation bill.[122] House Republicans, in favor of maintaining the current em-

bargo, eventually defeated, by a slim margin, the amendment in a conference committee.[123] But the victory in the Senate for embargo supporters showed growing support in Congress for lifting sanctions on Cuba. Hence, the anti-embargo movement continued its efforts with renewed confidence. A lobbyist from the U.S. Chamber of Commerce stated, "The Cuba amendment is dead for now, but we are not going to give up."[124]

The campaign against the embargo in 2000 was the most successful ever, with large victories in both the Senate and the House. The push in Congress started around May 2000, although senators from farm-states and other actors opposed to the embargo had been laying the groundwork for the new fight in Congress for several months.[125] On March 23, 2000, Senator Jesse Helms (R-N.C.) dropped his opposition to the sale of food and medicine under mounting pressure from Republican farm-state senators. He allowed the Senate Foreign Relations Committee, which he chaired, to vote for the authorization of such sales. An indication of the force of the anti-embargo campaign was the inability of Senator Helms to prevent the vote. The Helms–Burton law bears his name, and he has been a staunch supporter of maintaining the status quo on the embargo.[126] On May 9, the Senate Appropriations Committee also voted in favor of the sales, allowing their financing by private U.S. institutions. On May 10, the House Appropriations Committee also approved the sale of food and medicines to the Cuban government.[127] By May 16, legislators backing the measure were already predicting that this time they would prevail.[128] The Cuban government agreed. Ricardo Alarcón, president of the Cuban National Assembly, thought that there was a good chance that the U.S. Congress would put an end to the embargo because of mounting support among legislators.[129] On June 5, a delegation of the American Association of Wheat Growers went to Havana to check if Cuban mills and ports could efficiently process U.S. wheat.[130] The optimism about the eventual success of the anti-embargo campaign was well founded. On June 20, the House voted 232 in favor and 186 against to eliminate funds for the enforcement of the restrictions on travel to Cuba by Americans and 301 for and 116 against the lifting of sanctions on the sale of agricultural products and medications to the Cuban government.[131] The same day, the Senate also voted to end the bans on the sale of food and medicines by a vote of 78 to 13. The House version was attached to the Treasury Appropriations bill, which went to a conference committee. As in 1999, supporters of the embargo were able to defeat the weakening of the embargo in the conference committee. The measures easing the embargo on

154   *Democracy Delayed*

Cuba were taken out the House Treasury Appropriations bill on July 27, and the action by the conference committee was ratified on the House floor by a vote of 274 in favor and 270 against.[132] Yet the strength of the anti-embargo movement became more obvious than ever.

Finally, a measure was passed by both chambers in Congress to allow sale of food to Cuba and to make sale of medicines easier; before then, licenses for the sale of medicines and medical equipment were possible. The compromise measure passed the House, as part of the agriculture funding bill, on October 11 and was approved by the Senate on October 18. President Clinton signed the bill into law on October 28. However, financing for such sales from U.S. banks or with credit guarantees from the U.S. government was prohibited. Imports from Cuba or barter for U.S. products was also prohibited. In addition, the prerogative of the executive to lift a ban on U.S. tourism to Cuba was eliminated. The decision on allowing tourism to Cuba was placed in the hands of Congress.[133] Lincoln Díaz-Balart (R-Fla.), Tom DeLay (R-Tex.), and other strong supporters of the embargo convinced the Republican leadership of the House to require such restraints for passage in the House of the measure allowing sales to Cuba. On October 5, 2000, members of the House and Senate conference committee agreed on all the restrictions supported by the House Republican leadership.[134]

Even with the limitations imposed by the Republican leadership in the House, advocates of lifting the ban on the sale of food and medicines predicted that, once such sales were permitted, Cuba would buy significant amounts because Cuba wanted to buy U.S. products and would save a lot of money in shipping costs. Representatives of U.S. agricultural businesses recited what Cuban government officials were telling them in the attempt to get them to push for a weakening of the embargo. John Kavulich, president of the U.S.-Cuba Trade and Economic Council, estimated that sales during the first year would be in the range of $28 million to $45 million.[135] Yet after lifting the embargo on the sale of food and medicines, the Cuban government ruled out any trade with U.S. businesses unless the embargo is totally lifted. *Granma*, the newspaper of the Cuban Communist Party, stated that, with the restrictions on the sales to Cuba, Cuba would not buy one cent of food or medicines from the United States.[136] The experience of lifting restrictions on the sale of food and medicines to Cuba showed that what the Cuban government is really interested in is not to have the ability to buy from the United States but rather to have access to financial resources. Cuba gets most of its food imports, about

The Economic Embargo   155

$700 million a year, through credits or barter deals because the Castro government has insufficient amounts of hard currency.[137]

Between December 2001 and January 2002, Cuba made an exception to its promise not to buy U.S. products until the embargo is completely lifted. The Castro government bought about 220,000 tons of agricultural products from U.S. producers at a cost of about $35 million, paid in cash. The Cuban government stated that the purchase was due to a special circumstance. Hurricane Michelle had passed by Cuba on November 4, 2001, causing extensive damage. Even if the commercial transaction was justifiable in economic terms, the Cuban government and the anti-embargo movement in the United States used the purchase for political purposes. Fidel Castro conditioned further purchases on the continuing softening of the embargo. He reiterated his opposition to the ban on financing from U.S. sources. At the end of 2001, there were ongoing efforts in the U.S. Congress to weaken the embargo. After the purchase, the anti-embargo campaign intensified.

In January 2002, a series of anti-embargo advocates traveled to Cuba, including about one hundred members of the Young Presidents Organization, U.S. Senators Arlen Specter (R-Pa.) and Lincoln Chafee (R-R.I.), and seven members of the U.S. House of Representatives. Marc Carey, an executive of the Lexington Institute, which organized the congressmen's trip to Cuba, declared that it was part of a broad effort to lift the embargo. Kirby Jones, a major figure in the anti-embargo movement in the United States, stated after the sale of foodstuffs that the sale had energized people in the United States about Cuba because now Cuba had done some real business.

In Illinois, Governor George Ryan, another opponent of the embargo, announced his second trip to Cuba, set for January 24, 2002. The governor was making the trip to Cuba under a license held by the Americans for Humanitarian Trade with Cuba, an anti-embargo organization with ties to Archer Daniels Midland (ADM), based in Illinois. ADM was one of the main suppliers of foodstuffs sold to Cuba in December 2001–January 2002. Ryan had joined executives of ADM in New Orleans in December 2001 for a ceremony commemorating the shipment of agricultural products to Cuba.[138]

Lifting some economic sanctions on Cuba generates pressures to expand the demolition of the embargo. This is what at least some of the anti-embargo advocates have had in mind all along when they asked for the end of the ban on the sale of food and medicines. In the words of Shawn Malone, coordinator of the Cuba Program of the Caribbean Project of Georgetown University,

156   *Democracy Delayed*

"in terms of policy, the ability to sell anything to Cuba is significant because it opens a hole in a blanket prohibition. A lot of people would see that as a way to get a foot in the door."[139] After committees in the House and the Senate had approved legislation to allow the sale of food and medicines to the Cuban government, the U.S.-Cuba Trade and Economic Council asked the U.S. Congress to normalize banking relations between the United States and Cuba for sales of agricultural products to Cuba.[140] The same demand was made by various individual U.S. firms to the Office of Foreign Assets Control (OFAC).[141] When an agreement was reached in the House on allowing the sale of food and medicine but to prohibit credits to the Cuban government to finance the sales, anti-embargo lobbyists and the Cuban government screamed in disapproval.

After the agreement was made in the House, the Cuban government said that under those terms it could not buy.[142] The American Farm Bureau Federation then argued that sales to Cuba would be jeopardized if the Cuban government could not have access to credits from U.S. private banks. Other individuals and business associations involved in the push to lift sanctions on the sale of food and medicines added their voices in the chorus of pleas to have Cuba gain access to credits from U.S. sources.[143] Also, it is not a coincidence that the attempt to lift sanctions on the sale of agricultural products and medicines to Cuba accompanied the effort to end restrictions on tourism from the United States to Cuba. Knowing that the Cuban government is short on foreign currency and that tourism is the major source of foreign currency earnings for the Cuban government, it was not hard for U.S. businessmen to figure out that the more revenue from tourism the better able the Cuban government would be to pay for food imports. Moreover, the more tourists going to Cuba, the more food Cuba would need. In July 1999, at the U.S. Grains Council annual meeting, the vice president of the Cuban food import agency, Alimport, said that Cuba needed food for its growing tourist industry and predicted that by the year 2010 Cuba would need to feed 10 million tourists annually.[144]

Conclusions

Given the nature of the Castro regime, neither the embargo nor engagement can be expected to lead to political liberalization. If the effectiveness of the embargo is judged in terms of its ability to change the political policies of the Cuban government, then the embargo is not an effective measure. The in-

ternational relations literature on economic sanctions tends to evaluate the effectiveness of unilateral sanctions by the criterion of whether they change the policies or behaviors of target countries. But unilateral economic sanctions might not have this purpose. The U.S. embargo on the Castro government, for example, does not have this aim. Rather, the main goal is to help bring about the demise of the Castro regime. Consistent with previous findings on the successes of economic sanctions in destabilizing target governments, the U.S. embargo, at this juncture in Cuban history, weakens the Castro government by reducing its financial resources. The main concern of the Cuban government about the embargo is not with constraints on trade but with curtailment of revenue to the state. Scholars writing on the effects of economic sanctions and others studying the relationship between economic performance and regime changes agree in observing that economic problems undermine dictatorships. In Cuba in the 1990s, economic deterioration went together with the development of civil society, spontaneous popular protests triggered by economic grievances, and greater discontent among government cadres fueled by decreases in material resources. Reversing the situation, and helping Cuba's economy improve by lifting the embargo, is not bound to promote democracy. First of all, the comparative data do not support the hypothesis that economic growth causes transitions to democracy. And second, the high degree of government control over the economy prevents the spread of wealth among actors independent of the state, a key assumption in modernization theory, which argues that economic development brings about democracy.

Yet the embargo by itself is not enough to cause a political transition in Cuba. For this to occur, the U.S. government has to supplement the embargo with material assistance to the internal opposition and with the technical improvements in Radio and TV Martí that are needed to surmount the jamming done by the Cuban government. But these additional measures have not yet been implemented. As Hufbauer, Schott, and Elliott conclude, unilateral economic sanctions can undermine governments if complemented with other policies.

Even if a negotiated political transition might be possible in Cuba after Fidel Castro dies or becomes physically or mentally incapable of ruling, a reduction in the resources available to the ruling elite would help increase the probability of a transition by fostering the emergence of softliners able and willing to negotiate. As the literature on transitions to democracy from authoritarian rule has emphasized, crises, including economic ones, tend to mo-

158   *Democracy Delayed*

tivate softliners to implement political liberalization and also strengthen them in confronting hardliners. Thus, even under a different type of dictatorial regime, the embargo would help rather than hinder a transition in Cuba. For a negotiated transition, viable softliners are necessary, and it is when authoritarian or mature post-totalitarian regimes face serious difficulties that they tend to appear.

The anti-embargo lobby, long impotent, made a great leap in power by getting corporate American to join its ranks. Its success in weakening the trade embargo has shown that what the Castro government needs and wants is financial resources. Now, many U.S. businessmen, blinded by the glitter of promised profits and misguided about the political consequences of their actions, want to give Castro what he wants, on the assumption that then he will be able to pay for U.S. goods. The next battle cry of the anti-embargo movement is to lift the ban on U.S. tourism to the island an on financial credits to the Castro government. If they succeed, the Castro regime will receive a significant increase in its income, a boost that would help the dictatorship endure.

CHAPTER 7

Conclusions

Some scholars analyzing the demise of communist rule in Eastern Europe argue that the problems those dictatorships faced were so severe that they had to fall.[1] Yet while those problems or underlying conditions were necessary for the transitions, they were not sufficient. The list of conditions presented was incomplete. In the 1990s, Cuba confronted similar or worse difficulties, and the dictatorship endures. The explanation I have offered for the non-transition in Cuba points to factors that are necessary but missing. These conditions were taken for granted by many scholars in explaining the Eastern European transitions. The missing conditions can be created, manufactured by human determination. They depend on the strategies that the relevant actors pursue.

The typical distinction made in the literature on transitions between "conditions" and the strategic behavior of actors is not clear cut. Actors can create conditions. Even if all the necessary conditions are in place, there is certainly a role for the strategic behavior of key actors. One cannot predict the demise of communist dictatorships solely by pointing to underlying conditions. As Przeworski, Huntington, and others have indicated, democracies are created

160   *Democracy Delayed*

by individuals.[2] (That is where this book has policy implications for bringing about a political transformation in Cuba.) Since the creation of necessary conditions and the utilization of opportunities presented by those conditions depend on the strategies pursued by actors, whether a transition will take place in Cuba is uncertain. This indeterminacy is typical of all transition processes, as O'Donnell and Schmitter have argued.[3]

The Cuban case points to the crucial importance of two factors for a transition: (1) a widespread belief in the population that change is possible, a belief in political efficacy among people, and (2) the ability of independent sources of communication to reach a large percentage of the population regularly. Independent means of communication are vital to developing a sense of political efficacy among citizens. In Cuba, in contrast to the Eastern European cases at the end of the 1980s, these two factors are missing. The feeling of efficacy spread in Eastern Europe at the end of the 1980s. It was scarce before that time. The belief in political efficacy can be created under some conditions.

Except for the work of Opp, Voss, and Gern, scholars analyzing the transitions in Eastern Europe tend to make only casual reference to the role that beliefs in political efficacy played in the transitions from communism. Although studies conducted before the end of the 1980s concluded that citizens in Eastern European countries did not feel efficacious in their ability to achieve political change, the situation was different at the end of the 1980s. By that time, a widespread sense of political efficacy had developed among the citizens of those countries. Przeworski refers to the sequence of transitions in Eastern Europe as a domino effect and argues that as the process of transition took place in one country people elsewhere updated their probabilities of success in toppling their own dictatorship.[4] The implication is that people developed a sense of efficacy. But although Przeworki says that demonstration effects are important in transitions to democracy, very little attention is paid to this factor. The strength of the sense of political efficacy in the population is underestimated and its development is taken for granted. That Eastern Europeans would know what was happening in their neighboring countries is minimized. Huntington argues that transitions via regime collapse, what he refers to as transitions by replacement, occur when some triggering event exposes the weakness of the regime, thereby disclosing and galvanizing popular disaffection.[5] But for an event to have this consequence, it must be widely known. Thus Huntington's argument presupposes that some means of communication independent from the regime could reach,

Conclusions 161

without much delay, a large percentage of the population. Such a condition is missing in Cuba.

My main arguments can be summarized as follows. A transition from communism requires certain underlying conditions, specifically, serious problems faced by the regime. These problems include a decay of ideological legitimacy among regime cadres and poor economic performance, which further erode support for the system among members of the regime. One of the consequences of a decline in support from cadres is that the ability of the regime to repress acts of defiance by dissidents and the general population declines. This does not mean that repression is not considerable, especially in hardline regimes. Support for the regime in the population is also low, but that may have been so for a long time before the regime became brittle. However, the decay in ideological legitimacy and the deterioration of economic conditions further reduce whatever popular support the regime still enjoys. Also, what these crises do is weaken the dictatorship, making it more vulnerable when confronted with pressures from below.

I have indicated that all of these conditions are present in Cuba. There is an association between the economic quagmire since 1990 and increasing signs of discontent with the regime among citizens and regime cadres. Dissatisfaction with economic conditions has induced citizens to show their grievances in public spontaneously and to engage in collective action to demand resources from the government. If news about these actions was disseminated in the population, it would help generate a sense of political efficacy. Thus, discontent with economic conditions is not only a latent motivation that can induce people to join demonstrations to demand political changes once the numbers of citizens in the streets is large. The unhappiness with the economic situation can also act as a catalyst in the onset of protests.

Then, the regime must experience pressure from below. This pressure has to be more intense in hardline regimes, like the ones I have focused on in this book, than in regimes that liberalize as a step prior to transitions. Large and repeated mass demonstrations are necessary for transitions by regime collapse. For these kind of protests to occur, a sense of political efficacy must be widespread in the population. People must believe that their participation in public acts of defiance can bring about political changes.

What really matters for mass demonstrations is what people in the general population think. While courageous civil society activists defy the regime, without repeated, large-scale demonstrations by the general population, those

who thus far have not been involved in any independent or opposition activities, there cannot be a transition from below. Democratic activists comprise a small percentage of the population and therefore cannot by themselves produce mass protests of the magnitude that brought about the collapse of regimes in East Germany, Czechoslovakia, and Romania.

A belief that political change is possible does not necessarily mean that people expect to achieve a transition to democracy. The expected change could be only political liberalization in a hardline regime. But once a continuous uprising takes place, the regime might fall. A sense of political efficacy in the population can be developed in more than one way. In Eastern Europe, the contagion effect contributed to the spread of such belief among the citizens of countries in the region. A demonstrated strong commitment by the United States to help opposition groups in Cuba bring about change can foster confidence that a political transformation can take place. Domestic actors can also generate a widespread sense of efficacy. The actions of democratic activists and spontaneous protests in the population triggered by acts of injustice on the part of the regime and out of socioeconomic grievances in the population convey messages of popular discontent and defiance.

Since civil society activists can foster a sense of efficacy in the population, the strength of civil society as well as their strategic behaviors are important for the prospects of a transition. Civil society groups by themselves do not topple communist dictatorships, but they can serve as both catalysts and leaders for democratic revolutions. But to develop a sense of political efficacy in the population, it is necessary for independent sources of communication to reach a large percentage of the population on a regular basis. People have to receive the kinds of information that can lead them to believe that acts of defiance can be effective.

International factors play a more important role in transitions from communism than in transitions from other types of dictatorships. International actors can help or hinder the process of transition. The policies of the United States and the former Soviet Union have been vital in determining transitions, even when the impetus for the transitions emanates from the countries under dictatorial rule. The end of the Brezhnev doctrine lifted a crucial constraint to change in Eastern Europe. Also, to the extent that foreign actors provide material assistance to civil society groups under communism, the role played by these groups as catalysts of change is facilitated. Even more important for the prospects of transition has been whether foreign radio and television broad-

casts serve as effective means of independent communication. The role of these foreign stations is particularly important in transitions from communism, in comparison to transitions from authoritarian regimes, because of the extent to which channels of communication are controlled by the state under communism. The role of foreign radio and television stations is even more crucial in transitions from hardline communist regimes, which are transitions by collapse.

Once an uprising occurs in a hardline regime, those with guns face the choice of whether to shoot. If people are not shot, the regime collapses. If some members of the regime shoot and units of the armed forces or the political police join the people and succeed in defeating the forces that try to save the regime, a political transition from communism takes place. If brute force succeeds in ending the uprising, the regime survives, at least for a time. Whether the first two scenarios occur depends on the deterioration of support for the regime among cadres and on whether the people in the streets protest peacefully.

Following Linz and Stepan's typology of dictatorships, I classify the Castro regime as a mixture of frozen post-totalitarianism and sultanism. Consistent with theoretical arguments connecting regime types and likely transition paths, Fidel Castro and other hardliners dominate and adamantly oppose political liberalization.[6] No political softliners are visible in the regime. A political transition, initiated and negotiated by regime elites, is impossible in Cuba under the current regime. However, if the type of regime changes, then a political transition in which softliners play an important role might be possible. But given the nature of the Castro regime, only a transition by collapse seems possible, that is, a transition initiated and pushed by civil society and the population at large. If large numbers of people do not decide to participate in protests, a transition from below cannot occur. Mass demonstrations to demand democratization are necessary, although not sufficient. The relevancy of the transition paths of East Germany, Czechoslovakia, and Romania for Cuba is shown by the intense concern of the Castro regime about losing control of the streets. Even small acts of public defiance are routinely repressed. This behavior on the part of the Cuban government indicates that it considers the development of mass protests to be a serious threat to its survival.

A transition from below is objectively possible in Cuba under the government of Fidel Castro, as it fits the common pattern in the other cases when dictatorships faced one or more types of "crisis" prior to their downfall. Since the

164   *Democracy Delayed*

1990s, the strength of civil society, in terms of numbers of groups and of activists, is similar to or greater than in the Eastern European cases of transition by collapse. There is widespread discontent with the regime among the population, including young people. Dissatisfaction among young people is particularly threatening to the regime. It was the young who spearheaded the 1989 revolutions in Eastern Europe. At times, social unrest publicly bursts out. The Cuban economy is in shambles, even worse than the stagnant or declining economies in Eastern Europe at the end of the 1980s. The government is unable to meet the basic needs of the population under the economic system that Fidel Castro refuses to change.[7] The standard of living of the population sharply declined in the 1990s, with no significant improvement in sight. Poor economic performance further reduces whatever legitimacy the regime still enjoys. Cuba, as did Eastern European countries under communist rule, is experiencing a high degree of social decay indicated by widespread alcoholism, suicide, abortions as a means of birth control, prostitution, and divorce.[8] The social decay is a sign of intense discontent with prevailing conditions.

Faith and commitment to the official ideology have disintegrated. One factor involved in the decay of ideology has been the growing disjunction between official ideology and reality, as Linz and Stepan observe in transformations from totalitarian to post-totalitarian regimes.[9] Corruption in all spheres of the government and at all levels of hierarchies is pervasive. There is dissatisfaction with the regime among civilian cadres and military officers. The Party is having difficulties recruiting new members. The number of party members who have turned in their party cards or otherwise ceased their membership in the Party might be even larger than is assumed. Being a member of the Party does not necessarily imply ideological commitment. Most of those who join the Communist Party do so to seek personal benefits, jobs, or access to higher education. A sign of the ideological decay in Cuba is the concern the Cuban government shows about the paucity of ideological fervor. The government carries out campaigns to build "political culture," maintaining that the "battle of ideas" will be fought every day. Yet the discrimination of the regime against its own citizens in favor of foreigners reduces government appeals for support based on nationalism. Reports from Cuba and interviews with recent refugees show that the majority of people do not pay attention to nationalist appeals by the Cuban government based on its confrontation with the United States.[10]

The key to understanding the non-transition in Cuba is to explain why recurrent mass demonstrations developed in Czechoslovakia, East Germany, and Ro-

Conclusions   165

mania and not in Cuba. In addressing this query, I point to differences between Cuba and these other countries that really matter in accounting for the transitions and the non-transition. I agree with the logical argument that a transition has not taken place in Cuba because Cuba is different from Eastern Europe. The problem in the literature on Cuba is that the differences between Cuba and Eastern European cases that have been presented are the wrong ones. Some are empirically incorrect. In Cuba there has been no mass defection from the Communist Party, but that did not happen in the hardline regimes in Eastern Europe until they were already falling apart just before the end of communism. The contrast between Cuba and Eastern Europe in terms of the origins of the dictatorships cannot explain why in Cuba mass demonstrations to demand political changes have not taken place as they did in Czechoslovakia and East Germany. The argument that in Cuba the Castro regime resulted from a national revolution while in Eastern Europe communism was imposed by Soviet power implies that the Cuban dictatorship endures because it enjoys popular support. This is a flawed assumption. As in Cuba, communism was imposed in the Soviet Union after a national revolution; yet the overwhelming rejection of the Soviet regime was evident in the transition process of that country. Also, one should not lose sight of the fact that the revolutionary struggle in Cuba against Batista was made in the name of democracy, not Marxism-Leninism. The case of Nicaragua also shows that homegrown communist regimes can be rejected by the majority of the population. When the Sandinista government allowed a free election in 1990, it lost.

I have found the numerous explanations for the endurance of the Castro government to be mistaken or inadequate. The non-transition in the 1990s cannot be explained by the loyalty of members of the Communist Party or by the alleged legitimacy of the regime among the population. Under dictatorships there are no reliable survey data to measure the degree of support that the regime has among the population. Nonetheless, in the Cuban case there are various indirect signs, such as repeated waves of rafters desperately risking their lives to leave Cuba, which show pervasive aversion toward the regime. The very poor economic performance in Cuba since the beginning of the 1990s has increased the grievances of the population. Although there might still be a percentage of the population that genuinely supports the Castro government, most likely such a percentage is very small. The data cited in the introduction show that democratic activists in Cuba believe that the majority of the population does not support the regime. One group estimates that more than 80 percent of the population is against the government.

166   *Democracy Delayed*

The current numbers of independent groups and of civil society activists in Cuba do not preclude a transition to democracy. By these criteria, civil society in Cuba is not weak. Actually, from this perspective civil society in Cuba is stronger than it was in Romania and similar to the strength of independent groups in Czechoslovakia and East Germany in 1989. Nor is civil society in Cuba "atomized," as some claim. Independent groups have collaborated in carrying out various activities, and the proclivity for coordinated action is increasing. The Castro government is constantly monitoring and repressing activists. Civil society has become a permanent challenge to the regime.

Neither the objectives nor the strategies nor the timing that many opposition activists have in mind appear to be obstacles to the development of a transition process. There is a wide consensus among opposition groups that the goals are to achieve transitions to democracy and to markets. With respect to strategies, groups want to demand changes peacefully and have a fairly clear idea of what has to be done to achieve a transition. The idea of promoting peaceful street demonstrations to demand political changes is also commonly accepted by opposition groups in Cuba. These strategic views are in line with the types of activities that would foster a transition from below. Those groups that participated in the CEON study think that it is not necessary to wait for Fidel Castro to die of natural causes. Hence what is holding up a transition in Cuba is not the time frame that opposition groups have for pushing the transition process.

Other hypotheses for the non-transition in Cuba are that repression is too strong and civil society is too weak. Often this weakness of civil society is directly attributed to the repression. Some scholars argue that these factors are the key reasons for the endurance of the Castro dictatorship. The repressive apparatus, however, does not assure the survival of the regime in Cuba. The degree of repression in Romania before the end of 1989 was more intense than in Cuba today. In terms of government repression, Cuba is similar to East Germany and Czechoslovakia. The survival of the regime apparently rests only on the ability of the repressive apparatus to prevent the emergence of peaceful, massive, and repeated demonstrations to demand democratization. The Castro regime has been winning the battle for the streets because only small numbers of people, usually only democratic activists, engage in public protests. In the hardline regimes of East Germany, Czechoslovakia, and Romania, when dissidents were alone in confronting the forces of repression, they got routed. Yet when massive demonstrations developed, the dictatorships collapsed. The

Cuban dictatorship cannot be defeated in the battle for the streets without the participation of thousands of people. While repression is certainly an important pillar of the Castro regime, it is an inadequate explanation for the absence of continuous, peaceful mass protests. Repression cannot explain the endurance of the Cuban government unless two things happen: (1) large public demonstrations take place and the government massacres people in the streets, and (2) the outcome is a Chinese scenario rather than a Romanian one—that is, people are shot and the possibility of transition is aborted.

One cannot predict with certainty whether those with guns in Cuba will shoot people if large and repeated protests to demand political changes take place. Various indications from Cuba suggest that the Chinese solution at Tiananmen is not likely to be implemented. Even if some units of the political police fire on the population in Cuba, segments of the military or of the security apparatus might side with the population, as occurred in Romania. The military as an institution is not involved in repressing civil society. O'Donnell and Schmitter argue that the less the military is involved in repression, the less it should fear a transition to democracy.[11] The discontent with the regime among military officers in Cuba, indications of disloyalty among members of the political police, and the generalized decay of ideology make it doubtful that orders to fire on the population will be obeyed. Most of the security forces might allow the regime to collapse rather than fire on people protesting in the streets.[12] Thus far, in the few large spontaneous protests that have occurred in Cuba, involving from a few hundred to a few thousand people, no one has fired. If some units of the security forces fire on the population, other units might join the people. Most members of opposition groups in Cuba do not think that those with guns will fire on peaceful protesters. Democratic activists perceive that the population thinks likewise.

The fundamental obstacle to a transition in Cuba is that people feel incapable of inducing a political transformation. This is a key difference between Cuba today and Eastern European countries at the end of the 1980s. Unless people believe that their participation in public protests to demand democratization will bring about political changes, there are no regular mass demonstrations and hence no transition by regime collapse. Large-scale participation in protests to demand democratization does not occur in Cuba basically because the majority of the population feels that their political participation in opposition activities would be ineffective in achieving change; most people feel politically inefficacious. For a political transition to occur in Cuba, a large

168   *Democracy Delayed*

percentage of the population will have to develop a sense of political efficacy.

I question the conventional wisdom about Cuba, which assumes that fear of repression is the main explanation for the very low level of citizen participation in opposition activities. Despite the repression in Cuba, people have shown that they are able to overcome their fear by participating in spontaneous protests against the regime. These spontaneous protests have been controlled by the government because they have been ephemeral, have not spread simultaneously throughout Cuba, and have not involved very large numbers of people (in comparison to the mass demonstrations in Eastern Europe on the eve of the political transitions there). The survey conducted by Opp, Voss, and Gern in Leipzig soon after the end of communist rule in East Germany indicates that people decided to participate in protests despite their fear of repression.[13] People can overcome their fears under certain conditions. Repression in Romania under Ceauşescu was harsher than in Cuba today and yet an uprising occurred.

Repression in itself is insufficient to explain the shortcomings of civil society in Cuba at the turn of the millennium. In Cuba, the space of freedom, although very limited, increased in the 1990s. Democratic activists and other independent actors have had more room to operate without fear of execution or imprisonment as in earlier times. This greater space for independent activism seems to have resulted from a combination of societal conquest and regime decay.[14] Although the fall of communism in Eastern Europe was not sufficient to produce a domino effect in Cuba, the example of Eastern Europe encouraged Cuban activists. At the same time, with the economic decline in the 1990s, the capacity of the Cuban government to exert control over the population has declined. One indication is the government's inability to stop the pervasive theft of government property. As discontent among regime cadres has increased, in part due to the decay of the economy, the zeal for surveillance and repression among cadres has declined. A sign of this is the deterioration in the functioning of the Committees to Defend the Revolution. Moreover, with greater dependence on market relations with democratic countries, the Castro government has become more vulnerable to pressures from foreign actors to respect human rights. Although such pressures have not led to respect for human rights or to political liberalization, denunciations of human rights violation in international forums have helped to reduce repression. The Cuban case supports the argument that international norms concerning human rights and the desirability of democracy can decrease repres-

sion in dictatorships facing such pressures. However, where hardliners dominate and softliners have no chance to emerge, as in Cuba, even strong pressures to respect international norms are not decisive in bringing about political transitions. The Cuban case is relevant in assessing how important the Helsinki Accords of 1975 were in fostering transitions in the hardline regimes of Eastern Europe.

Although, as Saxonberg argues, civil society groups in Eastern Europe in the late 1980s by themselves did not topple the dictatorships, there is evidence that, even in the hardline regimes of Czechoslovakia and East Germany, democratic activists served as catalysts to the mass demonstrations.[15] This was so even in cases, like East Germany, where the uprising is said to have occurred spontaneously. Democratic activists can help to develop a sense of political efficacy in the population and lead the opposition to the regime once mass demonstrations surge. What is important is the dissemination of signals that change is possible: messages of popular defiance and of partial successes against autocratic regimes. In principle, these messages do not have to be diffused from abroad; they can come from sources and events internal to a particular country. In the case of Romania, a sense of efficacy was created by the diffusion effect. But even there, individual dissidents played a role. The Timisoara revolt was triggered by a dissident priest. By their acts of opposition, activists can provide a model to the population and show them that there are individuals willing to defy the regime. The larger the protests organized by dissidents, the greater the impact these protests should have in building a sense of efficacy. The occurrence of demonstrations, even if some people are beaten up or arrested, show that large numbers of citizens can overcome their fear and participate in acts of opposition. Activists can also let people know about reprehensible actions of the regime. Outrage can induce some people in the general population to protest. Dissidents can also spread information about spontaneous protests, raise the consciousness of the population about the importance of their participation in demonstrations, and provide political and economic alternatives to those under the dictatorship. Democratic activists can help organize citizens into non-political groups, such as farmers' cooperatives or neighborhood associations with social aims. Although the original intent of these groups is non-political, they can channel their members into activities to push for democratization at some point in time.

In Cuba, civil society has the potential to play a catalytic role, but the realization of that potential is frustrated by the absence of effective independent

170   *Democracy Delayed*

channels of communication. Civil society activists and grassroots initiatives have achieved what can be considered victories over the Castro government. The regime regularly commits grave injustices, not only against dissidents but also against regular citizens. Small, spontaneous protests often take place. If all of these things were widely known, people could start to believe that their participation in protests would be effective in bringing about political change. In Eastern Europe, the diffusion effect was important in building the belief in political efficacy among the populations in the region. Since the Eastern European contagion effect did not extend to Cuba, the task of civil society activists in cultivating political efficacy among the Cuban population is even more crucial for the prospect of a transition in the island.

The dearth of popular participation in activities promoted by civil society activists in Cuba could be seen as a weakness of civil society, as an incapacity to induce mass protests in the struggle for democracy. Repression in itself is insufficient to explain this shortcoming of civil society. In contrast to Eastern Europe, the lack of effective independent channels of communication in Cuba hinders the ability of civil society groups to play the catalytic role that independent groups did in fostering mass protests in Eastern Europe. Independent communication is a crucial determinant of mass protests.

A fundamental factor in the production of a widespread sense of political efficacy among the population is the ability of independent sources of communication to let people know what civil society activists are doing and saying, what acts of opposition are taking place, what outrageous acts the regime is committing, and other news and information that can motivate individuals to participate in popular protests to demand political changes. It is not just a matter of independent sources of communication being able to reach a large percentage of the population on a regular basis. The content of the communication matters. The activities of civil society in Eastern Europe, mass demonstrations in neighboring countries, acts of repression against demonstrators, and the caving in of dictatorships starting with Poland conveyed messages that there were people willing to confront the dictatorships publicly to demand respect for human rights and democratization, that successes were possible, and that rulers had carried out outrageous acts (e.g., the rumor that a student had been killed in the demonstration of November 17, 1989, in Czechoslovakia).

The role of Radio Free Europe and of samizdat publications should not be underestimated in explaining the Eastern European transitions. They are often

Conclusions   171

overlooked in pointing to the importance of the snowball or domino effect in the transitions. Radio Free Europe/Radio Liberty reached large percentages of the populations in Eastern European countries and influenced public opinion. East Germans received West German radio and television broadcasts. West German transmissions could be picked up in parts of Czechoslovakia and Hungary. The same can be said of Austrian news.[16] Hungarian television broadcasts were seen by Hungarian-speaking Romanians; this helped spread important information in Romania as Hungary underwent political liberalization. It is indicative of the role of communication in developing a sense of political efficacy that the Romanian revolution started with protests by the Hungarian minority. Timisoara, the birthplace of the revolution, is close to Hungary. Also, in many Eastern European countries (including Czechoslovakia and East Germany), in contrast with Cuba, the production and dissemination of samizdat literature was quite developed.

RFE/RL served as surrogate stations for dissidents. Democratic activists played a catalytic role in fostering mass demonstration by disseminating their views and calls to action among the population via samizdat and foreign radio and television broadcasts. This is a role that civil society groups in Cuba could play if they were able to communicate widely with the people. People in Cuba crave news and information from independent sources. In Cuba, as opposition groups have grown and increased their coordination, as they have stepped up their activities since the mid-1990s, their ability to communicate with the population has declined. An indication of the importance of independent channels of communication for the prospects of a transition from communism is that the Castro government has spared no effort or expense to forestall the ability of independent channels of communication to reach most of the population reliably. The intense jamming of Radio and TV Martí is a prime example. The government has progressively jammed Radio Martí since 1990.

In Cuba civil society activists lack the ability to convey news and information to the majority of the population on a regular basis. The independent means of communication are either missing or effectively jammed by the Cuban government. The total blackout of TV Martí, the poor channel effectiveness of Radio Martí, and the practically nonexistent samizdat literature produced in Cuba are key obstacles to the development of a sense of political efficacy and thus a key impediment to a political transition. In Cuba one finds the conjunction of two factors: (1) the lack of independent channels of communication able to reach most of the population on a regular basis, and (2) the

172   *Democracy Delayed*

absence of a widespread sense of political efficacy in the population. I contend that these missing factors are fundamental components in accounting for the non-transition in the island.

The main obstacle to the production of samizdat in Cuba is lack of resources in the hands of the opposition. Activists are simply not getting the necessary money and equipment from abroad. Opposition groups in East Germany and Czechoslovakia had more resources than their Cuban counterparts to produce samizdat. A significant increase in humanitarian assistance and resources for the production and distribution of samizdat would considerably boost the effectiveness of civil society activists in fostering a transition.

Greater material assistance would increase the size and strength of civil society in Cuba. In Cuba, more people would join independent groups if they knew that they could provide for basic necessities. Democratic activists in Cuba suffer greater economic repression than their counterparts in Czechoslovakia and East Germany under communist rule. The Cuban government closes all employment opportunities to members of civil society groups. Self-help networks in Cuba are hindered by the poor economic conditions of the general population. Private entrepreneurship, including independent farms, is severely curtailed by the government. The population is economically very dependent on the state. Self-help networks were established in Poland, but in that country the population was less dependent on the state. For example, the agricultural sector was mostly in private hands. In Cuba, the agricultural sector continues to be almost completely dominated by the government. Also, the material assistance sent to Eastern European countries from abroad was more focused on humanitarian assistance than is the case for Cuba. Besides the importance of humanitarian assistance for the sustenance of civil society activists and their families, to the extent that independent groups are able to distribute humanitarian assistance among the population, opposition activists gain the admiration and support of the population; people are more willing to defend them against the repressive apparatus. With more funds activists would also be better able to travel and coordinate efforts among themselves in different parts of the country.

Scholars who analyzed the transitions in Latin America and Southern Europe in the 1970s and 1980s concluded that international factors were of minor importance and focused on the strategic interactions of domestic actors. But in transitions from communist dictatorships international actors have played crucial roles, even though the impetuses for the political changes

Conclusions 173

have been internal. The foreign policies of the regional hegemonic power have been of major importance. For the Eastern European transitions, Gorbachev's decision to let Eastern European countries go their own way without having to face Soviet tanks lifted a vital constraint. In the Western Hemisphere, U.S. foreign policies were a critical determinant of the transitions in Grenada and Nicaragua. In Grenada, the transition was a consequence of a U.S. military invasion. In Nicaragua, the U.S. economic embargo and material assistance to the anti-communist insurgency, the "Contras," was part of the pressure that drove the Sandinistas to hold free elections in 1990.

Following the pattern, U.S. policies toward Cuba have proven to be the single most important factor in explaining the non-transition. The Soviet Union and the United States influenced the transition processes in each other's backyards—the United States by sponsoring Radio Free Europe/Radio Liberty and providing material assistance to civil society groups in Eastern Europe. The disintegration of the Soviet Union, resulting in the end of Soviet subsidies to the Cuban economy, has contributed to the weakening of the Castro regime by substantially worsening its economic performance. So, the end of the Soviet Union is an underlying condition of the potential transition in Cuba.

Besides the United States and the Soviet Union, other international factors have been important in transitions from communism. In Eastern Europe, the contagion effect that successively toppled the communist dominos played a crucial role. Gorbachev's domestic policy of glasnost contributed to the diffusion effect, but events in Poland, Hungary, and other countries were also part of the diffusion phenomenon. In the case of Cuba, the actions or inactions of important Cuban American actors are important in accounting for the prospects of a transition in the island. The importance of external actors is one more reason why Eastern Europe is more relevant to the Cuban case than transitions from authoritarian regimes in Latin America or Southern Europe, where the role of international factors was of marginal importance.

The amounts and kinds of material assistance reaching civil society groups in Cuba and the ability of Radio and TV Martí to reach the population depend on strategic decisions made by both domestic and international actors, especially the latter. The meager amounts of humanitarian aid and resources for the production of samizdat that the Cuban opposition has received seems ironic given that the U.S. government has a program of assistance to civil society groups in Cuba and many Cuban Americans are well-off economically.

174   *Democracy Delayed*

The Catholic Church in Cuba has adopted a position of accommodation with the regime and has refused to provide democratic activists with resources, in contrast to the Catholic Church in Poland and the Protestant Church in East Germany. Yet the strategy of accommodation toward the Castro government followed by the Catholic hierarchy in Cuba has not been very fruitful for the Church. The degree of pluralism for the Church has remained quite limited, and by mid-2001 the government seemed poised to roll back the spaces of freedom that the Church has conquered in its efforts to evangelize. Thus, it is conceivable that the Catholic hierarchy might modify its strategy to be more lenient and helpful toward civil society activists, even at the cost of increased tensions with the government. But so far the Catholic Church in Cuba has not played a facilitating role in the process of transition.

The Cuban American community has considerable economic resources and political power to influence U.S. foreign policies toward Cuba. Thus, the position of important actors in this community toward providing material assistance to independent groups in Cuba is an important determinant of the resources that opposition groups in Cuba receive. So far, the exile community has not provided significant material assistance to independent groups in Cuba. An adequate account of this behavior requires survey research. Yet, personal conversations with a number of members of this community leads me to believe that part of the explanation is a strategic myopia on the part of some opposition leaders, both in Cuba and in the United States. On the one hand, many activists in Cuba have publicly advocated positions which are supported by the Cuban government, such as opposition to the embargo. This behavior hinders trust and sympathy among part of the exile community toward the internal opposition. Attacking the embargo is not necessary for independent groups in Cuba to appeal to the population since the majority of the people in Cuba think that the main source of their problems is the Castro government and not the embargo. On the other hand, exile leaders in Miami lost sight of the fact that the internal opposition wants a transition to democracy, as the exiles do, and that the people in Cuba will play the predominant role in the transition. The most important thing is not the position of opposition activists in Cuba with respect to the embargo, but their quest for democracy and their activities to make this goal a reality.

The Cuban American National Foundation, the wealthiest exile organization, had not provided much assistance to the internal opposition until 2002. One reason seems to be that CANF had only been willing to help groups in Cuba on the condition that they follow CANF's directives. This is a mistaken

strategy at the pre-transition stage, in which opposition groups, both inside and outside Cuba, should overlook their differences and join forces in the struggle against the dictatorship. CANF might see some democratic activists in Cuba as potential rivals in the leadership of a transition government and in the post-transition period. It is premature for CANF to advance its aspirations for leadership in a post-transition period.

CANF and the Cuban Americans in the U.S. House of Representatives seem to have been hesitant, despite claims to the contrary, to push for a significant increase in material assistance to opposition groups in Cuba from the U.S. government. The irresolution on the part of these key Cuban American actors in Washington may have been due to the negative perception of dissidents in Cuba among exiles and the strategic calculations of CANF. However, recent developments indicate that the behavior of exiles, including CANF, is becoming more favorable to the idea of providing substantial material assistance to civil society groups in Cuba.

Something that has been going on for some time, and may explain at least in part the change in attitude among some exiles toward the internal opposition, is an international campaign to publicize the courageous activities of civil society activists in Cuba and show that their goals are to achieve transitions to democracy and to markets. The realization of the merit and the need to help these civil society activists in Cuba has started to sink into the consciousness of the Cuban American community in Miami. The idea of providing substantial material assistance to the opposition in Cuba is gaining popularity. The possible objections to doing so among exiles are receding. This phenomenon shows how the strategic behavior of important actors can change over time.

The U.S. government could, without military intervention, make a transition in Cuba possible. It would take relatively small expenditures to provide enough material assistance to opposition groups in Cuba to increase significantly their ability to confront the regime, including the production and distribution of samizdat. Hence, civil society could play a more effective role in developing a sense of political efficacy among the population. Likewise, it is relatively easy, in terms of the amount of money and the available technology, for the U.S. government to make it possible for Radio and TV Martí to reach most of the population in Cuba regularly. Policy makers in the Clinton administration were unwilling to pursue such actions. This was particularly inopportune for the prospects of a transition because during the Clinton years

176　*Democracy Delayed*

conditions in Cuba became very favorable for a transition. What could have been done to promote a transition was left undone. President George W. Bush has promised to do what Clinton did not.

The prevailing assumption in the scholarly literature is that President Bill Clinton wanted to topple the Castro dictatorship. This view was certainly supported by the rhetoric of the Clinton administration expressing wishes to promote a speedy transition to democracy in Cuba. Yet I argue that the Clinton administration actually sought to maintain the status quo in Cuba and therefore avoided doing anything that could undermine the Castro regime. Those who determined the administration's policies toward Cuba, such as Samuel Berger, the national security adviser, wanted to prevent the collapse of the Castro government out of fear of a migration wave and possibly for other reasons as well. Huntington indicates that the United States played an important role, by various means, as a promoter of transitions in a number of countries during the third wave of democratization.[17] The Clinton administration decided not to do so in Cuba.

The Cuban case is one more example in the history of U.S. foreign policy in which the United States has preferred stability over democracy. The Clinton years at the White House saw the end of the two main principles of U.S. policies toward Castro since 1959: the aim of the Eisenhower administration to remove Castro from power and the policy of containment followed by every president since Eisenhower. With the disintegration of the Soviet Union and the end of communist rule in Russia, the Castro government became unable to foster communism internationally. Thus, containment was no longer justifiable. Clinton stood Eisenhower on his head and tried to avoid any measure that could jeopardize the survival of Castro's regime.

Apparently, the intention of those who determined the Clinton administration's Cuba policies was to maintain stability in Cuba while Castro was alive and wait until his natural death to see if the regime type could change to make a transition from above possible, along the Nicaraguan path. In the meantime, efforts to collaborate with Cuban officials were apparently aimed at establishing personal connections with individuals who might turn out to be softliners in a post-Castro government, something that is impossible to predict since no latent softliners dare to make their views known under the current regime.

The debate about the utility of the U.S. embargo on the Castro government has paid little attention to the scholarly literature on economic sanctions and on transitions to democracy. One of the consequences is that critics of the embargo

base their arguments on hypotheses that are empirically wrong or on misreadings of scholarly findings. Supporters of the embargo, in turn, do not point to flaws in anti-embargo arguments with as much evidence and insight as possible.

The various engagement hypotheses are untenable in the Cuban case. The evidence cited in chapter 6 shows that economic development does not lead to democracy. Moreover, rather than being agents of political change, foreign investors in Cuba are likely to become supporters of the dictatorship. Foreign capitalists at the time of the transition to democracy will face legal and political problems that will likely entail considerable financial losses and/or impair their ability to continue doing business in Cuba. Hence, U.S. firms should not be concerned with their ability to compete and do business in Cuba once a transition takes place. The desire of some U.S. firms to establish businesses in Cuba now, seeking to get a hold on the market in preparation for the post-transition period, is shortsighted.

Given the nature of the Cuban dictatorship, neither engagement nor the embargo will move the Castro government toward political liberalization or democratization. Ending the embargo would not foster a negotiated political transition under the current regime nor induce the Castro government to have greater respect for human rights. Engagement between Cuba and countries in Latin America and Western Europe has failed to move the dictatorship toward political liberalization, despite countless pleas by leaders of countries in those regions. Castro has remained an intransigent hardliner. An incisive indicator of this fact is the refusal of the Cuban government to accept an economic co-operation agreement with the European Community in exchange for greater respect for human rights and indications of political liberalization. But regime changes, even peaceful ones, are possible without previous political liberalization, as the East German and Czechoslovak cases show.

Unilateral economic sanctions can be effective. The U.S. economic embargo works in two ways. One is by reaffirming a commitment to international norms of democracy and justice. Another is by weakening the Castro government and thus promoting a change of political regime. Indeed, the objective of U.S. economic sanctions against the Cuban government is to bring about a transition to democracy, not to change the policies or behaviors of the dictatorship.

The U.S. sanctions entail significant economic costs for the Castro government, especially given Cuba's low GDP per capita. The embargo weakens the Cuban regime by reducing the amount of hard currency it has available to sus-

178   *Democracy Delayed*

tain acquiescence in the population and distribute benefits among regime cadres. Although economic crises are not the only determinant of the demise of dictatorships, the probability of transitions to democracy increases when autocracies experience serious economic deterioration.[18] Dictatorships, and regimes with command economies, are more dependent than democracies on their capacity to deliver material resources to supporters in the regime and to the general population. The Cuban case supports this hypothesis by showing an association between poor economic performance and increased discontent among regime cadres (including officers in the military) and overt opposition to the regime in the population. In addition, there is a positive association between the deterioration of economic conditions in the 1990s and the emergence of numerous civil society groups and independent journalists that pose challenges to the government. By contrast, there is little evidence for the position that the end of the embargo would promote the demise of the Castro regime.

Yet a transition in Cuba has not occurred. One explanation in the literature, for example, in Haggard and Kaufman's *The Political Economy of Transitions*, for the ability of dictatorships to endure economic crisis is that socioeconomic actors, such as workers, are organizationally weak and have little access to resources independent from the state.[19] While I agree that in Cuba the scarcity of material resources in the hands of civil society groups is a factor in accounting for the non-transition, I argue that this is not an insurmountable obstacle. The dearth of resources and the organizational weakness of independent groups can be a remedy to a significant degree if external actors decide to provide the necessary resources.

The Cuban case shows that poor economic performance helps but is insufficient to dislodge dictatorships from power. While the U.S. embargo certainly contributes to weakening the Castro government, the embargo is not enough to bring about a political transition. The experience of Cuba supports the argument by Hufbauer, Schott, and Elliott that complementary policies are necessary for the success of economic sanctions in destabilizing target governments. The U.S. government has not implemented the supplementary measures of greater material assistance to civil society groups and improvement in the ability of Radio and TV Martí to reach the population.

The main cause of the poor state of the Cuban economy and of the economic hardship common citizens face is the refusal of the Castro dictatorship to implement significant market-oriented reforms. As Mesa-Lago concluded in

Conclusions   179

his analysis of problems and prospects of the Cuban economy, the implementation of market-oriented reforms is the only realistic way to overcome the economic crisis.[20] In its quest to maintain power, the Castro government is immersed in a dilemma. On one hand, by refusing to carry out more market-oriented economic reforms (such as letting small private enterprises surge), poor economic performance weakens support for the regime. Given the decay of ideology, the regime could benefit from performance "legitimacy" by a significant improvement in the economy and in the standard of living of the population. On the other hand, Castro thinks that moving the economy farther in a market direction threatens his political control. Castro has refused to follow the Chinese model for fear that an increase in economic independence among citizens will energize the internal political opposition. His stance against further economic reforms is not due to adherence to anti-capitalist ideology; it is a political calculus with regime survival as the foremost goal. As I have argued, one of the most effective means of repression in Cuba is the attempt to deprive dissidents and their families of means of subsistence. Civil society activists are prevented from holding any jobs with the state and are even denied licenses to work on their own. Thus, joining independent groups means taking the road to misery. Democratic activists and their families basically survive out of public charity, both from people in Cuba and from support groups abroad. Given this situation, many people who would like to join civil society groups refrain from doing so for fear of the economic consequences.

The very limited space that the government allowed after 1993 for citizens to engage in private entrepreneurship has been substantially stifled since 1996.[21] The capitalism that Castro came to accept because of the halt of Soviet subsidies is fundamentally contained in joint-venture enclaves in which the key actors and beneficiaries are foreign capitalists and the Cuban state, with little diffusion of wealth in the population. Lifting the embargo would not mean that the Castro government would allow a significant expansion of market reforms or that there would be considerable improvements in the living conditions of the population. For those who believe that the spread of market forces brings about democratization, lifting the embargo would not produce even the first part of the equation. Scholars who maintain that economic development fosters transitions to democracy see the intervening mechanism in the spread of wealth and economic independence outside state control, which in turn empowers and strengthens social actors such as capitalists or a middle class. Then these actors supposedly push for democratiza-

tion.[22] The Cuban case does not fit this model. This is why lifting the embargo would not produce this scenario. In Cuba, state control over economic activities would not lead to any social group becoming economically well-off and independent of the state. Thus no social actor would be empowered, and hence development would not foster democracy but would strengthen the state.

Besides handing a moral and political victory to the Cuban government, the end of the embargo would increase the regime's hard currency income. The state would have more resources to distribute benefits among regime cadres, to finance its extensive repressive apparatus, and to try to achieve acquiescence among the population. The dictatorship's strategy is to obtain enough foreign exchange to continue to muddle through the economic quagmire and prevent a political transition. Lifting the embargo would help the Castro regime endure.

Anyone, as the Clinton administration intended, willing to lift the embargo to help the Castro regime survive until the natural death of Fidel (which could take a decade or more) for the sake of a possible negotiated transition after his death is making a costly and unreasonable bet. Under the best outcome in this scenario, after Fidel Castro dies, a different type of regime could emerge in which a negotiated transition might be possible. But it is also possible that his younger brother, Raúl, or one of the younger members of the Politburo, could maintain the current regime type. Even in the best-case scenario, if the goal is to achieve a transition to democracy, lifting the embargo is unjustified. As has been shown in the literature on transitions from authoritarian rule in Latin America and Southern Europe, it is pressure on dictatorships, including poor economic performance, rather than relaxation of tensions that motivates and strengthens softliners to implement political liberalization.

If the precipitating conditions for transitions that are missing in Cuba materialize, then one can predict the end of the dictatorship. What is harder to predict is whether those conditions will be realized, because they depend on strategies of actors. For example, will George W. Bush, in contrast to Bill Clinton, decide to increase material aid substantially to the opposition in Cuba and enable the Martís to reach most of the people in the island on a regular basis? Uncertainty about how key actors will behave creates unpredictability in the processes of transition. If President George W. Bush does not deliver on his promises to overcome the jamming of Radio and TV Martí, and if civil so-

Conclusions 181

ciety groups in Cuba do not receive greater quantities of what they need so that they and their families can eat, produce and distribute samizdat, and carry out other activities in their struggle for democratization, probably Fidel will die in power. If so, the regime type might change and a negotiated transition might become possible, with powerful softliners playing an important role. If this is the outcome, there will be those who will claim that a political transition in Cuba required the "biological solution," that Fidel had to die before change could happen. Cuba will be compared with Spain, Fidel with Franco. Spain rather than Eastern European countries will be seen as the model that was relevant for Cuba all along. And a deterministic construction of history will appear. But all of these arguments would be true only by default. It would be false to claim that such outcomes had to happen. This book will then serve to deconstruct history and point to missed historical possibilities that did not materialize due to the strategic mistakes by some opposition actors and the unwillingness on the part of U.S. policy makers to foster a transition while Castro was alive.

Notes

Introduction

1. In a subsequent book, co-authored with Mark R. Thompson and Steven Saxonberg, we will compare the transitions in Eastern Europe with transitions and non-transitions in other parts of the world. The book is tentatively entitled *Transitions and Nontransitions from Communism: Eastern Europe, Asia, Latin America and Africa*.

2. O'Donnell, "Introduction to the Latin American Cases," in O'Donnell, Schmitter, and Whitehead, eds., *Transitions from Authoritarian Rule: Latin America*, 10; Saxonberg, *The Fall*, chaps. 8 and 10.

3. Mark Thompson, "Whatever Happened to Democratic Revolutions?"

4. Przeworski, "Transition to Democracy," 48.

5. Fearon, "Counterfactuals," 169, 176, 177, 193, and 194.

6. Huntington, *The Third Wave*, 45–46 and 106–8.

7. An example is Przeworski, *Democracy and the Market*.

8. Collier and Mahoney, "Insights and Pitfalls," 64, 67, 72, and 73.

9. López, "Theory Choice."

10. Domínguez, "Why the Cuban Regime Has Not Fallen," 697.

11. Saxonberg, *The Fall*, 158.

12. Grupo de Trabajo de la Disidencia Interna Cubana, "Cuba: Una propuesta sensata," 27.

13. Victor Rolando Arroyo, "La UJC no supera crisis de deserciones y apatia," *CubaNet,* January 11, 2001.

14. Lorenzo Téllez, "Visas seguras para aparentes miembros del partido," *CubaNet,* March 6, 2000.

15. Rui Ferreira, "Lanzan campaña de readoctrinamiento en Cuba," *El Nuevo Herald,* July 4, 2000.

16. "Homegrown" stands for some type of legitimacy, nationalism being the most obvious. As with other types of legitimacy, the association between nationalism and the regime can deteriorate, for example as in Cuba.

17. Jorge Domínguez argues that an important factor explaining why the Castro government has not fallen is that, in contrast to countries in Eastern Europe, the Cuban

Notes to Pages xviii–xxii 183

regime enjoys legitimacy among the population; see Domínguez, "The Secrets of Castro's Staying Power," 97–98.

18. Przeworski, "Transition to Democracy," 50–53.

19. This argument is made quite frequently; see, for example, Domínguez, "Why the Cuban Regime Has Not Fallen," 698; Schultz, "Introduction," 2; González, *Cuba Clearing Perilous Waters?* 79–80; and Alejandro Portes, "Under Helms–Burton: Cuba Struggles But It's Not Vanquished," *Miami Herald,* November 25, 1996.

20. Bunce, *Subversive Institutions,* 132.

21. Ricardo Alarcón, president of the National Assembly, stated that Helms–Burton is very useful for the Castro regime in ideologically motivating young people. Larry Rohter, "Cuba Taking a Harder Line," *New York Times,* March 31, 1996.

22. José Rivero García, "La Verdad Desnuda," *CubaPress,* March 2, 1996; declaration of the Partido Liberal Democrático de Cuba, April 8, 1997, distributed by *CubaNet;* "Cuba en la VI cumbre iberoamericana," *Revista Contacto* (November 1996); Roberts et al., "Measuring Cuban Public Opinion: Project Report," v.

23. Eyal, "Why Romania Could Not Avoid Bloodshed," 155.

24. "Revista católica lamenta discriminación económica," *El Nuevo Herald,* October 29, 1999.

25. Roberts et al., "Measuring Cuban Public Opinion: Project Report," v, 63, and 107.

26. González and Ronsfeldt, *Storm Warnings for Cuba;* and Centeno, "Cuba's Search for Alternatives." For a description of obstacles put by the state on Cuban private entrepreneurs, see Ulises Cabrera, "Cronica de un cuentapropista," *Agencia de Prensa Independiente de Cuba,* August 14, 1996, and Juan O. Tamayo, "Cuban Inspectors Crack Down on Home Businesses," *Miami Herald,* March 27, 1997.

27. According to Brown, in the German Democratic Republic and Romania, two regimes very unreceptive to perestroika, the state's refusal to reform antagonized the population to the point of open rebellion; Brown, *Surge to Freedom,* 127.

28. Domínguez, "Why the Cuban Regime Has Not Fallen," 693.

29. For a list of dissident/opposition organizations, as of March 31, 1998, see "Lista de organizaciones disidentes, opositoras y de derechos humanos," compiled by the Christian Democratic Party of Cuba (http://www.pdc-cuba.org/lista.htm). For one estimate of the number of political prisoners as of July 1999, see "Fin de 40 días de ayuno y crean el Foro Nacional," *Diario las Américas,* July 17, 1999.

30. Domínguez, "Why the Cuban Regime Has Not Fallen," 694.

31. Here is an illuminating example. In November 1999, the police conducted massive home search operations in the municipality of Morón, looking for people who had beef or lobster in their refrigerators. Heavy fines were imposed on citizens who had these foods and their refrigerators were confiscated; Ramón Negrín Jiménez, "Registros policiales y decomisos masivos en Ciego de Avila," *CubaNet,* December 9, 1999.

32. Aguirre, "Culture of Opposition and Collective Action in Cuba," 43 and 62.

33. Domínguez, "Why the Cuban Regime Has Not Fallen," 694; Walker and González, "Cuba Today," 3; del Aguila, "The Politics of Dissidence," 174 and 178.

34. González and Ronsfeldt, *Storm Warnings for Cuba,* 36; Walker and González, "Cuba Today," 3.

35. Saxonberg, *The Fall,* chap. 7.

36. For the role of civil society in the Southern European transitions, see Schmitter, "An Introduction to Southern European Transitions from Authoritarian Rule," in

184   *Notes to Pages xxiv–2*

O'Donnell, Schmitter, and Whitehead, eds., *Transitions from Authoritarian Rule: Southern Europe,* 6–7.

37. Saxonberg, *The Fall,* chap. 8.

38. Ibid., chap. 7.

39. Whitehead, "International Aspects of Democratization," in O'Donnell, Schmitter, and Whitehead, eds., *Transitions from Authoritarian Rule: Comparative Perspectives,* 4 and 20.

40. Whitehead, "Three International Dimensions of Democratization," 16 and 23.

41. Przeworski, *Democracy and the Market,* 5.

42. Bunce, *Subversive Institutions,* 133. Geoffrey Pridham also maintains that Gorbachev's policies of economic and political liberalization in the Soviet Union undermined the rule of communist regimes in other Eastern European countries; Pridham, "The International Dimension of Democratisation," 17–18.

43. Light, "The USSR/CIS and Democratization in Eastern Europe," 140, 142.

44. Saxonberg, *The Fall,* 127, 131–34, and 137–42.

45. For an assessment of anti-embargo arguments, see López, "Implications of the U.S. Economic Embargo for a Political Transition in Cuba."

46. Przeworski, "Transition to Democracy," 53–56; O'Donnell and Schmitter, *Transitions from Authoritarian Rule: Tentative Conclusions.*

47. Pzeworski, *Democracy and the Market,* 56–57.

48. Ibid., 6.

49. Saxonberg, *The Fall,* chap. 10.

50. Friedheim, "Democratic Transition Through Regime Collapse."

51. For example, see O'Donnell and Schmitter, *Transitions from Authoritarian Rule: Tentative Conclusions,* 24–25.

52. Karklins and Petersen, "Decision Calculus of Protesters and Regimes."

53. Millar, *Politics, Work, and Daily Life in the USSR,* vii.

54. Ibid., ix, 4, 19.

55. Thompson, "Why and How East Germans Rebelled," 266–67.

ONE. The Castro Regime and Political Transition

1. Przeworski, *Democracy and the Market,* 57.

2. Huntington, "How Countries Democratize," 593. Samuel Huntington points to the following factors that induce the emergence of regime softliners by making them believe that democratizing would produce benefits for their country: (1) reduction of U.S. or other sanctions against their regime, and (2) opening the door to economic assistance and International Monetary Fund (IMF) loans. These two factors are relevant for Cuba since by law the U.S. embargo would be lifted upon democratization and Bill Clinton's "Support for a Democratic Transition in Cuba" commits U.S. assistance to transitional and democratic governments in Cuba.

3. Haggard and Kaufman, *The Political Economy of Democratic Transition,* 31–32.

4. O'Donnell and Schmitter, *Transitions from Authoritarian Rule: Tentative Conclusions,* 16.

5. Mark Thompson, "To Shoot or Not to Shoot."

6. Przeworski and Limongi, "Modernization," 159–60.

7. Ibid., 167 and 169.

Notes to Pages 2–5   185

8. Halpern, "Economic Reform, Social Mobilization, and Democratization in Post-Mao China," 51.

9. Haggard and Kaufman, *The Political Economy of Democratic Transition*, 13, 37.

10. Ibid., 33–34.

11. Linden, "Analogies and the Loss of Community," 28–30.

12. Saxonberg, *The Fall*, 67–69; Judt, "Metamorphosis: The Democratic Revolution in Czechoslovakia," 96–97; Brown, *Surge to Freedom*, 209.

13. Remmer, "The Process of Democratization in Latin America," 10–12.

14. Saxonberg, *The Fall*, 69–70.

15. Ibid., 71, and Bruszt, "1989: The Negotiated Revolution in Hungary," 383.

16. Joppke, *East German Dissidents and the Revolution of 1989*, 144–45.

17. Saxonberg, *The Fall*, 128–29.

18. Haggard and Kaufman, *The Political Economy of Democratic Transition*, 29–32.

19. Linz and Stepan, *Problems of Democratic Transition*, 49.

20. Mesa-Lago, "Economic Effects on Cuba," 181–84, 187; Domínguez, "Why the Cuban Regime Has Not Fallen," 691.

21. González and Ronfeldt, *Storm Warnings for Cuba*, 12.

22. Mesa-Lago, "Assessing Economic and Social Performance in the Cuban Transition of the 1990s," 860.

23. For an example of the deterioration in the health care system, see "La Salud Pública de Pinar del Río requiere de un saneamiento de urgencia," *CubaNet*, June 12, 2000.

24. Mesa-Lago, "Assessing Economic and Social Performance in the Cuban Transition of the 1990s," 870.

25. Roberts et al., "Measuring Cuban Public Opinion: Project Report," 58–63.

26. Claudia Márquez Linares, "Encuesta informal sobre la atención médica primaria en Cuba," *CubaNet*, March 23, 2001.

27. Pérez, "The Pension System of Cuba," 526; and Mesa Lago, "Comments," on Pérez's work in the same volume, 535.

28. Mesa-Lago, "Assessing Economic and Social Performance in the Cuban Transition of the 1990s," 870.

29. "Aumentan los cortes de electricidad en Cuba," *CubaNet*, March 22, 2000; "Verano caliente para Cuba por falta de electicidad," *El Nuevo Herald*, March 22, 2000; "Cuba Announces Fuel Restrictions," EFE, June 27, 2000; "Crisis de combustible afecta a camioneros de La Habana," *CubaNet*, August 29, 2000; "Escasez de combustible afecta severamente zona de Camagüey," *CubaNet*, August 29, 2000.

30. For the scarcity of food in the government retail system available to the general population (using ration books), see Adalberto Yero, "Journalist Describes How the Government Starves Cubans," *Cuba Free Press*, March 2000; regarding the economic problems of individuals receiving social security, including inability to access basic goods, see Oscar Espinosa Chepe, "Social Security Reaps Frustration," *Cuba Free Press*, November 1999.

31. Pérez, "The Pension System of Cuba," 526; and Mesa Lago, "Comments," on Pérez's work in the same volume, 535.

32. Roberts et al., "Measuring Cuban Public Opinion: Project Report," 52.

33. Larry Rohter, "Cuba Taking a Harder Line," *New York Times*, March 31, 1996.

34. Dalia Acosta, "Food Shortfall Continues," *InterPress Third World News Agency*, September 23, 1996.

186   *Notes to Pages 5–9*

35. Carlos Batista, "Mejora la economia de la isla, pero no para el pueblo," *El Nuevo Herald,* November 26, 1999; José Melendez, "Reconoce Cuba que el crecimiento de su economía no se traducirá en beneficios para la población" *El Excelsior* (Mexico), August 10, 1999.

36. According to González and Ronsfeldt, *Storm Warning for Cuba,* xiii, 55, 57, if the Castro regime is to survive, it will need to improve economic performance at the micro level.

37. "Reclamo popular obliga al Partido Comunista a tomar medidas," *CubaNet,* April 21, 1998.

38. For example, see Pablo Alfonso, "Cuba por dentro," *El Nuevo Herald,* March 5, 1997.

39. Emily Rodriguez, "Los Jovenes Cubanos y su Frustración," *CubaNet,* February 12, 1998.

40. Hector Maseda, "La Habana, la capital del turismo sexual en el Caribe," *CubaNet,* June 2, 2000.

41. Haydeé Rodríguez, "El suicidio en Cuba," *CubaNet,* March 24, 2000; Oscar Espinosa Chepe, "Alcoholismo en Cuba," *CubaNet,* July 12, 2001.

42. Mesa-Lago, "Assessing Economic and Social Performance in the Cuban Transition of the 1990s," 857, 866–69.

43. Mesa-Lago, "The State of the Cuban Economy," 4.

44. A. Cawthorne, "Economistas disidentes no creen en las cifras de crecimiento," *El Nuevo Herald,* December 16, 2000. It is commonly acknowledged that data from the Cuban government are unreliable; see, for example, Mesa-Lago, "Assessing Economic and Social Performance in the Cuban Transition of the 1990s," 858–59. Professor Antonio Jorge raises serious doubts about the growth data of the Cuban government; see Ariel Remos, "Castro acorralado," *Diario las Américas,* March 29, 1996.

45. "Analizarán el fracaso de la zafra," *El Nuevo Herald,* July 7, 2001.

46. Mesa-Lago, "Assessing Economic and Social Performance in the Cuban Transition of the 1990s," 863.

47. For data on the decline in merchandise imports and negative trade balances in the 1989–97 period, see Mesa-Lago, "The Cuban Economy in 1997–1998," 2–3.

48. "Aumenta el déficit comercial y bancario de la isla," *El Nuevo Herald,* July 5, 2001.

49. Nelson del Castillo, "Débil la relación económica cubana con el Caribe," *Diario las Américas,* June 16, 1997; "Cuba consiguió refinanciaciones a su deuda," EFE (Havana), December 17, 1999.

50. "Cuba reestructura la deuda con Japón," *El Nuevo Herald,* February 16, 2000.

51. Pablo Alfonso, "Cuba suspende pagos de su deuda a España," *El Nuevo Herald,* May 22, 2001.

52. "Cuban Debt Discord Sours Japan Trade Mission," Reuters, November 24, 1995. Chronology of Cuban Events, 1994, Information Resources Branch, Radio Martí Program, March 22 and November 1. Cuba's officially declared trade deficits have been increasing. In 1994, the deficit was $624 million; in 1996, it was $1.7 billion.

53. Mesa-Lago, "Strategies for the 1990s," 187.

54. "Alza petrolera costó 92 millones de dólares a Cuba en 1999," *Diario las Américas,* March 18–19, 2000.

55. "Se venden en La Habana ropa vieja donada por extranjeros," *CubaNet,* March 14, 2000; Leonicio Pérez, "Se vende rantilla donada," *Cuba Free Press* (www.cubafreepress.

Notes to Pages 9–12   187

org), November 12, 1999; Adalberto Yero, "Ropa nueva? Reciclada? Donada? Y de Uso, en Dólares," *Cuba Free Press,* November 14, 1999; CubDest Information Service, "Pax Christi: Cuban Regime Diverts the International 'Humanitarian Aid' to Its Own Advantage" (www.cadpnyc.org/manuscripts/new%20manuscripts/pax_christi.htm); Juan Clark, "La Visita del Papa a Cuba y su Repercusión," Miami, Fla.: Centro de Estudios para una Opción Nacional, 1999, 22.

56. Mesa-Lago, "Assessing Economic and Social Performance in the Cuban Transition of the 1990s," 869–70. For a discussion of the stifling by the Cuban government of the small, private enterprises in Cuba, see Ritter, "Entrepreneurship, Microenterprise, and Public Policy in Cuba: Promotion, Containment, or Asphyxiation?"

57. "Obligado dulcero a romper su horno por mandato policial," *CubaNet,* November 24, 1999.

58. "Controles estatales ponen en crisis a trabajadores por cuenta propia," *CubaNet,* March 30, 2000; "Ofensiva de confiscaciones y multas contra cuentapropistas capitalinos," *CubaNet,* March 23, 2000.

59. "Retiran la licencia a veinte trabajadores por cuenta propia," *CubaNet,* April 17, 2000.

60. "Ofensiva del gobierno contra trabajadores por cuenta propia," *CubaNet,* May 5, 2000.

61. "Suspenden licencia de trabajo a más de cien cuentapropistas," *CubaNet,* July 19, 2000.

62. "Reprimen a cuentapropistas y vendedores ambulantes en la capital cubana," *CubaNet,* December 12, 2000; "Nueva reglamentación limita el comercio en los mercados agropecuarios," *CubaNet,* December 26, 2000; "Hostigan a trabajadores por cuenta propia," *CubaNet,* November 21, 2000; Rui Ferreira, "El gobierno cubano en plena ofensiva contra los paladares," *El Nuevo Herald,* September 30, 2000; Oscar Espinosa Chepe, "¿Fin del cuentapropismo?" *CubaNet,* December 22, 2000.

63. After I had reached this conclusion, I found out that Jaime Suchlicki has made the same observation; see his "Castro's Cuba," 124.

64. Dalia Acosta, "Food Shortfall Continues," *InterPress Third World News Agency,* September 23, 1996.

65. Mesa-Lago, "Assessing Economic and Social Performance in the Cuban Transition of the 1990s," 863–65. For a detailed account of the lack of incentives in the UBPCs from the viewpoint of a farmer, see Reylando Hernández Pérez, "Política de precios y compra de los productos agrícolas por parte del Estado al sector campesino," *CubaNet,* May 5, 1998.

66. Oscar Espinosa Chepe, "La eficiencia no llega," *CubaNet,* March 31, 2000.

67. Ibid.

68. Santiago Santana, "Son bienvenidos periodistas independientes," *CubaNet,* March 13, 2000; "El Talón de Aquilles de la agricultura cubana," *CubaNet,* March 3, 2000; "Sorprende a funcionarios gubernamentales éxito de cooperativa independiente," *CubaNet,* November 10, 1998; Emily Rodríguez, "En la cooperativa independiente Transición la naturaleza premia el esfuerzo," *CubaNet,* August 18, 1998.

69. "Impide el gobierno a campesinos abastecer de leche a la población," *CubaNet,* December 31, 2000; "Funcionarios estatales estafan a campesinos de Florencia," *CubaNet,* July 28, 2000; "Declaración de la Alianza Nacional de Agricultores Independientes de Cuba," *CubaNet,* September 16, 1999; Alvarez, "Independent Agricultural Cooperatives in Cuba?" 159–62.

188   *Notes to Pages 12–15*

70. Baloyra, "Where Does Cuba Stand?" 3; Frank Calzón, "Is Canada Aware of Evil in Cutting Deals with Cuba?" *Miami Herald,* April 15, 1996.

71. Frances Kerry, "Cuba Tourism Sector Tries to Stamp Out Prostitution," Reuters, December 12, 1995.

72. "Cabezazos de la industria turística," *CubaNet,* June 8, 2000; Pablo Alfonso, "El turismo no genera tanta divisa," *El Nuevo Herald,* January 8, 1999.

73. Cuban government data on foreign investment in Cuba are inflated. According to Jorge Pérez-López, UN data show that foreign direct investment in Cuba from 1990 to 1994 was $60 million; see also Werlau, "Foreign Investment in Cuba."

74. Pérez-López and Travieso-Díaz, "The Contribution of BITs to Cuba's Foreign Investment Program," 473.

75. "Cuba Woos Small, Medium Foreign Businesses," Reuters, November 25, 1996.

76. Werlau, "Foreign Investment in Cuba," 481.

77. Ibid.

78. Linz and Stepan, *Problems of Democratic Transition,* chaps. 3 and 4.

79. Liberalization is the process of allowing individuals to have certain rights, including freedom of speech, of movement, and of association, and the right to a fair trial under rules of preestablished laws. Liberalization is a matter of degree; rights can be granted by the dictatorship to a lesser or greater degree (O'Donnell and Schmitter, *Transitions from Authoritarian Rule: Tentative Conclusions*).

80. The Castro regime seems quite similar to Romania under Nicolae Ceauşescu. Juan Linz classifies Romania as a mixed type of totalitarianism and sultanism; see Linz, "Transitions to Democracy."

81. Linz and Stepan, *Problems of Democratic Transition,* chap. 4. For a characterization of the Castro regime that points to features of frozen post-totalitarianism, see González, *Cuba Clearing Perilous Waters?* ix. The regime in Cuba is portrayed as being in a state of stasis, with limited market reforms, the Communist Party monopolizing power, and without feasible political alternatives.

82. "Cuba's Castro Endorses His Brother Raúl as Successor," *Miami Herald,* October 13, 1997; "Cuba's Castro Discusses Successor," Associated Press Online, June 28, 2001.

83. Pablo Alfonso, "Una andanada laudatoria para Castro," *El Nuevo Herald,* January 3, 2001.

84. For clear sultanistic features of Fidel Castro's unrestrained personal rule, see Baloyra, "Socialist Transitions and Prospects for Change in Cuba."

85. For the very unlikely emergence of viable softliners under the Castro regime and the elimination of potential regime softliners during 1990–91, see del Aguila, "The Party, the Fourth Congress, and the Process of Counter-Reform."

86. EFE, September 2, 1999.

87. Aguirre, "Culture of Opposition and Collective Action in Cuba," 35–36.

88. For a recent reaffirmation by members of opposition groups in Cuba of the refusal of the Castro government to take any steps toward political liberalization, see Olance Nogueras, "Oposición no ve voluntad de cambio en régimen," *El Nuevo Herald,* July 5, 1998.

89. In an unprecedented coalescing of opposition groups inside Cuba, Concilio Cubano was formed as an umbrella organization in October 1995. At the time of its inception, it brought together 130 organizations of various types (e.g., political, environmental, professional, labor unions, and human rights groups). Its central goal was to work for a peaceful transition to democracy.

Notes to Pages 16–24   189

90. For example, see Gunn, "In Search of a Modern Cuba Policy," 140.

91. At the meeting, Fidel Castro maintained that "socialism has no alternative in this country; the revolution has no alternative." *CubaHoy* 2, no. 142 (March 27, 1996).

92. Mimi Whitefield and Juan O. Tamayo, "Raul Castro's Attack on Intellectuals Stirs Backlash," *Knight-Ridder News Service,* April 12, 1996.

93. Baloyra, "Socialist Transitions," 49–51.

94. Domínguez, "The Political Impact on Cuba," 105.

95. For example, Mesa-Lago and Fabian, "Analogies," 369–70; Schultz, "Introduction," 2.

96. Domínguez, "The Political Impact on Cuba," 123–25.

97. Domínguez, "U.S. Policy toward Cuba in the 1980s and 1990s," 171–72.

98. On the low probability of these events, see Suchlicki, "Possible Scenarios" and "Castro's Cuba," 132.

99. In 2002, civil society groups collected more than ten thousand signatures from citizens to petition the National Assembly to hold a referendum on political changes in Cuba. This initiative is known as "the Varela Project." The Cuban constitution at the time allowed for such a petition. The response of the Castro government was to emphasize that the current regime is unalterable.

100. Linz and Stepan, *Problems of Democratic Transition,* chap. 4.

101. O'Donnell, "Transition to Democracy: Some Navigation Instruments," 73.

102. Enrique Baloyra also makes the observation that no peaceful transition has ever taken place in a *caudillo*-led regime; Baloyra, "Socialist Transitions and Prospects for Change in Cuba," 38.

103. González and Ronsfeldt, *Storm Warnings for Cuba,* 36; Walker and González, "Cuba Today," 3.

104. Mujal-León and Busby, "Much Ado about Something? Regime Change in Cuba."

105. Verdery and Kligman, "Romania after Ceaușescu," 120–21.

106. See the chapter on Romania in Brown, *Surge to Freedom;* Rady, *Romania in Turmoil,* 93–99; Ratesh, *Romania: The Entangled Revolution,* 33 and 35–36.

107. Rady, *Romania in Turmoil,* 93 and 96.

108. Verdery and Kligman, "Romania after Ceaușescu."

109. Ibid., 101–4 and 109.

110. Linz and Stepan, *Problems of Democratic Transition,* 359.

111. Ibid., 101–4 and 109.

112. Judt, "Metamorphosis: The Democratic Revolution in Czechoslovakia," 96.

113. Wheaton and Kavan, *The Velvet Revolution,* 25–26.

114. Czechoslovak Helsinki Committee, *Human Rights in Czechoslovakia,* 6.

115. Urban, "Czechoslovakia: The Power and Politics of Humiliation"; Helsinki Watch, *Toward Civil Society: Independent Initiatives in Czechoslovakia,* 38 and 43–45.

116. Wheaton and Kavan, *The Velvet Revolution,* 27–28.

117. Ibid., 39–42.

118. Urban, "Czechoslovakia: The Power and Politics of Humiliation."

119. Ibid.

120. Ibid.

121. Pehe, "Czechoslovakia: An Abrupt Transition," 349–50.

190   *Notes to Pages 24–33*

122. Linz and Stepan, *Problems of Democratic Transition,* 325–26.

123. Urban, "Czechoslovakia: The Power and Politics of Humiliation."

124. Ibid.; Pehe, "Czechoslovakia: An Abrupt Transition," 346–48.

125. Opp, Voss, and Gern, *Origins of a Spontaneous Revolution,* 149.

126. Joppke, *East German Dissidents and the Revolution of 1989,* 148.

127. Ibid., 21–23 and 196.

128. Joppke, *East German Dissidents and the Revolution of 1989,* 149–50.

129. Ibid., 19 and 196–98.

130. Ibid., 178.

131. Oberschall, "Protests, Demonstrations and the End of Communist Regimes in 1989," 12–13.

132. Friedheim, "Democratic Transition Through Regime Collapse." The coercive apparatus was comprised not only of the security forces (e.g., the Interior Ministry), but also of party members who oversaw the security forces and some government officials.

133. Opp, Voss, and Gern, *Origins of a Spontaneous Revolution,* 178.

TWO. Civil Society and Repression

1. Linz and Stepan, *Problems of Democratic Transition,* 51.

2. Karklins, *Ethnopolitics and Transition to Democracy,* 65.

3. Brown, *Surge to Freedom,* 210.

4. Linz and Stepan, *Problems of Democratic Transition,* 352.

5. Ibid.

6. Tismaneanu, "Nascent Civil Society," 109.

7. Opp, Voss, and Gern, *Origins of a Spontaneous Revolution,* 103; Mark Thompson, "No Exit," 271. Friedheim cites a figure of 2,500 overt dissidents in 1989 and maintains that there was no organized opposition until the formation of the New Forum; Friedheim, "Democratic Transition Through Regime Collapse," 423.

8. Sharlet, "Human Rights and Civil Society in Eastern Europe," 170.

9. Linz and Stepan, *Problems of Democratic Transition,* 321.

10. Pehe, "Czechoslovakia: An Abrupt Transition," 349.

11. Linz and Stepan, *Problems of Democratic Transition,* 319 and 321.

12. For example, the Committee of Cuban Mothers for the Freedom of Political Prisoners was created on May 17, 2000. "Creado comité de madres de presos políticos," *CubaNet,* May 18, 2000.

13. Helsinki Watch, *Toward Civil Society: Independent Initiatives in Czechoslovakia.*

14. Elise Ackerman, "Guerrilla Journalism: The Underground Press Fights for an Audience," *Washington Post,* March 9, 1997.

15. Ibid.; Cuban Democratic Revolutionary Directorate, *Steps to Freedom 1998,* 29.

16. Cuban Democratic Revolutionary Directorate, *Steps to Freedom 1999,* 7, and *Steps to Freedom 2000,* 4.

17. Cuban Democratic Revolutionary Directorate, *Steps to Freedom 1998,* 17.

18. Cuban Democratic Revolutionary Directorate, *Steps to Freedom 1999,* 9, 54, and *Steps to Freedom 2000,* 3.

19. Steve Fainaru, "Nine Months Later, Cuba Dissidents Still in Disarray," *Boston Globe,* November 12, 1996; Anita Snow, "Bruised by Crackdown, Cuban Opposition Vows to Fight On," *Associated Press,* March 24, 1997.

Notes to Pages 34–38   191

20. Interview of Hector Palacios Ruiz in Mercedes Moreno Martínez, "Concilio Cubano se define a si mismo," *Buro de Prensa Independiente de Cuba (BPIC)*, April 14, 1996.

21. Ibid.; interview of Hector Palacios Ruiz by Lucas Grave, *CubaNet*, December 8, 1996.

22. Cynthia Corzo, "Concilio Cubano Isn't Dead, Activist Says," *Miami Herald*, May 31, 1997.

23. Manuel David Orrio, "Concilio Cubano: entre tirios y troyanos," *Agencia de Prensa Independiente de Cuba (APIC)*, August 14, 1996; Manuel David Orrio, "Concilio Cubano: Dictamenes y ¿Agonia?" *Agencia de Prensa Independiente de Cuba*, October 8, 1996; Lázaro González Valdés, "Hacer es la mejor manera de decir," *CubaNet*, February 3, 1999.

24. Miguel Fernández Martínez, "Creación de Alianza Nacional Cubana," *CubaNet*, July 21, 1997.

25. "Conferencia de prensa en Tamarindo 34 culmina ayuno de 40 días," *CubaNet*, July 16, 1999; "Comunicado de la Liga Cívica Martiana leído por William Ernesto Herrera," *CubaNet*, July 16, 1999; "Anuncian en Tamarindo 34 creación de frente único opositor," *CubaNet*, July 13, 1999; "1,910 visitantes ha tenido Tamarindo 34," *CubaNet*, July 9, 1999.

26. "Entrevista a Migdalia Rosado y Rolando Muñoz Yyobre," *CubaNet*, July 20, 1999; "Fin de 40 días de ayuno y crean Foro Nacional," *Diario las Américas*, July 17–18, 1999; "Anuncian en Tamarindo 34 creación de frente único opositor," *CubaNet*, July 14, 1999; "Comunicado de la Liga Cívica Martiana leído por William Ernesto Herrera," *CubaNet*, July 16, 1999; "Se reunirán opositores para organizar Foro de la Oposición Pacífica," *CubaNet*, August 30, 1999.

27. Manuel David Orrio, "Al escándalo, el pecho!" *CubaNet*, September 10, 1999.

28. "Acuerdan 23 agrupaciones opositoras constituir el Foro Tercer Milenio," *CubaNet*, October 4, 1999.

29. "Se reúne Foro Tercer Milenio," *CubaNet*, November 12, 1999.

30. Opp, Voss, and Gern, *Origins of a Spontaneous Revolution*, 12.

31. Linden, "Analogies and the Loss of Community," 32.

32. Cuban Democratic Revolutionary Directorate, *Steps to Freedom 1998*, 27 and 29.

33. Cuban Democratic Revolutionary Directorate, *Steps to Freedom 1999*, 8–9.

34. "Grupos desidentes se unen y forman el Congreso Opositor Cubano," *CubaNet*, October 31, 2000; "Crean frente de desobediencia civil en la Habana," *CubaNet*, November 7, 2000.

35. For example, see Walker and González, "Cuba Today," 3.

36. Lázaro González Valdés, "Hacer es la mejor manera de decir," *CubaNet*, February 3, 1999.

37. Pablo Alfonso, "Disidentes celebrarán una cumbre opositora el próximo año," *El Nuevo Herald*, December 6, 1998.

38. Interview with Hector Palacios Ruiz, the president of the Party of Democratic Solidarity (Partido Solidaridad Democrática) in "Informe sobre las relaciones internacionales del Comité Ejecutivo Nacional del Partido Solidaridad Democrática," *CubaNet*, June 2, 1998; Pablo Alfonso, "Disidentes instan a 'cambio ineludible' en Cuba," *El Nuevo Herald*, February 8, 2000; interview with the new president of the Party of Democratic Solidarity, Fernando Sánchez López, "El Partido Solidaridad Democrática en el 2000," *CubaNet*, February 4, 2000.

192   *Notes to Pages 39–44*

39. Lázaro González Valdés, "Hacer es la mejor manera de decir," *CubaNet,* February 3, 1999.

40. "Comunicado de la Liga Cívica Martiana leído por William Ernesto Herrera," *CubaNet,* July 16, 1999.

41. "Marcha por las called de La Habana," *El Nuevo Herald,* November 10, 1999.

42. Tom Gibb, "Cuba pounces on anti-government protest," BBC News, November 11, 1999; Mario J. Viera González, "La praxis del error," *CubaNet,* November 12, 1999.

43. Luis Cino and Juan González Febles, "Lanzan a la calle a las turbas castristas," *Diario las Américas,* November 11, 1999.

44. For evidence on activities by groups in civil society, see Cuban Democratic Revolutionary Directorate, *Steps to Freedom 1998.*

45. Ibid.

46. There was widespread news coverage of government repression during the first half of November 1999; for example, see Graciela Alfonso, "Impiden una marcha pacífica en la Habana," *Diario las Américas,* November 10, 1999; "Permanecen confinados cuatro opositores al régimen de Fidel Castro," *CubaNet,* November 24, 1999.

47. For an example of an indoor activity, see "Disidentes habaneros efectúan acción cívica en pro de los presos políticos," *CubaNet,* May 18, 2000.

48. For example, see Ernesto Iturriaga, "Terminan huelga de hambre con la detención de participantes," *CubaNet,* October 10, 2000.

49. "En Matanzas, Cuba, el pueblo se une a la desobediencia civil," *CubaNet,* December 17, 1999, and "Cien residentes matanceros se unen a manifestación opositora," *CubaNet,* January 21, 2000.

50. Angel Pablo Polanco, "La candela fue cercada, pero no apagada," *CubaNet,* December 18, 1998; "Hostigamiento a opositores por el Día de los Derechos Humanos," *CubaNet,* December 10, 1999.

51. Amarilys Cortina and José A. Fornaris, "Impide Seguridad del Estado actividad ecopacifista," *CubaNet,* August 15, 1999.

52. Angel Pablo Polanco, "La candela fue cercada, pero no apagada," *CubaNet,* December 18, 1998.

53. Andrew Cawthorne, "Cuba Ends Trial of Dissidents amid Big Crackdown," Reuters, March 1, 1999.

54. "Arrestan a disidentes en vísperas del juicio a Biscet," *El Nuevo Herald,* February 25, 2000.

55. Pablo Alfonso, "Grave motín en Puerto Padre," *El Nuevo Herald,* July 8, 1999.

56. "Millar y medio de habaneros impiden en La Lisa el desalojo de una familia," *CubaNet,* December 11, 2000.

57. Karklins and Petersen, "Decision Calculus of Protesters and Regimes."

58. Huntington, "How Countries Democratize."

59. Karklins and Petersen, "Decision Calculus of Protesters and Regimes," 598, 602–4; Opp, Voss, and Gern, *Origins of a Spontaneous Revolution,* 174–75.

60. Opp, Voss, and Gern, *Origins of a Spontaneous Revolution,* 174–75.

61. Domínguez, "Why the Cuban Regime Has Not Fallen," 694; Walker and González, "Cuba Today," 3; del Aguila, "The Politics of Dissidence," 174 and 178.

62. On these points, see Przeworski, *Democracy and the Market,* 58–59.

63. The surveys were conducted between January 1979 and April 1982.

64. Karklins, "The Dissent/Coercion Nexus in the USSR," 333–34.

Notes to Pages 45–49   193

65. Ibid., 337.
66. Sharlet, "Human Rights and Civil Society in Eastern Europe," 172–73.
67. Ibid.
68. Childs and Popplewell, *The Stasi*, 174.
69. Tismaneanu, "Nascent Civil Society," 106.
70. Opp, Voss, and Gern, *Origins of a Spontaneous Revolution*, 137.
71. Ibid., 149. For a similar observation about repression in East Germany, see Naimark, "Ich will hier raus," 81–82.
72. Tismaneanu, "Nascent Civil Society," 106–7.
73. Friedheim, "Democratic Transition Through Regime Collapse," 431–32.
74. Sharlet, "Human Rights and Civil Society in Eastern Europe," 170; Helsinki Watch, *Toward Civil Society*, 1–2.
75. Helsinki Watch, *Toward Civil Society*, 1–2.
76. Czechoslovak Helsinki Committee, *Human Rights in Czechoslovakia*.
77. Thomas, "The Helsinki Accords," 224.
78. For example, see "Despido laboral y robos, modalidades represivas contra disidentes," *CubaNet*, May 22, 2001.
79. Interview by Raúl Rivero, "Waiting for Another August," *Cuba Free Press*, September 1999.
80. For example, see "Entierro de preso de conciencia se realiza bajo agresión de la policia," *CubaNet*, May 22, 2001; Mercedes Moreno, "La solidaridad del pueblo con los periodistas," *Buró de Prensa Independiente de Cuba*, February 13, 1997; Manuel David Orrio, "Defienden vecinos a sindicalistas independientes," *CubaNet*, February 17, 1997; Cuban Democratic Revolutionary Directorate, *Steps to Freedom 1997*, 6.
81. Tomás Regalado, "Redoblan la vigilancia a los cubanos," *Diario las Américas*, April 30, 1997.
82. "Aparece un foco de debate en la Habana," *El Nuevo Herald*, April 7, 2001.
83. Friedheim, "Democratic Transition Through Regime Collapse."
84. Personal communication with the director of an organization in the United States that works closely with dissident groups in Cuba.
85. See Ricardo A. Puerta, "Sociedad Civil en Cuba: Coyunturas" (http://www.sigloxxi.org).
86. "Desertan otros cinco agentes cubanos," *El Nuevo Herald*, July 24, 2000; "Arrestan a civiles y militares por salida del país," *CubaNet*, September 4, 2000; "Enjuiciarán a militares por deserción," *El Nuevo Herald*, June 12, 2001.
87. Walker and González, "Cuba Today," 3.
88. Amuchastegui, "Cuba's Armed Forces," 112–13.
89. Cathy Booth, "The Surprising Emergence of Raúl," *Time* 144, no. 20 (November 14, 1994).
90. Andres Oppenheimer, "Cuban Forces Cut in Half, General Says," *Miami Herald*, February 21, 1998.
91. Millett, "From Triumph to Survival," 142.
92. Olance Nogueras, "Periodista cubano dice KGB quiso derrocar a Castro," *El Nuevo Herald*, June 27, 1998.
93. See, for example, Tomás Regalado, "Comunismo cubano admite corrupción amplia del gobierno," *Diario las Américas*, March 26, 1997. For a report of corruption among

194   *Notes to Pages 50–57*

top-ranking members of the state security apparatus (the Ministry of the Interior), see "Impugnados por corrupción dos altos funcionarios militares cienfuegueros," *CubaNet News,* August 1, 1997.

94. Friedheim, "Democratic Transition Through Regime Collapse," 190–92.

95. Huntington, "How Countries Democratize," 579–616.

96. Armando Correa, "Ejército cubano no asusta a Castro ni a Clinton," *El Nuevo Herald,* April 20, 1997.

97. Frank Calzón, "Los funerales del Líder Maximo," *El Nuevo Herald,* January 24, 1997.

98. Karklins and Petersen, "Decision Calculus of Protesters and Regimes," 589 and 593–97.

99. Walker and González, "Cuba Today," 3.

100. Ibid.

101. Jesús Zúñiga, "Nosotros los Independientes," *CubaNet,* November 16, 1998.

102. "Raúl Castro arremete contra dirigentes políticos," *El Nuevo Herald,* April 10, 1997; "Despiden a cien maestros por disentir del Ministerio de Educación," *CubaNet,* November 8, 2000.

103. Juan O. Tamayo, "Will Albright Make a Move on Cuba Policy?" *Miami Herald,* June 19, 1997.

104. France Presse, "Preocupa al Partido Comunista de Cuba su pérdida de influencia," July 1, 1999; Oswaldo de Céspedes, "Capitalismo en Cuba: Ya viene llegando?" *CubaNet,* October 15, 1998; Víctor Rolando Arroyo, "La debilidad del partido en Cuba," *CubaNet,* June 2, 1999; "La Isla," *El Nuevo Herald,* May 14, 2001.

105. Tomás Regalado, "Redoblan la vigilancia a los cubanos," *Diario las Américas,* April 30, 1997.

106. "Cederistas defienden a disidente agredido por un desconocido," *CubaNet,* September 28, 2000.

THREE. Political Efficacy and Independent Communication

1. Campbell, Gurin, and Miller, *The Voter Decides.*

2. Ibid., 187.

3. Renshon, *Psychological Needs and Political Behavior,* 32.

4. Marsh, *Protest and Political Consciousness,* 1 and 64–65.

5. Seligson, "Unconventional Political Participation," 134–36 and 142–43.

6. Opp, Voss, and Gern, *Origins of a Spontaneous Revolution,* 139–41 and 150.

7. Oberschall, "Protests, Demonstrations and the End of Communist Regimes in 1989," 12.

8. Opp, Voss, and Gern, *Origins of a Spontaneous Revolution,* 73–77 and 151.

9. Przeworski, "Transition to Democracy," 54–55.

10. Oberschall, "Rational Choice," 80.

11. Karklins and Petersen, "Decision Calculus of Protesters and Regimes," 590.

12. Thompson, "Why and How East Germans Rebelled," 264–65.

13. For example, Urban, "Czechoslovakia: The Power and Politics of Humiliation."

14. Saxonberg, *The Fall,* 326.

15. Stokes, *The Walls Came Tumbling Down,* 155–56; Wheaton and Kavan, *The Velvet Revolution,* 24; Huntington, *The Third Wave,* 104.

Notes to Pages 57–67   195

16. Karklins and Petersen, "Decision Calculus of Protesters and Regimes," 595; Przeworski, *Democracy and the Market,* 3–4 and footnote 4 on page 55; Thompson, "Why and How East Germans Rebelled," 264–65.

17. Przeworski, *Democracy and the Market,* 3–4 and footnote 4 on page 55.

18. Hirschman, "Exit, Voice and the Fate of the German Democratic Republic."

19. Urban, "Czechoslovakia: The Power and Politics of Humiliation"; Opp, Voss, and Gern, *Origins of a Spontaneous Revolution.*

20. Saxonberg, *The Fall,* 326.

21. Ibid., 326–27.

22. Karklins and Petersen, "Decision Calculus of Protesters and Regimes," 592; Opp, Voss, and Gern, *Origins of a Spontaneous Revolution,* 105.

23. Saxonberg, *The Fall,* chap. 10.

24. Joppke, *East German Dissidents and the Revolution of 1989,* 145–52.

25. Wheaton and Kavan, *The Velvet Revolution,* 39–42.

26. Kusin, "Challenge to Normalcy," 27; Ash, *The Uses of Adversity,* 63.

27. Eyal, "Why Romania Could Not Avoid Bloodshed," 140.

28. Radio Free Europe, "Czechoslovak, Hungarian and Polish Expectations Concerning Domestic Developments," October 1985, 10.

29. Lago, "The Human Cost of Social Revolution."

30. Raul Rivero, "En Cuba, balsas o resignación," *El Nuevo Herald,* June 30, 1998; Olance Nogueras, "Escasez y represión agobian a cubanos," *El Nuevo Herald,* June 25, 1998; Oswaldo Céspedes, "Un plebiscito sin urna ni bandera. El desenfreno de la inmigración," Cooperativa de Periodistas Independiente, *CubaNet,* June 29, 1998; Armando Añel Guerrero, "Viendo la vida pasar," *CubaNet,* November 6, 1998.

31. I am borrowing the concepts of exit, voice, and loyalty from Hirschman, *Exit, Voice, and Loyalty.*

32. Pablo Alfonso, "La crisis moral juvenil alarma a las autoridades," *El Nuevo Herald,* August 1, 1999.

33. The document can be viewed at www.lanuevacuba.com/pantalones.htm.

34. Roberts et al., "Measuring Cuban Public Opinion: Project Report," 115 and 117.

35. Ibid., 110.

36. Ibid., 95.

37. Huntington, *The Third Wave,* 102.

38. Karklins and Petersen, "Decision Calculus of Protesters and Regimes," 590–92 and 599–601.

39. See survey data in Roberts et al., "Measuring Cuban Public Opinion: Project Report," 93–95 and 119.

40. Cuban Democratic Revolutionary Directorate, *Steps to Freedom 1999,* 42–43.

41. Ibid., 13.

42. Pablo Alfonso, "Cuba por dentro," *El Nuevo Herald,* March 5, 1997. For the continued success of actions by workers and grassroots initiatives in getting government authorities to meet some economic demands, see Cuban Democratic Revolutionary Directorate, *Steps to Freedom 1999,* 10–11.

43. Ramón Humberto Colás, "Paro laboral, salarios y trenes," *CubaNet,* February 14, 2000.

196   *Notes to Pages 67–71*

44. *Diario las Américas,* July 8, 1998; Mery Miranda, "Protesta pública de cocheros en las Tunas," *CubaNet,* November 24, 1999; "Obreros pinareños obtienen parte de sus demandas por vía de la resistencia cívica," *CubaNet,* December 19, 2000.

45. "Reclamo popular obliga al Partido Comunista a tomar medidas," *CubaNet,* April 21, 1998.

46. "Concluye en el Santuario peregrinaje de madres y familiares de presos políticos," *CubaNet,* July 20, 1998.

47. Oswaldo de Céspedes, "Victoria de la disidencia cubana," *CubaNet,* December 6, 1999; Mario J. Viera González, "Diciembre caliente: de la Santa Bárbara hasta San Lázaro," *CubaNet,* December 21, 1999.

48. "Impiden a opositores de Villa Clara viajar al santuario de la Caridad," *CubaNet,* September 9, 1999; "Arrestos y amenazas en Santiago de Cuba," *CubaNet,* February 16, 1999; Oswaldo de Céspedes, "Ola represiva por Día de San Lázaro," *CubaNet,* December 17, 1999.

49. Philipsen, *We Were the People,* 84.

50. Tismaneanu, "Nascent Civil Society," 110.

51. Skilling, *Samizdat and an Independent Society in Central and Eastern Europe,* 11–12.

52. Helsinki Watch, *Toward Civil Society,* 29.

53. Ibid., 1–2.

54. Ibid., 38 and 43–45.

55. Board of International Broadcasting, *Annual Report* (1988), 19 and 36–37.

56. Board of International Broadcasting, *Annual Report* (1989), 21 and 24.

57. East European Area Audience and Opinion Research, "Two Measurements of RFE's 'Uniqueness' in the Eyes of Its Audience," 1 and 4.

58. East European Area Audience and Opinion Research, "Listeners Assess RFE's Influence on Themselves, on Public Opinion and on the Government of Their Country," 1, 5, 7, and 8.

59. Polish Helsinki Watch Committee, *Poland Under Martial Law,* 78.

60. U.S. Congress, "Authorizing Additional Appropriations," 7.

61. For quotes by Solidarity activists and government officials about the importance of foreign radio broadcasts for the pro-democracy movement, see Nelson, *War of the Black Heavens,* 158–60.

62. John Omicinski, "Pope More Involved in Freedom Movement Than Known, Book Reveals," Gannett News Service, September 2, 1997.

63. Board of International Broadcasting, *Annual Report* (1989), 42; Nelson, *War of the Black Heavens,* 170.

64. Nelson, *War of the Black Heavens,* 169.

65. Skilling, *Samizdat and an Independent Society in Central and Eastern Europe,* 8.

66. Sakwa, *Gorbachev and His Reforms,* 65–70.

67. Nelson, *War of the Black Heavens,* 169.

68. Sakwa, *Gorbachev and His Reforms,* 207.

69. Nelson, *War of the Black Heavens,* 170; Sakwa, *Gorbachev and His Reforms,* 69.

70. Karklins, "Explaining Regime Change in the Soviet Union," 35.

71. Nelson, *War of the Black Heavens,* 163.

72. Saxonberg, *The Fall,* 311.

73. Ibid., 184.

74. I owe this observation to Daniel Friedheim.

75. Buhl, "Window to the West," 8.

Notes to Pages 71–73 197

76. Ibid., 1, 6, 7, and 8.

77. Radio Free Europe, "Listening to RFE Programs in Czechoslovakia Before and After August 21st," April 1969, 5.

78. East European Area Audience and Opinion Research, "Reasons for Not Listening to Radio Free Europe in Czechoslovakia," 2 and 8.

79. East European Area Audience and Opinion Research, "Czechoslovak Listeners' Exposure to and Evaluation of RFE Programs," 2 and 7.

80. Helsinki Watch, *Toward Civil Society,* 1–2.

81. Board of International Broadcasting, *Annual Report* (1989), 67.

82. Nelson, *War of the Black Heavens,* 183.

83. Thomas, "The Helsinki Accords," 27.

84. Wheaton and Kavan, *The Velvet Revolution,* 49.

85. U.S. Congress, "Authorizing Additional Appropriations," 7.

86. Rady, *Romania in Turmoil,* 95.

87. Ratesh, *Romania: The Entangled Revolution,* 21.

88. Ibid., 33 and 35–36; Rady, *Romania in Turmoil,* 95 and 99.

89. Nelson, *War of the Black Heavens,* 182–83.

90. Roberts et al., "Measuring Cuban Public Opinion: Project Report," 80–81.

91. Office of Research, International Broadcasting Bureau, "Research Memorandum," 8.

92. Radio Martí Program Office of Audience Research, "Cuban Audience Survey: Radio Martí and Its Competition," 5; Office of Cuba Broadcasting, "1991 Cuban Audience Survey Report: A Survey of Media Habits of Cuban Arrivals," 13–15; Office of Research and Media Reaction, "Radio Martí Audience Assessment. A Survey of Cuban Travelers in Miami, December 1994 thru February 1995," 4. In contrast to survey data from interviews in Miami, questionnaires filled out by visa applicants at the United States Interests Section in Havana suggest that the availability of short-wave radios among the population is much less. Twenty percent to 26 percent of respondents from two surveys reported that they had access to a short-wave radio. Office of Research, International Broadcasting Bureau, "UHF Access and TV Martí Viewership in Cuba," 3; Office of Research, International Broadcasting Bureau. "Media Habits Among Visa Applicants at the U.S. Interests Section in Havana, Cuba," 8.

93. Roberts et al., "Measuring Cuban Public Opinion: Project Report," 84.

94. Office of Cuba Broadcasting, "1991 Cuban Audience Survey Report: A Survey of Media Habits of Cuban Arrivals," 122–23 and 144–45. For interest in TV Martí as a potential source of news, see Office of Research and Media Reaction, Radio Martí Audience Assessment, "A Survey of Cuban Travelers in Miami, December 1994 thru February 1995," 10.

95. Roberts et al., "Measuring Cuban Public Opinion: Project Report," 83 and 85. CNN is available via cable in hotels for foreign tourists, something out of reach for the general population.

96. Office of Research, International Broadcasting Bureau, "Media Habits Among Visa Applicants at the U.S. Interests Section in Havana, Cuba," 1.

97. Office of Research, USIA, "U.S. Government Broadcasting to Cuba: An In-Country Assessment," 4–5.

98. Roberts et al., "Measuring Cuban Public Opinion: Project Report," 83 and 85.

99. PricewaterhouseCoopers LLP Evaluation of the USAID Cuba Program, July 21, 2000, 16.

198   *Notes to Pages 73–76*

100. Héctor Maseda and Leonel Pérez Bellette, "El correo electrónico en Cuba," *CubaNet,* May 31, 2000; Scott Doggett, "In Castro's Cuba, Internet Hookups Are Few and Far Between," *The Times,* May 1, 2000; Maria F. Durand, "Cuba Goes Online," ABCNews.com, July 24, 2000; Eduardo G. Estrada, "Internet: un imposible para la generalidad de los cubanos," *CubaNet,* May 31, 2000; Pablo Alfonso, "Cuba tiende la cortina de hierro por la internet," *El Nuevo Herald,* October 9, 2000.

101. William J. Drake, Shanthi Kalathil, and Taylor C. Boas, "Dictatorships in the Digital Age: Some Considerations on the Internet in China and Cuba," The Carnegie Endowment for International Peace, October 2000 (http://www.ceip.org).

102. Regular listeners are daily listeners except for 1991 and 1995. For 1991, the data are for people who listened an average of 5.5 days/week. For 1995, the data are for people who listened at least once a week.

103. Pablo Alfonso, "Instalan un campo de antenas que interfieren a Radio Martí," *El Nuevo Herald,* April 20, 1999; Ramon Alberto Cruz-Lima, "Continúa interferencia de Radio Martí," *Diario las Américas,* May 5, 1999.

104. Radio Martí Office of Audience Research, "Radio Martí Reception Study: Report on Survey Findings," tables 49 and 53.

105. Report by The Advisory Board for Radio Broadcasting to Cuba, 1989, 2; Radio Martí Program Office of Audience Research, "Cuban Audience Survey: Radio Martí and Its Competition," 4–6, 11, and 71; Office of Cuba Broadcasting, "1991 Cuban Audience Survey Report: A Survey of Media Habits of Cuban Arrivals," 5 and 24; Office of Research, USIA, "U.S. Government Broadcasting to Cuba: An In-Country Assessment," 4–5; Office of Research and Media Reaction, "Radio Martí Audience Assessment. A Survey of Cuban Travelers in Miami, December 1994 thru February 1995," 4; Office of Research, International Broadcasting Bureau, "UHF Access and TV Martí Viewership in Cuba"; Office of Research, International Broadcasting Bureau, "Media Habits Among Visa Applicants at the U.S. Interests Section in Havana, Cuba," i, 1, 5.

106. Office of Research and Media Reaction, "Radio Martí Audience Assessment. A Survey of Cuban Travelers in Miami, December 1994 thru February 1995," 3.

107. Office of Research, International Broadcasting Bureau, "Media Habits Among Visa Applicants at the U.S. Interests Section in Havana, Cuba," 5; International Broadcasting Bureau, "A Qualitative Research Study Among Recently-Arrived Cuban Immigrants to Gauge Reaction to Selected Radio Martí Programs," 4.

108. International Broadcasting Bureau, "A Qualitative Research Study Among Recently-Arrived Cuban Immigrants to Gauge Reaction to Selected Radio Martí Programs," 3.

109. For the dearth of domestic dissemination of news and information from independent sources, see Oswaldo de Céspedes y Angel Pablo Polanco, "Avanza desobediencia civil en Cuba," *CubaNet,* January 15, 1999.

110. The *Confederación de Trabajadores Democráticos de Cuba* published a bulletin, *El Sindical Haciendo Caminos,* on May 1, 1998 (see Ricardo González, "La Voz de los Trabajadores Que No Tienen Voz," *CubaNet,* May 5, 1998). The Union of Independent Journalists and Writers distributed a newsletter, *Transición,* in the streets of Havana on February 11, 1997 (see Cuban Democratic Revolutionary Directorate, "Steps to Freedom," 6). The Partido Liberal Democrático de Cuba published a bulletin, *El Liberal,* in January 1999 (see "Circula boletín El Liberal," *CubaNet,* January 15, 1999).

111. "Llaman a la desobediencia civil," *CubaNet,* November 27, 2000.

112. For example, see the "Resumen de Noticias," APIC, *CubaNet,* September 25, 1996; "Llueven volantes sobre la Habana," *El Nuevo Herald,* February 26, 1999.

Notes to Pages 76–80 199

113. Miguel Fernández Martínez, "Iglesia Apostólica de Jesucristo vigila violaciones de derechos humanos dentro de la isla," *Diario las Américas*, April 2, 1998.

114. Personal conversations with activists in Miami.

115. H. Gordon Skilling, *Samizdat and an Independent Society in Central and Eastern Europe*, 7–13.

116. One of the main channels for the writings of independent journalists in Cuba is the Internet. Journalists in Cuba send their articles to support groups in the United States, and the latter place the articles on the Internet. But access to the Internet in Cuba is under government control.

117. "Entrevista con Oscar Elías Biscet, directivo de la Fundación Lawton," *CubaNet*, January 21, 1999.

118. Mario J. Viera, "Una oposición desorientada," *CubaNet*, September 23, 1999.

119. Roberts et al., "Measuring Cuban Public Opinion: Project Report," 83.

120. Office of Research, International Broadcasting Bureau, "A Qualitative Research Study Among Recently-Arrived Cuban Travelers: Perceptions of Radio Martí and Reactions to Selected Programs," 4 and 7.

121. Roberts et al., "Measuring Cuban Public Opinion: Project Report," v, 28, and 93–95.

122. Ibid., vii, 2, 94–95, and 119.

123. Office of Research, International Broadcasting Bureau, "Research Memorandum," 1.

124. Radio Martí Program Office of Audience Research, "Cuban Audience Survey: Radio Martí and Its Competition," 71, 73; Office of Cuba Broadcasting, "1991 Cuban Audience Survey Report: A Survey of Media Habits of Cuban Arrivals," 68 and 88; Office of Research, "U.S. Government Broadcasting to Cuba: An In-Country Assessment," 4–5; Office of Research and Media Reaction, "Radio Martí Audience Assessment: A Survey of Cuban Travelers in Miami, December 1994 thru February 1995," 4–5; Roberts et al., "Measuring Cuban Public Opinion: Project Report," 83 and 85.

125. Radio Martí Program Office of Audience Research, "Cuban Audience Survey: Radio Martí and Its Competition," 71, 73, 103–14, and 123.

126. Office of Research and Media Reaction, "Radio Martí Audience Assessment: A Survey of Cuban Travelers in Miami, December 1994 thru February 1995," 3 and 22.

127. Office of Research, International Broadcasting Bureau, "A Qualitative Research Study Among Recently-Arrived Cuban Travelers: Perceptions of Radio Martí and Reactions to Selected Programs," 6; International Broadcasting Bureau, "A Qualitative Research Study Among Recently-Arrived Cuban Immigrants to Gauge Reaction to Selected Radio Martí Programs," 5.

128. Channel effectiveness is the percentage of the audience who can receive a clear, audible signal at any given time.

129. For technical means of surmounting jamming, see Board of International Broadcasting, *Annual Report* (1985), 23 and 25; Nelson, *War of the Black Heavens*, 219–20. Other ways that have been proposed to increase the reach of Radio and TV Martí are for RM to broadcast from the United States Naval Base at Guantanamo Bay and for TV Martí to transmit from a C-130 military airplane over international airspace off Cuba.

130. I reach this conclusion based on both the (in)actions of the administration regarding Radio and TV Martí and interviews with several individuals very familiar with the operations and politics of these stations.

200   *Notes to Pages 80–88*

131. "Statement by the President. Toward a Democratic Cuba," The White House Office of the Press Secretary, July 13, 2001.

132. Final Report of The Presidential Commission on Broadcasting to Cuba, September 30, 1982, 16 and 24.

133. Report by The Advisory Board for Radio Broadcasting to Cuba, 1989, 5 and 13.

134. Advisory Board for Broadcasting to Cuba, Report by the Advisory Board, 2–3.

135. *El Nuevo Herald,* November 9, 1999.

136. Ibid.; Manuel David Orrio, "Interferencias radiales no sufren 'apagon,'" *CubaNet,* December 7, 1999.

137. Board of International Broadcasting, *Annual Report* (1986), 5.

138. Richard Sammon, "Sending a (TV) Signal to Cuba," *Congressional Quarterly,* March 9, 1996, 633.

139. Board for International Broadcasting, *Annual Report* (1985), 21.

140. In 1987, the United States signed an agreement with Israel to install sixteen 500–kW transmitters to be used by the Voice of America, Radio Free Europe, and Radio Liberty. Such a transmitter facility in Israel was seen as enabling RFE/RL to penetrate massive Soviet jamming; Board of International Broadcasting, *Annual Report* (1988), 1.

141. Board for International Broadcasting, *Annual Report* (1986), 1.

142. Board of International Broadcasting, *Annual Report* (1988), 51.

143. I obtained some of the information about RFE/RL broadcasts from personnel at RFE/RL in Washington, D.C.

144. Information given to me personally from the technical department at RFL/RL in Washington, D.C.

145. William A. Buell, "Radio Free Europe/Radio Liberty in the mid 1980s," 71.

146. Board of International Broadcasting, *Annual Report* (1988), 51; Nelson, *War of the Black Heavens* 173.

FOUR. Assistance to Civil Society

1. Saxonberg, *The Fall,* 215 and 221.

2. Opp, Voss, and Gern consider the peace prayers in Leipzig as a necessary prerequisite for the emergence of spontaneous mass protests; Opp, Voss, and Gern, *Origins of a Spontaneous Revolution,* 123 and 198.

3. Ibid., 95, 104, and 122–23.

4. Ibid., 123 and 198.

5. I draw the observations about the role of the Catholic Church in Poland from Saxonberg, *The Fall,* 213–15.

6. Juan Tamayo, "Pope Likens Cuba Trip to Fateful Poland Visit," *Miami Herald,* January 29, 1998.

7. Rosa Townsend, "El obispo de la Habana advierte que su misión no es derribar a Castro," *El Pais,* June 17, 1998.

8. For a brief and incisive review of marriages of convenience between the Catholic Church and dictatorships at various times in the history of Cuba, see Jesús Zúñiga, "La salvación por la Iglesia?" *CubaNet,* June 9, 1998.

9. Information from a group in Miami that provides assistance to dissidents in Cuba.

10. *Diario las Américas,* March 25, 1998, 10–A.

Notes to Pages 88–94 201

11. In East Germany, the Church was allowed to run kindergartens, received state subsidies, and broadcast religious services on radio and television; Tismaneanu, "Nascent Civil Society," 95 and 105; Opp, Voss, and Gern, *Origins of a Spontaneous Revolution,* 121.

12. Omar Rodriguez Saludes, "Prohíben procesiones católicas en dos poblados habaneros," *Diario las Américas,* July 18, 1998; "Pope's Visit Changed Little in Cuba." *Miami Herald,* June 26, 1998; "Negan permiso para efectuar procesión religiosa," *CubaNet,* March 22, 2000; "Gobierno de Cuba prohíbe procesión de la Candelaria," *CubaNet,* February 7, 2000.

13. Clark, "La Visita del Papa a Cuba y su Repercusión," 19–22 and 26.

14. Pablo Alfonso, "Ofensiva contra el auge religioso," and "Se prepara el gobierno para dar una batida antireligiosa en la Habana," *El Nuevo Herald,* June 17, 2001.

15. Manuel David Orrio and Joaquín Torres Alvarez, "Opositores Ayunan for Libertad Ciudadana." *CubaNet,* February 26, 1998.

16. "Asiste la oposición a vigilia en la iglesia de Santa Bárbara," *CubaNet,* November 16, 1999.

17. "Seguirán las misas a favor de los prisioneros políticos en Cuba," *CubaNet,* March 23, 2000.

18. "Misa por prisioneros políticos cubanos," *CubaNet,* March 6, 2000.

19. "El Padre Oscar pide ruegos a favor de los presos políticos," *CubaNet,* March 10, 2000.

20. "Seguridad del Estado amenaza con arresto masivo en iglesia habanera," *CubaNet,* March 23, 2000.

21. "No admitirán más a disidentes en iglesia católica de Párraga," *CubaNet,* March 24, 2000.

22. "Siguen las oraciones por los presos políticos, pero en otra iglesia," *CubaNet,* March 31, 2000.

23. "Sacerdote cubano ofende y expulsa del templo a disidentes," *CubaNet,* May 12, 2000.

24. Pablo Alfonso, "Sacerdote exhorta a los fieles a disentir del gobierno," *El Nuevo Herald,* September 29, 1999; Rui Ferreira, "Sacerdote afirma el sistema cubano se ha vuelto impotente," *El Nuevo Herald,* June 27, 1998.

25. The document can be viewed at www.lanuevacuba.com/pantalones.htm.

26. "Una agencia del Vaticano denuncia campaña contra la iglesia católica," *El Nuevo Herald,* April 5, 2000; "Papa aboga por más libertades en Cuba," *El Nuevo Herald,* June 10, 1998; "Pide el Papa a Cuba más apertura y libertad para los cubanos," *Diario las Américas,* December 2, 1999.

27. Part of my knowledge about the story is based on personal conversation with the director of an NGO in the United States who works with opposition groups in Cuba.

28. "Furor Over Time Article," *Polish News Bulletin,* February 19, 1992.

29. Day, *The Velvet Philosophers,* 80, 92, 116–17, 121, 124, 127, 129, 131–33, and 160–66.

30. Ibid., 266–68.

31. Ash, *Freedom for Publishing,* 18–25 and 48.

32. National Endowment for Democracy, *Annual Report* (1984), 40–41.

33. National Endowment for Democracy, *Annual Report* (1985), 19 and 38–39.

34. National Endowment for Democracy, *Annual Report* (1987), 37–39.

202   *Notes to Pages 94–101*

35. National Endowment for Democracy, *Annual Reports* (1986), 18–20; (1987), 37–39; (1988), 23–24; (1989), 21–23.

36. National Endowment for Democracy, *Annual Reports* (1986), 21–23; (1987), 40–42; (1989), 24–26.

37. National Endowment for Democracy, *Annual Report* (1988), 26–29.

38. National Endowment for Democracy, *Annual Reports* (1986), 17–18; (1987), 36; (1988), 22; (1989), 20–21.

39. National Endowment for Democracy, *Annual Reports* (1986), 17–18; (1987), 36; (1988), 22; (1989), 20–21.

40. National Endowment for Democracy, *Annual Reports* (1987), 40; (1988), 25; (1989), 24.

41. National Endowment for Democracy, *Annual Reports* (1985), 37; (1986), 17 and 23; (1987), 34–35; (1988), 21–22; (1989), 19.

42. Interview by Oswaldo de Céspedes, "Cuba no ha cambiado porque los cubanos no se han determinado a hacerlo" *CubaNet,* March 15, 2000; for an example of economic repression against democratic activists, see "Niegan a opositora pacífica derecho al trabajo," *CubaNet,* June 9, 2000.

43. Personal conversation with the director of the Support Group to the Dissidence in Miami.

44. Ana Acle, "Cuba Comes Between Children, Church's Toys," *Miami Herald,* February 3, 2000.

45. Antonio Alonso, "Ayuda humanitaria preocupa a Seguridad del Estado," *CubaNet,* May 29, 2000.

46. Juan O. Tamayo, "Pope Summons Cuba's Bishops as Church-State Relations Stall," *Miami Herald,* May 31, 1998.

47. "Controversia entre el MINSAP y Caritas deja a enfermos sin medicinas," *CubaNet,* May 4, 2000; "Prohiben extender recetas para adquirir medicinas donadas a la Iglesia Católica," *CubaNet,* January 10, 2001.

48. "Suspenden sus operaciones humanitarias en Cuba Médicos Sin Fronteras-España," *Diario las Américas,* December 3, 1999.

49. See, for example, Childs and Popplewell, *The Stasi.*

50. National Endowment for Democracy, *Annual Reports* (1984–91).

51. This observation is based on personal conversations with numerous individuals whose organizations received USAID grants and with a former director of the USAID Cuba Program.

52. Personal conversation.

53. For the 1997 fiscal year, the amount was $1.5 million, and for 1998, it was $2 million.

54. PricewaterhouseCoopers LLP Evaluation of the USAID Cuba Program, July 21, 2000.

55. Personal conversations with the director of GAD.

56. The USAID Cuba Program is funded through the Economic Support Fund, which is appropriated to the Department of State. The Cuba Program is advised by an Interagency Working Group (IWG), which is the key decision-making body on grant awards. The IWG is co-chaired by the senior advisor/coordinator for Cuba at the USAID and the head of the Office of Cuban Affairs (the Cuba Desk) of the State Department. The State Department plays a central role in the implementation of the USAID Cuba Program.

57. Personal conversation with a former U.S. government official.

Notes to Pages 102–105   203

58. www.info.usaid.gov/countries/cu/mand-cub.htm.

59. See the U.S.-Cuba Business Council web page at: www.uscubabiz.org.

60. Pablo Alfonso, "Cuestionan destino del dinero para la democracia en Cuba," *El Nuevo Herald*, February 22, 2000.

61. Center for Development and Information Evaluation, 1999 Agency Performance Report (Washington, D.C., Center for Development and Information Evaluation, 2000), 6–7.

62. Public Law 105–174 and a Senate amendment to the foreign operations bill, S. 2334.

63. "CIA Drafts Covert Plan to Topple Saddam," *New York Times*, February 25, 1998.

64. For accounts of the weakness of Iraqi opposition groups and the divisiveness among those groups, see Cordesman and Hashim, *Iraq: Sanctions and Beyond*, 59–64; and comments by U.S. Marine Corps General Anthony Zinni in "Gulf Commander Criticizes Policy," *Chicago Tribune*, January 29, 1999, section 1, p. 3.

65. George Gedda, "Senators Seek $100M for Cuba Groups," Yahoo! Cuba News, May 17, 2001; Randall Mikkelsen, "Bush Supports Efforts to Fund Cuban Dissidents," Reuters, May 18, 2001.

66. Rafael Lorente, "Bill Seeks $100 Million for Direct Aid to Cuban Dissidents," *Chicago Tribune*, May 17, 2001.

67. Jim Burns, "Cuba Criticizes US Legislation to Aid Cuban Dissidents," CNSNews.com, May 18, 2001; Daniel Schweimler, "Cuba Blasts Bush over Dissidents," BBC News Online, May 24, 2001.

68. Rafael Lorente, "Bill Seeks $100 Million for Direct Aid to Cuban Dissidents," *Chicago Tribune*, May 17, 2001; Christopher Marquis, "Helms and Lieberman Seek to Aid Dissidents in Cuba," *New York Times*, May 16, 2001.

69. Jim Burns, "Senate Bill Seeks to Boost Cuban Democracy," CNSNews.com, May 17, 2001.

70. For about thirty years, I have had contacts with activists in organizations of exiles in various parts of the United States and have been in close contact with the Cuban American community in Chicago. Part of my knowledge comes from personal observations and conversations with a myriad of activists over the years.

71. "Recaudan fondos para apoyar acusados de asesinar a Castro," *Diario las Américas*, August 17, 1999.

72. Wilfredo Cancia Isla, "Abren un fondo legal para la defensa de Elián," *El Nuevo Herald*, March 8, 1999; "Recaudan más de 222.000 dólares para defensa legal caso Elián," *Diario las Américas*, March 13, 2000.

73. For evidence of opposition groups in Cuba attacking the embargo and supporting the return of Elián to Cuba, see the interview with the new president of the Party of Democratic Solidarity, Fernando Sánchez López, "El Partido Solidaridad Democrática en el 2000," *CubaNet*, February 4, 2000, and "Disidentes apoyan cese del embargo al gobierno de Cuba," *CubaNet*, July 4, 2000.

74. For example, the Mesa de Reflexión de la Oposición Moderada, an umbrella for several organizations, declared that it supported the immediate return of Elián González to Cuba; see, "Disidentes cubanos pidieron el regreso de Elián a Cuba," *CubaNet*, March 8, 2000.

75. Pablo Alfonso, "Payá desmiente declaraciones de otro disidente," *El Nuevo Herald*, May 25, 2000.

204   *Notes to Pages 105–115*

76. Pablo Alfonso, "Cuestionan destino del dinero para la democracia en Cuba," *El Nuevo Herald,* February 22, 2000.

77. I got this impression from personal contacts with some of the directors of CANF in Miami.

78. Maria Travierso, "Piden ley para enviar ayuda a la oposicíon de la isla," *El Nuevo Herald,* May 25, 2000.

79. Olance Nogueras, "40 grupos dicen no a modificar embargo a Cuba," *El Nuevo Herald,* February 17, 1998.

80. I was at the conference and observed this dynamic.

FIVE. U.S. Policies toward Cuba

1. Fontaine, *On Negotiating with Cuba,* 41–45; Bender, *Cuba vs. United States,* 12–17; Rabe, *Eisenhower and Latin America,* 162–63.

2. Rabe, *Eisenhower and Latin America,* 170.

3. Schlesinger Jr., *A Thousand Days,* 225.

4. Ibid., 233–34.

5. Ibid., 233.

6. Ibid., 225; Wyden, *Bay of Pigs,* 92.

7. Fontaine, *On Negotiating with Cuba,* 46; Wyden, *Bay of Pigs,* 100; Schlesinger Jr., *A Thousand Days,* 237. For a discussion of the possibility that the Bay of Pigs invasion and the internal resistance at the time could have toppled the Castro government, see Blight and Kornbluh, eds., *Politics of Illusion,* chaps. 1 and 2.

8. Blight and Kornbluh, eds., *Politics of Illusion,* 64; Wyden, *Bay of Pigs,* 100.

9. Thompson, *The Missiles of October,* 120.

10. Lazo, *Dagger in the Heart,* 265–77. At the time of the invasion, there were about 200 anti-Castro guerrillas in the Escambray Mountains, a group waiting for armaments to start another guerrilla force in the Sierra Maestra Mountains, and several hundred urban guerrillas throughout Cuba waiting to act in coordination with the invasion. Encinosa, *Cuba en Guerra,* 64 and 77.

11. Fontaine, *On Negotiating with Cuba,* 46; Schlesinger Jr., *A Thousand Days,* 270–74.

12. Fontaine, *On Negotiating with Cuba,* 48.

13. Lazo, *Dagger in the Heart,* 372–74; Blight and Welch, *On the Brink,* 270, 294, and 308.

14. Fontaine, *On Negotiating with Cuba,* 49–50.

15. Ibid., 51–60.

16. Brenner, *From Confrontation to Negotiation,* 18–19; LeoGrande, "From Havana to Miami," 70–71.

17. Brenner, *From Confrontation to Negotiation,* 19–23; Bender, *Cuba vs. United States,* 36–37; LeoGrande, "From Havana to Miami," 71.

18. Central American and Caribbean Program, "Report on Cuba: Findings of the Study Group on United States-Cuban Relations," 16.

19. Kagan, *A Twilight Struggle,* 174; Robert Pastor, "The Reagan Administration," 6.

20. See the remarks by Thomas O. Enders, assistant secretary for inter-American affairs, "Dealing with the Reality of Cuba," U.S. Department of State, Bureau of Public Affairs, December 14, 1982; and the address by Kenneth N. Skoug Jr., director of the Office of Cuban Affairs, "The United States and Cuba," United States Department of State, Bureau of Public Affairs, December 17, 1984.

Notes to Pages 115–117 205

21. Skoug, *The United States and Cuba under Reagan and Shultz,* ix–xi, 7, 9–10, and 75–76.

22. Ibid., ix–xi, 7, 17–23, 26–27, 207–8, and 212.

23. Vanderbush and Haney, "Policy toward Cuba in the Clinton Administration," 393; Domínguez, "U.S.-Cuban Relations," 61.

24. Vanderbush and Haney, "Policy toward Cuba in the Clinton Administration," 392–95.

25. There are some indications that Cuba has biological and chemical weapons, but most likely the United States is prepared to defend itself in case Castro orders an attack on the United States in a moment of desperation, as he perceives that his rule is about to end. I have seen what is presented as an intelligence report stating that there are biological and chemical weapons in Cuba. Also, Ernesto Betancourt, former director of Radio Martí, told me that he read a top-secret CIA report when he was director of Radio Martí, maintaining that Cuba has biological weapons. Betancourt also had a conversation with a defector from the Cuban military who told him about the existence of such weapons in Cuba. Brian Latell, former senior intelligence adviser for Latin America at the CIA, said in 1999 at a conference at the University of Miami that the Cuban government has biological weapons. In 1998, the Department of Defense released a report on an assessment of the Cuban threat to the national security of the United States. The report says that Cuba does not have biological weapons. Yet in a cover letter to the report by the then Defense Secretary William Cohen, addressed to Senator Strom Thurmond, chair of the Armed Services Committee, Cohen stated that he remains concerned about Cuba's potential to develop and produce biological agents, given Cuba's biotechnology infrastructure. Cohen adds that, after reviewing contingency plans, he finds them appropriate for the level and nature of the Cuban threat to the national security of the United States. For a newspaper article stating that Cuba has biological weapons, see Roberto Fabricio, "Pugnan agencias del gobierno sobre las armas bacteriológicas," *El Nuevo Herald,* June 23, 1999.

26. For examples of the emphasis by officials of the Clinton administration on the need for Cuba to move toward democracy, see the transcript of an interview with Michael Ranneberger, who was the head of the Cuba desk at the State Department, in http://usinfo.state.gov/regional/ar/us-cuba/rann15.htm; "EU seguirá presidonando a Cuba, dice funcionario," *El Nuevo Herald,* March 24, 1998; "The United States and Cuba," remarks by Charles S. Shapiro, who replaced Ranneberger, in http://usembassy.state.gov/posts/cu1/wwwhsh.html; speech by President Clinton on March 20, 1998, in "Ayuda humanitaria promoverá transición en Cuba, dice Clinton," *Diario las Américas,* March 20, 1998.

27. Domínguez, "U.S.-Cuban Relations," 55; LeoGrande, "From Havana to Miami," 68 and 73.

28. Domínguez, "U.S.-Cuban Relations," 57.

29. Members of the U.S. military and intelligence community have declared that Cuba does not represent a threat to the national security of the United States or to other countries in the region. For example, see declarations by Charles Wilhem, chief of the Southern Command, in "Militar norteamericano dice que Cuba no representa amenaza," Yahoo! Noticias, March 31, 2000. Also, see a report by the U.S. Defense Intelligence Agency in "DIA Report on Cuban Threat to U.S. National Security," (http://usinfo.state.gov/regional/ar/us-cuba/dia.htm). However, it turned out that a key U.S. intelli-

206   *Notes to Pages 117–120*

gence official on whom the American military relied for intelligence on Cuba was a Castro mole.

30. Gunn, *Cuba in Transition,* 25.

31. Vanderbush and Haney, "Policy toward Cuba in the Clinton Administration," 396.

32. Gunn, *Cuba in Transition,* 21–26.

33. LeoGrande, "From Havana to Miami," 77.

34. "The Clinton Administration's Reversal of U.S. Immigration Policy Toward Cuba," Hearing, Subcommittee on the Western Hemisphere, Committee on International Relations, House of Representatives, May 18, 1995 (Washington, D.C.: U.S. Government Printing Office, 1995), 13.

35. Vanderbush and Haney, "Policy toward Cuba in the Clinton Administration," 397–99.

36. Ibid., 400–402.

37. Christopher Marquis and Andres Oppenheimer, "Clinton Cut Spying on Cuba," *Miami Herald,* October 1, 1996.

38. Vanderbush and Haney, "Policy toward Cuba in the Clinton Administration," 403.

39. "Clinton Inclined to Sign Cuban Bill," Yahoo! News, June 28, 2000.

40. "The Clinton Administration's Reversal of U.S. Immigration Policy Toward Cuba," Hearing, Subcommittee on the Western Hemisphere, Committee on International Relations, House of Representatives, May 18, 1995 (Washington, D.C.: U.S. Government Printing Office, 1995), 61.

41. Christopher Marquis and Andres Oppenheimer, "Clinton Cut Spying on Cuba," *Miami Herald,* October 1, 1996.

42. Carroll J. Doherty, "Planes' Downing Forces Clinton to Compromise on Sanctions," *Congressional Quarterly,* March 2, 1996, 565–66; Vanderbush and Haney, "Policy toward Cuba in the Clinton Administration," 404–5.

43. Rick Pearson, "Ryan Blasts Embargo in Cuba Report," *Chicago Tribune,* December 12, 1999, sec. 4, p. 10.

44. Karen DeYoung, "U.S. Businesses Encouraged to Explore Trade with Cuba," *Washington Post,* July 28, 1999.

45. Christopher Marquis, "Senate Supports Sales of Food to Cuba if President Oks Them," *Miami Herald,* August 6, 1999.

46. "W. House Interested in Bill to Ease Cuba Sanctions," Reuters, July 24, 2000; Alan Fram, "House Votes to Lift Cuban Limits," Yahoo! News, July 21, 2000; "Clinton Inclined to Sign Cuban Bill," Yahoo! News, June 28, 2000.

47. Charles Abbott, "Clinton Sees 'Big Mistake' in Small Cuba Easing," Yahoo! News, October 6, 2000.

48. "Clinton Inclined to Sign Cuban Bill," Yahoo! News, June 28, 2000.

49. Anita Snow, "US, Cuba Trade Show Plans Finalized," *CubaNet,* October 4, 1999; "Satisfacción en Cuba por el acuerdo sobre la vacuna contra la meningitis B," CNN, September 6, 1999.

50. "Clinton Announces New Steps to Help Cuban People," http://usinfo.state.gov/regional/ar/us-cuba/c105.htm; "Senior U.S. Officials Speak on Cuba Policy," http://usinfo.state.gov/regional/ar/us-cuba/rom5.htm; "Ranneberger Testimony on U.S. Policy Toward Cuba March 24," http://usinfo.state.gov/regional/ar/us-cuba/ran24.htm; "Michael Ranneberger Speech on U.S. Policy Toward Cuba," http://usinfo.state.gov/regional/ar/us- cuba/ ran16.htm.

Notes to Pages 121–125 207

51. Agustín Blázquez, "Sacrificial Birds," www.amigospais-guaracabuya.org/oagaq021.html.

52. James M. O'Neil, "St. Joe's Students Get an Education in Trip to Cuba," *Philadelphia Inquirer*, February 16, 1999.

53. Personal conversation.

54. Personal conversation with Peter Orr on November 28, 1998; Institute for U.S. Cuba Relations, "The Cuban Solidarity (Solidaridad) Act of 1998," in U.S. CUBA Policy Report, vol. 5, no. 9., September 15, 1998.

55. United States Interests Section in Havana, "U.S. Policy Toward Cuba," http://usembassy.state.gov/posts/cu1/wwwh0012.html.

56. For example, see the remarks by Charles S. Shapiro, then coordinator for Cuban affairs at the State Department, in "The United States and Cuba," http://usembassy.state.gov/posts/cu1/wwwhsh.html.

57. For example, stability has taken precedence over democracy in U.S. foreign policy toward Mexico and Brazil; Lowenthal, "The United States and Latin American Democracy," 277.

58. "The Prospects for a Peaceful Transition in Cuba: Six Months after the Papal Visit," remarks by Michael Kosak at the Dallas Morning News conference on "Cuba in Evolution," September 28, 1998, http://www.usia.gov/abtusia/posts/CUI/wwwh0035.html.

59. "Ex diplomático de EEUU en Cuba pronostica caos en la isla," *Diario las Américas*, March 7, 2000.

60. http://www.usia.gov/regional/ar/us-cuba/ran9.htm.

61. "Michael Renneberger Speech on U.S. Policy Toward Cuba," http://usinfo.state.gov/regional/ar/us-cuba/ran16.htm.

62. Horowitz, *The Conscience of Worms and the Cowardice of Lions*, 6–7.

63. Ariel Remos, "EE.UU.: más vuelos, y más dinero para el pueblo de Cuba," *Diario las Américas*, January 5, 1999.

64. For support for this interpretation, see Tim Golden, "U.S., Avoiding Castro, Relaxes Rules on Cuba," *New York Times*, July 7, 1999.

SIX. The Economic Embargo

1. The embargo was originally imposed by the Eisenhower administration in October 1960 after the Castro government had confiscated Cuban and foreign-owned properties and showed signs of moving toward the establishment of a communist dictatorship.

2. For examples of the scholarly literature, see Brady, "The Utility of Economic Sanctions as a Policy Instrument," 298; Kaempfer and Lowenberg, *International Economic Sanctions*, 3 and 16. For examples of political criticism of the U.S. embargo, see the arguments cited in William R. Hawkins, "Big Business vs. National Security?" *The Weekly Standard*, January 18, 1999; Jacob Heilbrunn, "The Sanctions Sellout," *The New Republic*, May 25, 1998.

3. The main purpose of the sanctioner in a given case can change through time.

4. Hufbauer, Schott, and Elliott, *Economic Sanctions Reconsidered*, 38.

5. Brady, "The Utility of Economic Sanctions as a Policy Instrument," 298.

6. Despite the decline in the strength of the Cuban armed forces in terms of deteri-

208   *Notes to Pages 125–130*

oration in preparedness and equipment and claims by some U.S. government officials that the Castro government no longer poses a military threat to the United States, some sources indicate that the Cuban government has biological and chemical weapons that could be launched against the southern part of the United States.

7. My work is concerned with economic sanctions for noneconomic purposes. Economic sanctions can also be applied for economic reasons in trade disputes between countries.

8. Hufbauer, Schott, and Elliott, *Economic Sanctions Reconsidered.* USA Engage is an association of U.S. firms that carries out political campaigns and lobbying efforts against economic sanctions.

9. Ibid., 12, 91, and 92.

10. For the common view that economic sanctions have as their goal to pressure targets into policy changes, see, for example, Kaempfer and Lowenberg, "The Problem and Promise of Sanctions," 61 and 63; Martin, *Coercive Cooperation,* 4; Brady, "The Utility of Economic Sanctions as a Policy Instrument," 298.

11. Brady, "The Utility of Economic Sanctions as a Policy Instrument," 298; Kaempfer and Lowenbert, *International Economic Sanctions,* 3 and 16.

12. White House press release on March 12, 1996.

13. The value of U.S. properties seized by the Castro government was about $2 billion at the time of the expropriations in 1960. There are now about 1,000 claimants who are entitled to file suit under the Helms–Burton law. Arthur Gottschalk, "Putting Pressure on Cuba: U.S. Puts Embargo Ultimatum in the Mail," *Journal of Commerce,* June 13, 1996.

14. Subsequently, Grupo Domos divested itself from its business in Cuba.

15. Elena Moreno, "EEUU y UE Reconocen Fallaron sus Métodos Respecto a Cuba," *CubaNet,* February 2, 1997.

16. For example, see the article by Tom Raum, "Allies Criticize U.S. Sanctions on Trade with Outlaw Nations," *Miami Herald,* June 29, 1996.

17. According to the terms of the agreement made public, the EU pledged to adopt rules to inhibit new investment in confiscated property, and the United States promised to seek congressional approval to waive Title IV of the Helms–Burton law and to continue to suspend Title III. Under the Libertad Act, the president forfeited his foreign policy power to change the provisions of the Act without congressional approval. Christopher Marquis, "U.S., Europeans Strike Deal on Helms–Burton," *Miami Herald,* April 12, 1997.

18. "Robaina llama a la 'unión sagrada' de los cubanos," *El Nuevo Herald,* January 19, 1997.

19. Robert Evans, "Update from Geneva," Reuters, April 22, 1996.

20. Voice of America, March 5, 1996.

21. "Castro debe iniciar la transición, dice disidente cubano," *El Nuevo Herald,* December 17, 1996.

22. Mesa-Lago, "Strategies for the 1990s," 197.

23. Roberts et al., "Measuring Cuban Public Opinion: Project Report," 118.

24. For example, see Mesa-Lago and Fabian, "Analogies," 370. Liberalization is allowing individuals to have certain rights, including freedom of speech, of movement, and of association, and the right to a fair trial under rules of preestablished laws. Liberalization is not the same as democratization, which would entail, at least, the holding of free and fair elections to select candidates to the national government.

Notes to Pages 130–134   209

25. Thomas W. Lippman, "U.S. Allies to Seek Reforms in Cuba," *Washington Post*, August 17, 1996.

26. Mesa-Lago and Fabian, "Analogies," 370.

27. For the association between types of dictatorships and the modes of transition, see Linz and Stepan, *Problems of Democratic Transition*.

28. José Miguel Vivanco, executive director of Human Rights Watch/Americas, in an article published in 1996, states that while Europe's dialogue with Cuba has led to the periodic release of some political prisoners, European Union policy toward Cuba has had no effect whatsoever on the repression of basic liberties by the Castro regime; Christopher Marquis, "Rights Group: EU Economic Policy in Cuba Unjustified," *Miami Herald*, September 21, 1996.

29. Mesa-Lago, "Strategies for the 1990s," 194.

30. *Cuba al día* (June 1994) and the "Chronology of Cuban Events" (Washington, D.C.: Information Resources Branch, Radio Martí Program, 1994).

31. *CubaHoy* 2, no. 200 (November 12, 1996).

32. "Castro Again Rejects World Pleas for Reform," *Miami Herald*, November 26, 1996.

33. Reports of human rights violations come from Cuba on a daily basis by independent journalists; see *CubaNet* on the Internet. The Inter-American Commission on Human Rights, an agency of the Organization of American States (OAS), issued a report in 1997 stating that the Cuban government systematically tramples civil rights and political freedom, among other abuses. Pablo Alfonso, "Report Cites Abuses of Rights in Cuba," *Miami Herald*, April 30, 1997.

34. "No de Castro al llamado de apertura," *El Nuevo Herald*, November 17, 1999; David Adams, "Castro Defies Leaders' Push for Democracy," *St. Petersburg Times*, November 17, 1999.

35. "Cuba Cracks Down, New Attack Launched on Dissent," *Miami Herald*, February 17, 1999; Anita Snow, "Cuba Crackdown on US Collaboration," The Associated Press, February 16, 1999 (CubaNet); "US Rights Groups Assail 'Scandalous' New Cuban Law," *Miami Herald*, February 18, 1999.

36. "Cuba Announces Jail Sentences for Dissident Four," Reuters, March 15, 1999 (CubaNet).

37. Chronology of Cuban Events, 1994, Information Resources Branch, Radio Martí Program, January 26, 1994.

38. Juan O. Tamayo, "Europeans Get Tough in Policy on Cuba," *Miami Herald*, December 3, 1996.

39. "El canciller de Cuba ataca a la Unión Europea," *El Nuevo Herald*, April 30, 2000.

40. *CubaHoy* 2, no. 200 (November 12, 1996).

41. For Raúl's comments, see Reuters, November 18, 1995. For Fidel's position, see Mesa-Lago, "Strategies for the 1990s," 196–97.

42. Reuters, November 18, 1995.

43. Juan Tamayo and Andres Oppenheimer, "Cuba Keeps Stranglehold on Foreign Journalists, Visas for Pope's Visit Withheld," *Miami Herald*, January 17, 1998, p. 1.

44. "Castro amenaza a las agencias de prensa," *El Nuevo Herald*, January 19, 2001.

45. For example, Susan Bilello, an official of the New York–based Committee to Protect Journalists, was expelled from Cuba in June 1996 after being arrested and interrogated by Cuban security for "fomenting rebellion." Bilello was in Cuba meeting with Cubans attempting to practice independent journalism. All of her notebooks, personal

210   *Notes to Pages 134–139*

papers, and film were seized. Hector Palacio Ruiz, president of the Partido Solidaridad Democrática, was jailed after talking to Swedish journalists in December 1996. And envoys from the United States and Europe reaching out to dissidents are being harassed by Cuban authorities; see Christopher Marquis, "Havana Placing Bumps in Foreign Envoy's Way," *Miami Herald,* April 4, 1997.

46. "Policía política de Cuba detiene a turista belga," *CubaNet,* April 21, 2000.

47. "Protestan por arrestos de suecos," *CubaNet,* August 30, 2000.

48. Mimi Whitefield, "Two Detained Czechs May Face Trial in Cuba," *Miami Herald,* January 17, 2001.

49. Childs and Popplewell, *The Stasi,* 174–75.

50. For documentation on the international network helping the cause of human rights and democracy in Cuba, see the web page of the Cuban Committee Pro Human Rights at www.sigloxxi.org and the Cuban Democratic Revolutionary Directorate at www.directorio.org.

51. Thomas, "The Helsinki Accords."

52. Lipset, "Some Social Requisites of Democracy," 69–105.

53. Pzeworski and Limongi, "Modernization"; Armijo, "Mixed Blessing," 34.

54. For the empirical evidence, see Przeworski and Limongi, "Modernization."

55. Huntington, *The Third Wave,* 60–61.

56. Ibid., 65; see also Armijo, "Mixed Blessing," 34–36.

57. Werlau, "Foreign Investment in Cuba," 481.

58. Pablo Alfonso, "Cuba 'alquila' trabajadores al exterior," *El Nuevo Herald,* June 11, 2001.

59. Roberts et al., "Measuring Cuban Public Opinion: Project Report," 66.

60. Only very small private enterprises were allowed for Cubans after 1993 (e.g., a restaurant could not have more than twelve chairs).

61. For examples of government attacks against private enterprise in the general population, see Juan O. Tamayo, "Cuban Inspectors Crack Down on Home Businesses," *Miami Herald*, March 27, 1997; Gustavo Rafael Rodríguez, "Aumenta represión contra actividad privada en Villa Clara," *CubaNet,* September 15, 1997; David Abel, "Cuba's Control over Capitalism," *Orlando Sentinel,* January 24, 1999.

62. This is a common observation among individuals who follow Cuban affairs. For example, see Mesa-Lago, "The Cuban Economy in 1997–1998," 1.

63. Roberts et al., "Measuring Cuban Public Opinion: Project Report," iii, 16–17, and 50–51. Only 5 percent of respondents in the Roberts et al. survey blamed the U.S. embargo for shortages in the supply of basic necessities in Cuba. The vast majority of respondents (90 percent) attributed the shortages of supplies to policies of the Cuban government. In a survey done by the diocese of Santa Clara, only 2.7 percent of respondents considered the embargo a problem; "Publica encuesta la revista católica Amanecer," *CubaNet,* February 17, 2000.

64. U.S. Department of State, "The U.S. Embargo and Healthcare in Cuba," May 14, 1997.

65. "Cuba-Europe: EU Rejects Washington Deal," *InterPress Third World News Agency,* September 4, 1996.

66. Figure provided by James Foley from the State Department. "EU estudia aumentar los envíos humanitarios," *El Nuevo Herald,* January 15, 1998.

67. Hawkins, "Big Business vs. National Security?"

Notes to Pages 139–143 211

68. Werlau, "Foreign Investment in Cuba," 458, 468, and 475–79. For environmental degradation in Cuba, see also Díaz-Briquets and Pérez-López, "Socialism and Environmental Disruption."

69. On the resentment by Cubans in the island against foreigners see Werlau, "Foreign Investment in Cuba," 476.

70. Rui Ferreira, "Demandan a inversionistas por violar derechos," *Miami Herald*, June 25, 1999.

71. "Disidentes advierten a inversores extranjeros," *El Nuevo Herald*, July 19, 1998.

72. Jesús Zúñiga, "Cuba, inversiones y embargo" (Coorperativa de Periodistas Independientes), *CubaNet*, January 18, 1999.

73. Roberts et al., "Measuring Cuban Public Opinion: Project Report," iv and 70.

74. Hufbauer, Schott, and Elliott, *Economic Sanctions Reconsidered*, 6–7, 40, and 51.

75. Ibid., 52.

76. Ibid., 6–7, 40, and 51.

77. Przeworski, *Democracy and the Market*, 57; Huntington, "How Countries Democratize," 593.

78. Przeworski and Limongi, "Modernization."

79. Haggard and Kaufman, *The Political Economy of Democratic Transitions*, 33–34.

80. For example, see Bruszt, "1989: The Negotiated Revolution in Hungary," 383; Judt, "Metamorphosis: The Democratic Revolution in Czechoslovakia," 96–97; and Brown, *Surge to Freedom*, 209.

81. Remmer, "The Process of Democratization in Latin America," 10–12.

82. Haggard and Kaufman, *The Political Economy of Democratic Transition*, 29–32.

83. Ibid., 31–32.

84. The perception that substantial popular revolts can occur in Cuba as a consequence of the poor state of the economy is shared by top generals in the Cuban military and by dissident leaders in Cuba. Pablo Alfonso, "Plan abre vía a militares cubanos," *El Nuevo Herald*, February 6, 1997, and "Elizardo Sánchez ve cambio inminente en Cuba," *El Nuevo Herald*, January 19, 1997.

85. This point is made by Mesa-Lago, "Strategies for the 1990s," 197, and by Hufbauer, Schott, and Elliott, *Economic Sanctions Reconsidered*, 7.

86. Hufbauer, Schott, and Elliott, *Economic Sanctions Reconsidered*, 36, 47, 52, and 58.

87. Mesa-Lago, "The State of the Cuban Economy," 5.

88. Wilfredo Cancio Isla, "Académicos debaten el futuro económico de Cuba," *El Nuevo Herald*, March 20, 1999.

89. Cited in Purcell, "Cuba," 46.

90. Don C. Becker, "Cuba," *Journal of Commerce*, February 28, 1996; Frances Kerry, "U.S. Travel Executives Meet Cuban Tourism Minister," Reuters, December 12, 1995.

91. Don C. Becker, "Cuba," *Journal of Commerce*, February 28, 1996; Frances Kerry, "U.S. Travel Executives Meet Cuban Tourism Minister," Reuters, December 12, 1995; "Cuba espera recibir hasta 100 mil turistas en escala de cruceros," *El Nuevo Herald*, May 21, 2001.

92. Carlos Batista, "El turismo se prepara para el cese del embargo," *El Nuevo Herald*, May 11, 2000.

93. Rui Ferreira, "En manos del Senado el turismo de EU a Cuba," *El Nuevo Herald*, July 22, 2000.

212 *Notes to Pages 143–150*

94. *Time News Service,* March 7, 1996, and *CubaHoy* 2, no. 142 (March 27, 1996).

95. Pascal Fletcher, "Canada Sees 'Chill' Effect of U.S. Law on Cuba," Reuters, May 8, 1996.

96. Peter Morton, "Fear of U.S. Reaction Has Kept Banks from Lending to Commercial Consolidators for Its Cuban Operation," *National Post,* March 10, 2000.

97. Juan González Yuste, "Una cadena de hoteles española se retira de Cuba," *El Periódico,* June 12, 1996, and Juan O. Tamayo, "Foreign Firms Delay Plans for Cuba Hotels," *Miami Herald,* June 14, 1996.

98. "Cemex Leaves Cuba to Avoid U.S. Sanctions," Reuters, May 29, 1996. Cemex operated a cement plant in Cuba that once belonged to the U.S. company Lone Star Industries and had a contract to market cement produced in Cuba.

99. *Journal of Commerce,* March 6, 1996.

100. *Cuba Brief,* April 12, 1996. U.S. Assistant Secretary for International Affairs Jeffrey Davidow reported to Congress in July 1996 that, because of Title IV of the Libertad Act, a significant number of firms that were doing business involving confiscated U.S. properties were ending those business deals (Werlau, "Foreign Investment in Cuba").

101. "Mayor inversionista anunciaría su retirada de Cuba a fin de mes," *El Nuevo Herald,* March 3, 1997.

102. Werlau, "Foreign Investment in Cuba," 458–59; Mimi Whitefield, "Bill Puts Damper on Foreign Investments Initiatives," *Miami Herald,* April 1, 1996.

103. Werlau, "Foreign Investment in Cuba," 458–59; Mimi Whitefield, "Bill Puts Damper on Foreign Investments Initiatives," *Miami Herald,* April 1, 1996. On October 7, 1995, senior executives from more than forty major U.S. corporations, including Sears, Hyatt Corporation, General Motors, Samsonite Luggage, Kmart, Tandy Corporation, the Gap, Lowes, Rockwell, and Harley-Davidson, dined with Fidel Castro in Havana. Chronology of Cuban Events, 1995, Information Resources Branch, Radio Martí Program.

104. Przeworski, *Democracy and the Market,* 57.

105. Hufbauer, Schott, and Elliott, *Economic Sanctions Reconsidered,* 11; Leyton-Brown, "Lessons and Policy Considerations About Economic Sanctions"; Leyton-Brown, *The Utility of International Economic Sanctions,* 303.

106. Cited in Klotz, *Norms in International Relations,* 99.

107. Ibid., 100.

108. Agustin Blazquez, "Where Is the Condemnation of Castro's Apartheid?" *Houston Chronicle,* February 18, 1999.

109. Hufbauer, Schott, and Elliott, *Economic Sanctions Reconsidered,* 6–7, 40, and 51.

110. Horowitz, "An Ocean of Mischief," 553 and 556.

111. Karen De Young and Juliet Eilperin, "Anti-Castro Group Aims Ads at Sanctions Foes in Congress," *Washington Post,* June 18, 2000, A06.

112. Horowitz, "An Ocean of Mischief," 556; Pablo Alfonso, "U.S. Groups Spend Millions in Push to Ease Embargo, Build Ties to Cuba," *Miami Herald,* July 5, 1998; Pablo Alfonso, "Fundaciones dan millones para levantar el embargo," *El Nuevo Herald,* July 5, 1998; Pablo Alfonso, "Los donantes, los fondos y su empleo," *El Nuevo Herald,* July 5, 1998; Charles Abbott, "Bank Access Dispute Slows US-Cuba Sanctions Reform," Yahoo! News, June 21, 2000.

113. For a strong critique of the report, see Werlau, "The Effects of the U.S. Embargo on Health-sector Imports: A Critical Analysis of the Report by The American Association for World Health," paper presented at the American Economic Association annual meeting, Sheraton New York Hotel, January 3, 1999.

Notes to Pages 150–153 213

114. "Cámara de Comercio de EU visita Cuba," *El Nuevo Herald,* May 31, 2000; "Cámara de Comercio contra el embargo," *El Nuevo Herald,* June 3, 2000.

115. "Delegación cubana a Cancún para cumbre empresarial Estatos Unidos-Cuba," Yahoo! Noticias, June 6, 2000; "Empresarios de EEUU pierden con el embargo-Cuba," Yahoo! Noticias, June 9, 2000; Anita Snow, "Americans Explore Cuban Business," Yahoo! News, June 9, 2000; Doreen Hemlock, "Donations Offer Path into Cuba," *Sun-Sentinel,* September 10, 1998.

116. Kathy Seal, "Cuba Courts Radisson," *Hotel & Motel Management* 213, no. 11 (June 15, 1998), 1 and 68.

117. "Cuba Eager to Buy from US Farmers Cuba Official," Reuters, July 20, 1999.

118. Christopher Marquis, "Senate Supports Sales of Food to Cuba if President Oks Them," *Miami Herald,* August 6, 1999; Charles Abbott, "Change In U.S.-Cuba Embargo Hangs by Thread," Yahoo! News, September 29, 1999; Anne Fitzgerald, "Soybean Growers: Repeal the Embargo," *Des Moines Register,* May 6, 1999; Anita Snow, "U.S. Wheat Growers in Cuba," Yahoo! News, June 6, 2000.

119. Tim Loughran, "Los arroceros de Texas se van a la isla para hablar del embargo," *El Nuevo Herald,* August 29, 1999; "U.S. Farmers Visit Cuba, Back Easing of Sanctions," Reuters, May 30, 2000; Chris Anderson, "Farm Group Pushes Cuba Trade," *Pantagraph,* May 11, 1999.

120. Chris Anderson, "Soybean Growers Join Embargo Fight; Illinois Group Seeks Sales in Cuba," *Pantagraph* (Bloomington, Ill.), May 19, 1999.

121. Ray Long and John Diamond, "Cuba-Illinois Courtship on," *Chicago Tribune,* October 6, 1999; Dave McKinney, "Ryan Explores Autumn Trade Trip to Cuba," *Chicago Sun-Times,* August 14, 1999; Ana Mendieta, "Cuba Eyes Illinois as Trade Partner," *Chicago Sun-Times,* October 7, 1999; Chris Anderson, "Soybean Growers Join Embargo Fight; Illinois Group Seeks Sales in Cuba," *Pantagraph,* May 19, 1999; "Cuba amenaza Sección de Intereses de EE.UU," *Diario las Américas,* October 29, 1999.

122. Christopher Marquis, "Senate Supports Sales of Food to Cuba if President Oks Them," *Miami Herald,* August 6, 1999.

123. Charles Abbott, "Cuba Omitted in Plan to Ease Food, Medicine Bans," Reuters, September 22, 1999; Charles Abbott, "Change in U.S.-Cuba Embargo Hangs by Thread," Yahoo! News, September 29, 1999; Charles Abbott, "Leaders Near Win to Strip Down U.S. Farm Aid Bill," Yahoo! Finance, September 30, 1999.

124. William E. Gibson, "Legislation to Lift Cuban Embargo Was Close Call for Supporters," Sun-Sentinel.com, September 30, 1999.

125. Charles Abbott, "Senate Panel Backs U.S.-Cuba Food, Medicine Trade," Yahoo! News, March 23, 2000.

126. Philip Brasher, "Helms Softens Opposition to Cuban Trade," *Sun-Sentinel,* March 24, 2000.

127. Charles Abbott, "U.S.-Cuba Trade Wins Key Vote, Elian May Be Reason," Yahoo! News, May 10, 2000.

128. "US Lawmakers Confident Cuba Sanctions to Be Eased," Yahoo! Finance, May 16, 2000.

129. "Alarcón dice que existen oportunidades de que congreso norteamericano apruebe levantamiento del embargo," Yahoo! Nocitias, May 22, 2000.

130. Pablo Alfonso, "Abre hoy el congreso el debate del embargo," *El Nuevo Herald,* June 7, 2000.

214   *Notes to Pages 153–160*

131. "EEUU reacciona tibiamente ante levantamiento de restricciones de viajes a Cuba," Yahoo! Noticias, July 21, 2000.

132. Charles Abbott, " Not Yet on U.S.-Cuba Trade, Congress Leaders Say," Yahoo! News, July 27, 2000; Pablo Alfonso, "Frenan el suavizamiento del embargo," *El Nuevo Herald,* July 28, 2000.

133. Christopher Doering, "Congress Eases Cuban Embargo on Food and Medicine," Yahoo! News, June 27, 2000.

134. "GOP Leaders Agree to Ease Cuba Trade Rules," *Washington Post,* September 28, 2000; Rafael Lorente, "Deal to Ease Cuban Embargo Could Fizzle," *Sun-Sentinel,* September 28, 2000; Ana Radelat, "Deal Reached in Congress for U.S.-Cuba Food Sales," *Miami Herald,* October 6, 2000; "House Passes Plan to Ease Cuba Embargo," Yahoo! News, October 11, 2000; Rui Ferreira, "Senado aprueba las ventas a la isla," *El Nuevo Herald,* October 19, 2000; "Clinton firma ley que alivia el embargo," *El Nuevo Herald,* October 29, 2000.

135. Philip Brasher, "Senators Seek Cuba Trade Compromise," Associated Press Online, September 28, 2000; Andrew Cawthorne, "U.S. Embargo Seen Unlikely to Spur Quick Cuba Trade," Yahoo! News, October 6, 2000.

136. "Rechaza Cuba entablar relaciones comerciales con EEUU," Notimex, October 5, 2000; "Cuba afirma que sólo aceptará la anulación total del embargo," Noticias Yahoo!, October 6, 2000; "Cuba Calls for Protest March Against Embargo Move," Yahoo! News, October 17, 2000.

137. Charles Abbott, "Senate Panel Backs U.S.-Cuba Food, Medicine Trade," Yahoo! News, March 23, 2000.

138. "Castro fija condiciones a las nuevas compras," *El Nuevo Herald,* December 21, 2001; "Llegan 100 ejecutivos de EU," *El Nuevo Herald,* January 4, 2002; Nancy San Martin, "Piden buscar la ayuda de Cuba contra el terrorismo," *El Nuevo Herald,* January 7, 2002; "Hundreds of Americans Head to Cuba," AP, World News, January 3, 2002; "Estadounidences desbordan La Habana en primera semana del año," *La Nueva Cuba* (www.lanuevacuba.com), January 5, 2002; and Ray Long, "Ryan Set to Make 2nd Trip to Cuba," *Chicago Tribune,* January 9, 2002.

139. Charles Abbott, "Momentum Builds for Easing Embargo on Cuba," Yahoo! News, May 19, 2000.

140. "Piden Empresarios de EU Normalizar Relación Bancaria con Cuba," Yahoo! Noticias, May 16, 2000.

141. Pablo Alfonso, "La Habana y Washington buscan restablecer sus vínculos bancarios," *El Nuevo Herald,* June 14, 2000.

142. "Cuba dice plan del Congreso de EEUU endurecería el embargo," Yahoo! Noticias, June 29, 2000; Eudardo Yero, "Raúl Castro cree que los gobiernos de Cuba y de EU pueden llegar a entenderse," *El Nuevo Herald,* July 3, 2000.

143. Charles Abbott, "Bank Access Dispute Slows US-Cuba Sanctions Reform," Yahoo! News, June 21, 2000; Jim Landers, "Some Farm Groups, Democrats Slam Trade Compromise," *Dallas Morning News,* July 7, 2000.

144. "Cuba Eager to Buy from US Farmers Cuba Official," Reuters, July 20, 1999.

SEVEN. Conclusions

1. Chirot, "What Happened in Eastern Europe in 1989?" 26 and 31.

2. Przeworski, "Transition to Democracy"; Huntington, *The Third Wave,* 107.

Notes to Pages 160–180   215

3. O'Donnell and Schmitter, *Transitions from Authoritarian Rule: Tentative Conclusions.*

4. Przeworski, *Democracy and the Market,* 3–4, 55n4.

5. Huntington, "How Countries Democratize," 603.

6. Liberalization is the process in which the dictatorship allows citizens to have certain rights, such as freedom of speech and of association and the right to fair trials under preestablished laws. Individuals come to have certain protection from arbitrary acts committed by government officials. O'Donnell and Schmitter, *Transitions from Authoritarian Rule: Tentative Conclusions,* 7.

7. Chirot, "What Happened in Eastern Europe in 1989?" 26 and 31.

8. For the serious problem of alcoholism in Cuba, see "Altos los niveles de alcoholismo en Cuba," *El Nuevo Herald,* August 12, 2000; for a report stating that the rate of divorce is 43 percent, see "Aumentan los divorcios y las mujeres en Cuba," *El Nuevo Herald,* July 12, 2000.

9. Linz and Stepan, *Problems of Democratic Transition,* 48.

10. José Rivero García, "La Verdad Desnuda," *CubaPress,* March 2, 1996; declaration of the Partido Liberal Democrático de Cuba, April 8, 1997, distributed by *CubaNet;* "Cuba en la VI cumbre iberoamericana," *Revista Contacto* (November 1996); Roberts et al., "Measuring Cuban Public Opinion: Project Report," v.

11. O'Donnell and Schmitter, *Transitions from Authoritarian Rule: Tentative Conclusions,* 28.

12. Linz and Stepan, *Problems of Democratic Transition,* chap. 4. Interview data indicate that, among the coercive staff of the communist dictatorship in East Germany in 1989, there was a sharp erosion in the belief that it was legitimate to use force against protesters. This fact seems to explain why people were not shot when mass protests threatened the survival of the regime. Linz and Stepan, *Problems of Democratic Transition,* 323.

13. Opp, Voss, and Gern, *Origins of a Spontaneous Revolution.*

14. On factors involved in transformations from totalitarian to post-totalitarian regimes, see Linz and Stepan, *Problems of Democratic Transition,* 51 and 293.

15. Saxonberg, *The Fall,* chap. 7.

16. I owe these observations to Steven Saxonberg.

17. Huntington, *The Third Wave,* 91–98.

18. Haggard and Kaufman, *The Political Economy of Democratic Transition;* Laothamatas, *Democratization in Southeast and East Asia;* Przeworski and Limongi, "Modernization."

19. Haggard and Kaufman, *The Political Economy of Democratic Transition,* 36.

20. Mesa-Lago, "Strategies for Confronting the Crisis," 247, 250.

21. For examples of government attacks against private enterprise in the general population, see Gustavo Rafael Rodríguez, "Aumenta represión contra actividad privada en Villa Clara," *CubaNet,* September 15, 1997; Juan O. Tamayo, "Cuban Inspectors Crack Down on Home Businesses," *Miami Herald,* March 27, 1997; and Mauricio Vicent, "Fidel Castro acorrala a la iniciativa privada," *El País,* October 25, 1996.

22. For a review of arguments that economic development causes democracy, see Anek Laothamatas, "Development and Democratization: A Theoretical Introduction with Reference to the Southeast Asian and East Asian Cases."

References

Advisory Board for Broadcasting to Cuba. 1988. *Report by the Advisory Board for Radio Broadcasting to Cuba.* Washington, D.C.: Advisory Board for Broadcasting to Cuba.

Aguirre, B. E. 1998. "Culture of Opposition and Collective Action in Cuba." Manuscript. Department of Sociology, Texas A&M University.

Alonso, José F., and Ralph J. Galliano. 1999. "Russian Oil-for-Sugar Barter Deals 1989–1999." In Association for the Study of the Cuban Economy, ed., *Cuba in Transition,* vol. 9. Washington, D.C.: ASCE.

Alvarez, José. 1999. "Independent Agricultural Cooperatives in Cuba?" In Association for the Study of the Cuban Economy, ed., *Cuba in Transition,* vol. 9. Washington, D.C.: ASCE.

Amuchastegui, Domingo. 1999. "Cuba's Armed Forces: Power and Reforms." Paper presented at the annual meeting of the Association for the Cuban Economy, Miami, Fla.

Armijo, Leslie Elliot. 1999. "Mixed Blessing: Expectation about Foreign Capital Flows and Democracy in Emerging Markets." In Leslie Elliot Armijo, ed., *Financial Globalization and Democracy in Emerging Markets.* London: Macmillan.

Ash, Timothy Garton. 1993. *The Uses of Adversity: Essays on the Fate of Central Europe.* New York: Random House.

———, ed. 1995. *Freedom for Publishing, Publishing for Freedom: The Central and East European Publishing Project.* Budapest, Hungary: Central European University.

Baloyra, Enrique A. 1993. "Socialist Transitions and Prospects for Change in Cuba." In Enrique A. Baloyra and James A. Morris, eds., *Conflict and Change in Cuba.* Albuquerque: University of New Mexico Press.

———. 1994. "Where Does Cuba Stand?" In Donald E. Schulz, ed. *Cuba and the Future.* Westport: Greenwood.

Bender, Lynn-Darrell. 1981. *Cuba vs. United States: The Politics of Hostility.* San Juan, Puerto Rico: Inter American University Press.

Blight, James G., and Peter Kornbluh, eds. 1998. *Politics of Illusion: The Bay of Pigs Invasion Reexamined.* Bounder, Colo.: Lynne Rienner.

Blight, James G., and David A. Welch. 1989. *On the Brink: Americans and Soviets Reexamine the Cuban Missile Crisis.* New York: Hill and Wang.

218   *References*

Board of International Broadcasting. 1985. *Annual Report*. Washington, D.C.: BIB.
———. 1986. *Annual Report*. Washington, D.C.: BIB.
———. 1988. *Annual Report*. Washington, D.C.: BIB.
———. 1989. *Annual Report*. Washington, D.C.: BIB.
Brady, Lawrence J. 1987. "The Utility of Economic Sanctions as a Policy Instrument." In David Leyton-Brown, ed., *The Utility of International Economic Sanctions*. London: Croom Helm.
Brenner, Philip. 1988. *From Confrontation to Negotiation: U.S. Relations with Cuba*. Boulder, Colo.: Westview.
Brown, J. F. 1991. *Surge to Freedom: The End of Communist Rule in Eastern Europe*. Durham, N.C.: Duke University Press.
Bruszt, Laszlo. 1990. "1989: The Negotiated Revolution in Hungary." *Social Research* 57, no. 2 (summer): 365–87.
Buell, William A. 1986. "Radio Free Europe/Radio Liberty in the mid 1980s." In K. R. M. Short, ed., *Western Broadcasting over the Iron Curtain*. London: Croom Helm.
Buhl, Dieter. 1991. "Window to the West. How Television from the Federal Republic Influenced Events in East Germany." Discussion Paper D-5. The Joan Shorenstein Barone Center, John F. Kennedy School of Government, Harvard University.
Bunce, Valerie. 1999. *Subversive Institutions: The Design and the Destruction of Socialism and the State*. New York: Cambridge University Press.
Campbell, Angus, Gerald Gurin, and Warren Miller. 1954. *The Voter Decides*. Evanston, Ill.: Row Peterson.
Centeno, Miguel Angel. 1996. "Cuba's Search for Alternatives." In Miguel Angel Centeno and Mauricio Font, eds., *Toward a New Cuba? Legacies of a Revolution*. Boulder, Colo.: Lynne Riener.
Central American and Caribbean Program. 1984. "Report on Cuba: Findings of the Study Group on United States-Cuban Relations." SAIS Papers in International Affairs. Boulder, Colo.: Westview.
Childs, David, and Richard Popplewell. 1996. *The Stasi: The East German Intelligence and Security Service*. New York: New York University Press.
Chirot, Daniel. 1999. "What Happened in Eastern Europe in 1989?" In Vladimir Tismaneanu, ed., *The Revolutions of 1989*. New York: Routledge.
Clark, Juan. 1999. "La Visita del Papa a Cuba y su Repercusión." Miami, Fla.: Centro de Estudios para una Opción Nacional.
Collier, David, and James Mahoney. 1996. "Insights and Pitfalls : Selection Bias in Qualitative Research." *World Politics* 49, no. 1 (October): 56–91.
Cordesman, Anthony H., and Ahmed S. Hashin. 1997. *Iraq: Sanctions and Beyond*. Boulder, Colo.: Westview.
Cuban Democratic Revolutionary Directorate. 1998. *Steps to Freedom 1997*. Miami, Fla.: CDRD.
———. 1999. *Steps to Freedom 1998*. Miami, Fla.: CDRD.
———. 2000. *Steps to Freedom 1999*. Miami, Fla.: CDRD.
———. 2001. *Steps to Freedom 2000*. Miami, Fla.: CDRD.
Czechoslovak Helsinki Committee. 1989. *Human Rights in Czechoslovakia*. Washington, D.C.: U.S. Helsinki Watch Committee.
Day, Barbara. 1999. *The Velvet Philosophers*. London: Claridge.
del Aguila, Juan M. 1993. "The Politics of Dissidence: A Challenge to the Monolith." In Enrique A. Baloyra and James A. Morris, eds., *Conflict and Change in Cuba*. Albuquerque: University of New Mexico Press.

Díaz-Briquets, Sergio, and Jorge Pérez-López. 1998. "Socialism and Environmental Disruption: Implications for Cuba." In Association for the Study of the Cuban Economy, ed., *Cuba in Transition,* vol. 8. Washington, D.C.: ASCE.

Domínguez, Jorge I. 1993. "The Political Impact on Cuba of the Reform and Collapse of Communist Regimes." In Carmelo Mesa-Lago, ed., *Cuba After the Cold War.* Pittsburgh: University of Pittsburgh Press.

———. 1993. "The Secrets of Castro's Staying Power." *Foreign Affairs* (spring): 97–107.

———. 1994. "U.S. Policy toward Cuba in the 1980s and 1990s." *Annals of the American Academy of Political and Social Science* 533 (May): 165–76.

———. 1995. "Why the Cuban Regime Has Not Fallen." In Irving Louis Horowitz, ed., *Cuban Communism, 1959–1995.* 8th ed. New Brunswick, N.J.: Transaction.

———. 1997. "U.S.-Cuban Relations: From the Cold War to the Colder War." *Journal of Interamerican Studies and World Affairs* 39 (fall): 49–75.

East European Area Audience and Opinion Research. 1986. "Reasons for Not Listening to Radio Free Europe in Czechoslovakia" (May).

———. 1982. "Two Measurements of RFE's 'Uniqueness' in the Eyes of Its Audience" (June).

———. 1981. "Listeners Assess RFE's Influence on Themselves, on Public Opinion and on the Government of Their Country" (October).

———. 1980. "Czechoslovak Listeners' Exposure to and Evaluation of RFE Programs" (May).

Easton, David, and Jack Dennis. 1967. "The Child's Acquisition of Regime Norms: Political Efficacy." *American Political Science Review* 61.

Encinosa, Enrique. 1995. *Cuba en Guerra.* 2nd ed. Miami, Fla.: The Endowment for Cuban American Studies.

Eyal, Jonathan. 1990. "Why Romania Could Not Avoid Bloodshed." In Gwyn Prins, ed., *Spring in Winter: The 1989 Revolutions.* Manchester, U.K.: Manchester University Press.

Fearon, James D. 1991. "Counterfactuals and Hypothesis Testing in Political Science." *World Politics* 43, no. 2 (January): 169–95.

Fontaine, Roger W. 1975. *On Negotiating with Cuba.* Washington, D.C.: American Enterprise Institute for Public Policy Research.

Friedheim, Daniel V. 1997. "Democratic Transition Through Regime Collapse: East Germany in 1989." Ph.D. dissertation, Yale University.

González, Edward. 1996. *Cuba Clearing Perilous Waters?* Santa Monica, Calif.: RAND.

González, Edward, and David Ronsfeldt. 1992. *Cuba Adrift in a Postcommunist World.* Santa Monica, Calif.: RAND.

———. 1994. *Storm Warnings for Cuba.* Santa Monica, Calif.: RAND.

Grupo de Trabajo de la Disidencia Interna Cubana. 1996. "Cuba: Una propuesta sensata," online at http://www.sigloxxi.org/chuny.htm.

Gunn, Gillian. 1993. *Cuba in Transition: Options for U.S. Policy.* New York: Twentieth Century Fund.

Haggard, Stephan, and Robert R. Kaufman. 1995. *The Political Economy of Democratic Transition.* Princeton: Princeton University Press.

Halpern, Nina P. 1991. "Economic Reform, Social Mobilization, and Democratization in Post-Mao China." In Richard Baum, ed., *Reform and Reaction in Post-Mao China: The Road to Tiananmen.* New York: Routledge.

220   *References*

Helsinki Watch. 1989. *Toward Civil Society: Independent Initiatives in Czechoslovakia.* Washington, D.C.: Human Rights Watch.

Hirschman, Albert O. 1970. *Exit, Voice, and Loyalty: Responses to Decline in Firms, Organizations and States.* Cambridge, Mass.: Harvard University Press.

Horowitz, Irving Louis. 1998. "An Ocean of Mischief: The Cuba Lobby Then and Now." *Orbis* 42 (summer): 553–63.

———. 1992. *The Conscience of Worms and the Cowardice of Lions.* New Brunswick, N.J.: Transaction.

Hufbauer, Gary Clyde, Jeffrey J. Schott, and Kimberly Ann Elliott. 1990. *Economic Sanctions Reconsidered.* 2nd ed. Washington, D.C.: Institute for International Economics.

Huntington, Samuel P. 1991. *The Third Wave: Democratization in the Late Twentieth Century.* Norman: University of Oklahoma Press.

———. 1991. "How Countries Democratize." *Political Science Quarterly* 106, no. 4 (winter): 579–616.

International Broadcasting Bureau. 1999. "A Qualitative Research Study Among Recently-Arrived Cuban Immigrants to Gauge Reaction to Selected Radio Martí Programs." Washington, D.C.: USIA.

Joppke, Christian. 1995. *East German Dissidents and the Revolution of 1989: Social Movement in a Leninist Regime.* New York: New York University Press.

Judt, Tony R. 1992. "Metamorphosis: The Democratic Revolution in Czechoslovakia." In Ivo Banac, ed., *Eastern Europe in Revolution.* Ithaca, N.Y.: Cornell University Press.

Kaempfer, William H., and Anton D. Lowenberg. 1995. "The Problem and Promise of Sanctions." In David Cortright and George A. López, eds., *Economic Sanctions: Panacea or Peacebuilding in a Post-Cold War World?* Boulder, Colo.: Westview.

———. 1992. *International Economic Sanctions: A Public Choice Perspective.* Boulder, Colo.: Westview.

Kagan, Robert. 1996. *A Twilight Struggle: American Power and Nicaragua 1977–1990.* New York: The Free Press.

Karklins, Rasma. 1987. "The Dissent/Coercion Nexus in the USSR." *Studies in Comparative Communism* 20, nos. 3/4 (autumn/winter): 321–41.

———. 1994. "Explaining Regime Change in the Soviet Union." *Europe-Asia Studies* 46, no. 1, 29–45.

———. 1994. *Ethnopolitics and Transition to Democracy: The Collapse of the USSR and Latvia.* Baltimore: Johns Hopkins University Press.

Karklins, Rasma, and Roger Petersen. 1993. "Decision Calculus of Protesters and Regimes: Eastern Europe 1989." *Journal of Politics* 55, no. 3 (August): 588–614.

Klotz, Audie. 1995. *Norms in International Relations: The Struggle Against Apartheid.* Ithaca, N.Y.: Cornell University Press.

Kusin, Vladimir V. 1979. "Challenge to Normalcy: Political Opposition in Czechoslovakia, 1968–77." In Rudolf L. Tokes, ed., *Opposition in Eastern Europe.* Baltimore: Johns Hopkins University Press.

Lago, Armando. 2000. "The Human Cost of Social Revolution." Unpublished manuscript.

Laothamatas, Anek. 1997. *Democratization in Southeast and East Asia.* New York: St. Martin's.

Lazo, Mario. 1968. *Dagger in the Heart: American Policy Failures in Cuba.* New York: Funk & Wagnalls.

LeoGrande, William M. 1998. "From Havana to Miami: U.S. Cuba Policy as a Two-Level Game." *Journal of Interamerican Studies and World Affairs* 40 (spring): 67–86.

Leyton-Brown, David. 1987. "Lessons and Policy Considerations About Economic Sanctions." In David Leyton-Brown, ed., *The Utility of International Economic Sanctions.* London: Croom Helm.

Light, Margot. 1997. "The USSR/CIS and Democratization in Eastern Europe." In Geoffrey Pridham, Eric Herring, and George Sanford, eds., *Building Democracy? The International Dimension of Democratisation in Eastern Europe.* Rev. ed. London: Leicester University Press.

Linden, Ronald H. 1993. "Analogies and the Loss of Community: Cuba and East Europe in the 1990s." In Carmelo Mesa-Lago, ed., *Cuba After the Cold War.* Pittsburgh: University of Pittsburgh Press.

Linz, Juan J. 1990. "Transitions to Democracy." *Washington Quarterly* 13, no. 3 (summer): 143–64.

Linz, Juan J., and Alfred Stepan. 1996. *Problems of Democratic Transition and Consolidation: Southern Europe, South America, and Post-Communist Europe.* Baltimore: Johns Hopkins University Press.

Lipset, Seymour Martin. 1959. "Some Social Requisites of Democracy: Economic Development and Political Legitimacy." *American Political Science Review* 53, no. 1 (March): 69–105.

López, Juan J. 1992. "Theory Choice in Comparative Social Inquiry." *Polity* 25, no. 2 (winter): 267–82.

———. 1999. "Implications of the U.S. Economic Embargo for a Political Transition in Cuba." *Cuban Studies* 28: 40–69.

Lowenthal, Abraham. 1991. "The United States and Latin American Democracy: Learning from History." In Abraham Lowenthal, ed., *Exporting Democracy: The United States and Latin America, Case Studies.* Baltimore: Johns Hopkins University Press.

Mainwaring, Scott. 1989. "Grassroots Popular Movements and the Struggle for Democracy: Nova Iguaçu." In Alfred Stepan, ed., *Democratizing Brazil: Problems of Transition and Consolidation.* New York: Oxford University Press.

Marsh, Alan. 1977. *Protest and Political Consciousness.* Beverly Hills, Calif.: Sage.

Martin, Lisa L. 1992. *Coercive Cooperation: Explaining Multilateral Economic Sanctions.* Princeton: Princeton University Press.

Maybarduk, Gary H. 1999. "The State of the Cuban Economy 1998–1999." In Association for the Study of the Cuban Economy, ed., *Cuba in Transition,* vol. 9. Washington, D.C.: ASCE.

Mesa-Lago, Carmelo. 1993. "The Economic Effects on Cuba of the Downfall of Socialism in the USSR and Eastern Europe." In Carmelo Mesa-Lago, ed., *Cuba After the Cold War.* Pittsburgh: University of Pittsburgh Press.

———. 1993. "Cuba's Economic Policies and Strategies for Confronting the Crisis." In Carmelo Mesa-Lago, ed., *Cuba After the Cold War.* Pittsburgh: University of Pittsburgh Press.

———. 1995. "Cuba's Economic Policies and Strategies for the 1990s." In Irving Louis Horowitz, ed., *Cuban Communism, 1959–1995.* 8th ed. New Brunswick, N.J.: Transaction.

———. 1996. "The State of the Cuban Economy: 1995–96." In Association for the Study of the Cuban Economy, ed., *Cuba in Transition,* vol. 6. Washington, D.C.: ASCE.

222   *References*

———. 1998. "The Cuban Economy in 1997–1998: Performance and Policies." In Association for the Study of the Cuban Economy, ed., *Cuba in Transition*, vol. 8. Washington, D.C.: ASCE.

———. 1998. "Assessing Economic and Social Performance in the Cuban Transition of the 1990s." *World Development* 26, no. 5: 857–76.

Mesa-Lago, Carmelo, and Horst Fabian. 1993. "Analogies Between East European Socialist Regimes and Cuba: Scenarios for the Future." In Carmelo Mesa-Lago, ed., *Cuba After the Cold War*. Pittsburgh: University of Pittsburgh Press.

Millar, James R. 1987. *Politics, Work, and Daily Life in the USSR*. New York: Cambridge University Press.

Millett, Richard L. 1996. "From Triumph to Survival: Cuba's Armed Forces in an Era of Transition." In Richard L. Millett and Michael Gold-Biss, eds., *Beyond Praetorianism: The Latin American Military in Transition*. Miami, Fla.: University of Miami, North-South Center Press.

Morris, Emily. 2000. "Interpreting Cuba's External Accounts." In Association for the Study of the Cuban Economy, ed., *Cuba in Transition*, vol. 10. Washington, D.C.: ASCE.

Mujal-León, Eusebio, and Joshua W. Busby. 2001. "Much Ado about Something? Regime Change in Cuba." *Problems of Post-Communism* 48, no. 6 (November/December): 6–18.

Naimark, Norman M. 1992. " 'Ich will hier raus': Emigration and the Collapse of the German Democratic Republic." In Ivo Banac, ed., *Eastern Europe in Revolution*. Ithaca, N.Y.: Cornell University Press.

National Endowment for Democracy. 1984–89. *Annual Reports*. Washington, D.C.: National Endowment for Democracy.

Nelson, Michael. 1997. *War of the Black Heavens: The Battles of Western Broadcasting in the Cold War*. Syracuse, N.Y.: Syracuse University Press.

Oberschall, Anthony. 1994. "Protests, Demonstrations and the End of Communist Regimes in 1989." *Research in Social Movements, Conflicts and Change* 17: 1–24.

———. 1994. "Rational Choice in Collective Protests." *Rationality and Society* 6, no. 1 (January): 79–100.

O'Donnell, Guillermo. 1989. "Transition to Democracy: Some Navigation Instruments." In Robert A. Pastor, ed., *Democracy in the Americas: Stopping the Pendulum*. New York: Holmes & Meier.

———. 1986. "Introduction to the Latin American Cases." In Guillermo O'Donnell, Philippe C. Schmitter, and Laurence Whitehead, eds. *Transitions from Authoritarian Rule: Latin America*. Baltimore: Johns Hopkins University Press.

O'Donnell, Guillermo, and Philippe Schmitter. 1986. *Transitions from Authoritarian Rule: Tentative Conclusions about Uncertain Democracies*. Baltimore: Johns Hopkins University Press.

Office of Cuba Broadcasting. 1992. "1991 Cuban Audience Survey Report: A Survey of Media Habits of Cuban Arrivals." Washington, D.C.: USIA, May 29.

Office of Research, USIA. 1994. "U.S. Government Broadcasting to Cuba: An In-Country Assessment." Washington, D.C.: USIA, February.

———. 1995. "Radio Martí Audience Assessment: A Survey of Cuban Travelers in Miami, December 1994 thru February 1995." Washington, D.C.: USIA, June.

———. 1998. "UHF Access and TV Martí Viewership in Cuba." Washington, D.C.: USIA, April 3.

———. 1998. "A Qualitative Research Study Among Recently-Arrived Cuban Travelers: Perceptions of Radio Martí and Reactions to Selected Programs." Washington, D.C.: USIA.

———. 1999. "Media Habits Among Visa Applicants at the U.S. Interests Section in Havana, Cuba." Washington, D.C.: USIA, October 12.

———. 1999. "Research Memorandum," Washington, D.C.: USIA, January 6.

Opp, Karl-Dieter, Peter Voss, and Christiane Gern. 1995. *Origins of a Spontaneous Revolution: East Germany, 1989.* Ann Arbor: University of Michigan Press.

Pastor, Robert A. 1995. "The Reagan Administration: On Its Own Petard." In John D. Martz, ed., *United States Policy in Latin America: A Decade of Crisis and Challenge.* Lincoln: University of Nebraska Press.

Pehe, Jiri. 1992. "Czechoslovakia: An Abrupt Transition." In Lyman H. Legters, ed., *Eastern Europe: Transformation and Revolution, 1945–1991.* Lexington, Mass.: D. C. Heath.

Pérez, Lorenzo L. 1998. "The Pension System of Cuba." In Association for the Study of the Cuban Economy, ed., *Cuba in Transition,* vol. 8. Washington, D.C.: ASCE.

Pérez-López, Jorge F. 1996. "Cuban Military Expenditures: Concepts, Data and Burden Measures." In Association for the Study of the Cuban Economy, ed., *Cuban in Transition,* vol. 6. Washington, D.C.: ASCE.

———. 1997. "The Cuban Economy in Mid-1997." In Association for the Study of the Cuban Economy, ed., *Cuban in Transition,* vol. 7. Washington, D.C.: ASCE.

Pérez-López, Jorge F., and Matías F. Travieso-Díaz. 2000. "The Contribution of BITs to Cuba's Foreign Investment Program." In Association for the Study of the Cuban Economy, ed., *Cuban in Transition,* vol. 10. Washington, D.C.: ASCE.

Philipsen, Dirk. 1993. *We Were the People: Voices from East Germany's Revolutionary Autumn of 1989.* Durham, N.C.: Duke University Press.

Polish Helsinki Watch Committee. 1983. *Poland Under Martial Law.* Washington, D.C.: U.S. Helsinki Watch Committee.

Pridham, Geoffrey. 1997. "The International Dimension of Democratisation: Theory, Practice and Inter-regional Comparisons." In Geoffrey Pridham, Eric Herring, and George Sanford, eds., *Building Democracy? The International Dimension of Democratisation in Eastern Europe.* Rev. ed. London: Leicester University Press.

Przeworski, Adam. 1986. "Some Problems in the Study of Transition to Democracy." In Guillermo O'Donnell, Philippe C. Schmitter, and Laurence Whitehead, eds., *Transitions from Authoritarian Rule: Comparative Perspectives.* Baltimore: Johns Hopkins University Press.

———. 1991. *Democracy and the Market: Political and Economic Reforms in Eastern Europe and Latin America.* New York: Cambridge University Press.

Przeworski, Adam, and Fernando Limongi. 1997. "Modernization: Theories and Facts." *World Politics* 49 (January): 155–83.

Purcell, Susan Kaufman. 1998. "Cuba." In Richard N. Haass, ed., *Economic Sanctions and American Diplomacy.* New York: The Council on Foreign Relations.

Rabe, Stephen G. 1988. *Eisenhower and Latin America: The Foreign Policy of Anticommunism.* Chapel Hill: University of North Carolina Press.

Radio Martí Program Office of Audience Research. 1990. "Radio Marti Reception Study: Report on Survey Findings." Washington, D.C.: USIA, October.

———. 1991. "Cuban Audience Survey: Radio Marti and Its Competition." Washington, D.C.: USIA, July.

Rady, Martyn. 1992. *Romania in Turmoil: A Contemporary History.* London: IB Tauris.

Ratesh, Nestor. 1991. *Romania: The Entangled Revolution.* New York: Praeger.

Remmer, Karen L. 1992. "The Process of Democratization in Latin America." *Studies in Comparative International Development* 27, no. 4 (winter): 3–24.

Renshon, Stanley Allen. 1974. *Psychological Needs and Political Behavior: A Theory of Personality and Political Efficacy.* New York: The Free Press.

Ritter, Archibald, R. M. 1998. "Entrepreneurship, Microenterprise, and Public Policy in Cuba: Promotion, Containment, or Asphyxiation?" *Journal of Interamerican Studies and World Affairs* 40 (summer): 63–94.

Roberts, Churchill, Ernesto Betancourt, Guillermo Grenier, and Richard Scheaffer. 1999. "Measuring Cuban Public Opinion: Project Report." University of Florida.

Sakwa, Richard. 1990. *Gorbachev and His Reforms 1985–1990.* New York: Philip Allan.

Saxonberg, Steven. 2001. *The Fall: A Comparative Study of the End of Communism in Czechoslovakia, East Germany, Hungary and Poland.* Amsterdam, The Netherlands: Hardwood Academic.

Schlesinger, Arthur M., Jr. 1965. *A Thousand Days: John F. Kennedy in the White House.* Boston: Houghton Mifflin.

Schmitter, Philippe C. 1986. "An Introduction to Southern European Transitions from Authoritarian Rule: Italy, Greece, Portugal, Spain, and Turkey." In Guillermo O'Donnell, Philippe C. Schmitter, and Laurence Whitehead, eds., *Transitions from Authoritarian Rule: Southern Europe.* Baltimore: Johns Hopkins University Press.

Schulz, Donald E. 1994. "Introduction." In Donald E. Schultz, ed., *Cuba and the Future.* Westport: Greenwood.

Seligson, Mitchell A. 1979. "Unconventional Political Participation: Cynicism, Powerlessness, and the Latin American Peasant." In Mitchell A. Seligson and John A. Booth, eds., *Political Participation in Latin America.* New York: Holmes & Meier.

Sharlet, Robert. 1989. "Human Rights and Civil Society in Eastern Europe." In William E. Griffith, ed., *Central and Eastern Europe: The Opening of the Curtain?* Boulder, Colo.: Westview.

Skilling, Gordon. 1989. *Samizdat and an Independent Society in Central and Eastern Europe.* Columbus: Ohio State University Press.

Skoug, Kenneth N., Jr. 1996. *The United States and Cuba under Reagan and Shultz.* Westport: Praeger.

Smith, Peter H. 2000. *Talons of the Eagle: Dynamics of U.S.–Latin American Relations.* 2nd ed. New York: Oxford University Press.

Stokes, Gale. 1993. *The Walls Came Tumbling Down: The Collapse of Communism in Eastern Europe.* New York: Oxford University Press.

Suchlicki, Jaime. 1992. "Possible Scenarios of Change in Cuba." In Endowment for Cuban American Studies, ed., *Cuba's Transition to Democracy.* Miami: Endowment for Cuban American Studies.

———. 2000. "Castro's Cuba: More Continuity than Change," *Studies in Comparative International Development* 34, no. 4 (winter): 123–35.

Thomas, Daniel. 1999. "The Helsinki Accords and Political Change in Eastern Europe." In Thomas Risse, Stephen C. Ropp, and Kathryn Sikkink, eds., *The Power of Human Rights: International Norms and Domestic Change.* New York: Cambridge University Press.

Thompson, Mark R. 1996. "No Exit: 'Nation-stateness' and Democratization in the German Democratic Republic." *Political Studies* 44: 267–86.

———. 1996. "Why and How East Germans Rebelled." *Theory and Society* 25: 263–99.

———. 2000. "Whatever Happened to Democratic Revolutions?" *Democratization* 7, no. 4 (winter): 1–20.

———. 2001. "To Shoot or Not to Shoot: Post-Totalitarianism in China and Eastern Europe." *Comparative Politics* 34, no. 1 (October): 63–83.

Thompson, Robert Smith. 1992. *The Missiles of October: The Declassified Story of John F. Kennedy and the Cuban Missile Crisis.* New York: Simon & Schuster.

Tismaneanu, Vladimir. 1989. "Nascent Civil Society in the German Democratic Republic." *Problems of Communism* 38 (March–June): 90–111.

Todorova, Maria N. 1992. "Improbable Maverick or Typical Conformist? Seven Thoughts on the New Bulgaria." In Ivo Banac, ed., *Eastern Europe in Revolution.* Ithaca, N.Y.: Cornell University Press.

Urban, Jan. 1990. "Czechoslovakia: The Power and Politics of Humiliation." In Gwyn Prins, ed., *Spring in Winter: The 1989 Revolutions.* Manchester, U.K.: Manchester University Press.

U.S. Congress, House, Subcommittee on International Relations of the Committee on Foreign Affairs. 1980. "Authorizing Additional Appropriations for the Board for International Broadcasting and Grants to Radio Free Europe/Radio Liberty for Fiscal Years 1980 and 1981." Hearings, 96th Cong., 2d sess., March 26 and April 16.

Vanderbush, Walter, and Patrick J. Haney. 1999. "Policy toward Cuba in the Clinton Administration." *Political Science Quarterly* 114, no. 3 (autumn): 387–409.

Verdery, Katherine, and Gail Kligman. 1992. "Romania after Ceauşescu: Post-Communist Communism?" In Ivo Banac, ed., *Eastern Europe in Revolution.* Ithaca, N.Y.: Cornell University Press.

Walker, Phyllis Greene, and Edward González. 1999. "Cuba Today and Prospects for Peaceful or Violent Change." The RAND Forum on Cuba, Conference Proceedings. Santa Monica, Calif.: RAND.

Werlau, María C. 1996. "Foreign Investment in Cuba: The Limits of Commercial Engagement." In Association for the Study of the Cuban Economy, ed., *Cuba in Transition,* vol. 6. Washington, D.C.: ASCE.

Wheaton, Bernard, and Zdenek Kavan. 1992. *The Velvet Revolution: Czechoslovakia, 1988–1991.* Boulder, Colo.: Westview.

Whitehead, Laurence. 1986. "International Aspects of Democratization." In Guillermo O'Donnell, Philippe C. Schmitter, and Laurence Whitehead, eds., *Transitions from Authoritarian Rule: Comparative Perspectives.* Baltimore: Johns Hopkins University Press.

———. 1996. "Three International Dimensions of Democratization." In Laurence Whitehead, ed., *The International Dimensions of Democratization: Europe and the Americas.* New York: Oxford University Press.

Wyden, Peter. 1979. *Bay of Pigs: The Untold Story.* New York: Simon & Schuster.

Index

Abrams, Elliot, 119
Agreement for Democracy, 63
American Center for International Labor Solidarity, 102
American embargo, 113–115, 119, 125–127, 130, 138–139, 141, 176–178; economic effect on Cuba, 12, 142–145, 177–178, 212n. 100; perception of, in Cuba, 139, 210n. 63. *See also* anti-embargo movement; economic sanctions, effectiveness of; engagement policy; Helms-Burton Act
Andreas, Dwayne, 147
Andrei Sakharov Foundation, 135
anti-embargo movement: aims of, 119, 155–156; composition of, 147–148, 151–152; and Cuban government, participation in, 119, 121, 148, 150–151; funding for, 149–150; victories of, 119, 147–149, 152–154. *See also* American embargo; anti-embargo movement, arguments of
anti-embargo movement, arguments of: economic growth promotes democracy, 2, 137; the embargo causes hardship, 12, 139, 150; the embargo harms American firms, 125, 154; the embargo increases repression, xxvii, 16–17, 129; the embargo is ineffective, 125, 126, 127, 130; engagement promotes democracy, 125, 130, 132–133; foreign capitalists promote democracy, 139–140. *See also* economic performance and transitions to democracy; economic reforms in Cuba; engagement policy; foreign investment in Cuba
Arca Foundation, 147, 149–150
Archer Daniels Midland, 147, 152, 155
Armstrong, Fulton, 119

Ashcroft, Sen. John, 152
assistance to civil society from abroad: Cuban, xxii, 31–32, 36, 46–47, 60, 62, 65, 86, 95–108, 172–175; Eastern European, 92–95
Aznar, José María, 131–132

Basulto, José, 105
Bay of Pigs invasion, 111–113, 204nn. 7, 10
Berger, Samuel, 119
Biscet, Oscar Elías, 34–35, 41, 78, 136
Blyth, Peter T., 151
Bowles, Chester, 111
Brothers to the Rescue, 90, 105, 118–119
Buhl, Dieter, 71
Bunce, Valerie, xix, xxvi
Bush (41st) administration, policies toward Cuba, 17, 78, 116. *See also* U.S. policies toward Cuba
Bush (43rd) administration, policies toward Cuba, xiv, 78, 80, 103–104, 176, 180. *See also* U.S. policies toward Cuba

Campbell, Angus, 55
Carter, Pres. Jimmy, 129
Carter administration, policies toward Cuba, 114–115. *See also* U.S. policies toward Cuba
Castro, Fidel, ix–x, xix–xx, 14–18, 104, 124, 127, 131–133, 145, 166, 180. *See also* Castro regime
Castro, Raúl, ix, 14, 16, 18, 132–133, 180
Castro regime: credit-worthiness of, 8; economic data of, 7, 186n. 44, 188n. 73; and legitimacy, xviii–xix, 2, 10, 44, 47–48, 133, 164; and nationalism, xi, xix–xx, 44, 164; nature of, x, xvi, xxviii–xxix, 13–17, 127,

228   *Index*

Castro regime (*cont.*)
163, 188n. 81; signs of discontent within,
xvii, 48–52, 164, 168; troubles faced by, ix,
xvii–xviii, xx–xxi, 2, 4–6, 164; U.S. national
security, threat to by, 205nn. 25, 29
Catholic Church. *See* Roman Catholic Church
Ceauşescu regime, and nationalism, xx, 44
Center for a Free Cuba, 101
Center for Democracy, 94–95
Center for the Study of a National Option
(CEON), xii, xxxi, 77
Central and East European Publishing Project,
93–94
church. *See* Protestant Church, in East Germany; Roman Catholic Church
civil society, in Cuba: ix, xxii–xxiii, 20, 29–33,
46, 64, 67, 74, 76–77, 86, 89–90, 92, 97,
166, 168; assistance to from abroad, xxii,
31–32, 36, 46–47, 60, 62, 65, 86, 95–108,
172–175; coordination within, 33–37,
46–47; and the Cuban-American community, 97–99, 104–108, 174–175; economic
repression against, xxii, 10, 46, 86, 96–97,
137; numbers of groups and members in,
xxii, 32–33; objectives and strategies of,
37–39, 65, 164; petitions to the government for political change by, 15, 189n. 99;
struggle for the streets, 33, 38–42, 67–68,
166–167. *See also* democracy, transitions to:
in Cuba; U.S. material assistance, to anti-
apartheid activists
civil society, in Eastern Europe: assistance to
from abroad, 92–95; in Czechoslovakia,
xxiii, 22–23, 30, 32, 58–59, 68–69; in East
Germany, xxiii, 25, 30, 32, 58–59, 68, 190n.
7; in Romania, 20–21, 31, 32. *See also*
democracy, transitions to; political efficacy
Clinton administration, policies toward
Cuba, xiv, xxvii–xxviii, 80, 93, 100–102,
110, 116–124, 128, 146, 154, 175–176. *See
also* U.S. policies toward Cuba
Committee in Support of Solidarity, 94
communication, independent: in Cuba, xiv,
xxiv, xxvii, 20, 32, 46–47, 60–62, 64, 66–68,
72–82, 171; in Eastern Europe, xxiii–xxv,
xxvii, 20–26, 66, 68–72, 77. *See also* assis-

tance to civil society from abroad; Clinton
administration, policies toward Cuba;
Martí, Radio and TV; Radio Free Europe
Communist Party of Cuba, xvii–xix, 12, 51,
89, 164
comparative analysis: cross-regional, of Eastern
European transitions, xvi, xxv–xxvi; relevance of this study, beyond Castro and Cuba,
ix–xiii, xv–xvi, xxiii–xxiv, xxvii, 18–20, 126,
144–145, 159–160, 169, 176, 178, 181
Concilio Cubano, 15, 34–35, 37, 89, 116
corruption, in the Cuban government, 48,
49, 51–52
counterfactuals, xiv–xv
Cuba. *See* American embargo; Castro regime;
Communist Party of Cuba; Cuba, non-transition to democracy in; Cuban economy;
Cuban military; foreign investment in
Cuba; popular discontent in Cuba; Roman
Catholic Church: in Cuba
Cuba, non-transition to democracy in: explanations for, of the author, ix, xi–xvi, xxii,
xxiv, xxvii, 20, 31–32, 39, 44, 60–62, 66–67,
86, 159–161, 164–165, 167–172; explanations for, of others, ix, xiii, xvii–xxii, 29,
44–45, 56, 62–65, 165–168; origin of
regime (homegrown) explanation,
xviii–xix, 44. *See also* civil society, in Cuba:
assistance to from abroad; Clinton administration, policies toward Cuba; communication, independent: in Cuba; democracy,
transitions to: in Cuba; political efficacy
Cuba Democracy Act, 17, 100, 116, 122, 133,
143
CubaNet, xxx, 99
Cuba Solidarity Act of 2001, 103–104, 106
Cuban American National Foundation, 63–64,
100, 104, 106–107, 140, 148–149, 174–175
Cuban economy, 4–9, 11–12, 164, 178–179;
credit-worthiness of, 8; reforms, scarceness
of, xx, 6, 8–13, 138, 179; sugar, 7–8;
tourism, 8–9, 12–13, 143; unreliability of
data on, 7, 186n. 44, 188n. 73. *See also*
American embargo; economic performance
and transitions to democracy; economic
sanctions; foreign investment in Cuba

Index 229

Cuban Internal Opposition Act of 2000, 106, 107

Cuban Liberty and Democratic Solidarity Act of 1996. *See* Helms-Burton Act

Cuban military, 48–50, 167

Cuban Revolutionary Directorate (Directorio Revolucionario Democratico Cubano), 107–108

CREMONA Foundation, 95

Czechoslovakia: civil society in, xxiii, 22–23, 30, 32, 58–59, 68–69; transition to democracy in, xxii–xxiii, 19, 22–24, 43, 50

data sources, xxx–xxxii

DeLay, Rep. Tom, 154

democracy, transitions to, xxiv, xxviii–xxix, 66, 85–87, 159–163; in Cuba, possibility of, x, xiii, xxii–xxiii, xxvii, xxix–xxx, 4, 13–21, 31, 42, 44, 47–49, 60, 85, 159–164, 167–170, 175, 180–181; in Czechoslovakia, xxii–xxiii, 19, 22–24, 43, 50; in East Germany, xxii–xxiii, 19, 24–26, 43, 47, 50, 56, 58; by regime collapse, x–xi, xiii–xiv, xxi–xxii, xxix, 16, 18–20, 42–44, 66, 85–87, 161–163; by regime collapse, without shooting, xxix–xxx, 26, 42–43, 47–50, 56, 163, 167; regime types and modes of, xxix, 13–14, 18; in Romania, xxii–xxiii, 19–22; and splits in ruling blocs, x, xxviii–xxix, 1, 13, 16. *See also* Cuba, non-transition to democracy in; economic performance and transitions to democracy; international factors in transitions to democracy; political efficacy

demonstrations, antigovernment, in Cuba, 6, 42, 44, 47. *See also* civil society, in Cuba: struggle for the streets

Díaz-Balart, Rep. Lincoln, 106–107, 154

Dodd, Sen. Christopher, 107, 147

Domínguez, Jorge, 110, 117, 182n. 17

double standard, toward cause of democracy in Cuba, 145–146

Duval, Lázaro Constantín, 41

East Germany: civil society in, xxiii, 25, 30, 32, 58–59, 68, 190n. 7; Protestant Church

in, xxv, 20, 25, 59, 68, 87–88, 201n. 11; repression, overcoming fear of in, 56, 168; transition to democracy in, xxii–xxiii, 19, 24–26, 43, 47, 50, 56, 58

Eastern Europe: civil society in, xxii–xxiii, 92–95; cross-regional comparability of transitions to democracy, xxv–xxvi; economic performance, and transitions to democracy, 2–3, 141–142, 183n. 27; independent communication in, xxiii–xxv, xxvii, 20–26, 66, 68–72, 77; political efficacy in, xiv, xxii–xxiv, 22, 30–31, 56–60, 66, 69–72, 160, 169–170. *See also* Czechoslovakia; East Germany; Romania

economic performance and transitions to democracy, 1–3, 137, 141–142, 178; in Cuba, xxi, 4, 6, 11, 128, 137–142, 161, 178, 211n. 84; in Eastern Europe, 3, 141–142, 183n. 27; in Latin America, 3, 142

economic reforms in Cuba, scarcity of, 6, 8–13, 138, 179

economic sanctions, effectiveness of, 125–128, 141–142, 144–146, 177

Eisenhower administration, policies toward Cuba, 110–113, 176. *See also* U.S. policies toward Cuba

Eizenstat, Stuart, 123

Elliott, Kimberley, 125–127, 141–142, 146, 178

embargo. *See* American embargo

engagement policy, effects of, 128–134, 138–141, 177, 179–180, 209nn. 28, 45. *See also* anti-embargo movement, arguments of; Castro regime: nature of; economic reforms in Cuba

European Union, 129, 132

fear of repression, overcoming: in Cuba, xxi, 6, 42, 47, 67, 168; in East Germany, 56, 168

Fearon, James, xv

Ford administration, policies toward Cuba, 114–115. *See also* U.S. policies toward Cuba

Ford Foundation, 93, 147, 149–150

foreign investment in Cuba, 11–13, 137–144, 177

foreign investors in Cuba, likely future backlash against, 139–140, 177
Foreign Policy Research Institute, 95
Franco, Francisco, x
Freedom House, 95, 101, 122
Friedheim, Daniel, xxix, 26, 47, 196n. 74
Fulbright, Sen. J. William, 111

García, Reynaldo Alfaro, 41
General Services Foundation, 149–150
Gern, Christiane, xxxii, 25–26, 43, 56, 87
González, Felipe, 131
Gorbachev factor, xxv–xxvi
Graham, Sen. Bob, 116
Groth, Carl-Johan, 129
Gutierrez-Menoyo, Eloy, 129

Haggard, Stephan, 2–3, 178
Haig, Alexander, 115
Halperin, Morton, 119
Halpern, Nina, 2
Havel, Vaclav, 23, 24, 30, 31, 131
Helms-Burton Act (Cuban Liberty and Democratic Solidarity Act of 1996), xxvii, 16–17, 101, 118–120, 122, 125–126, 208n.13; controversy about, 129–130, 208n. 17; legal text of, 50, 98, 100, 107, 119, 120, 122, 128–129; main purpose of, 127–128. See also American embargo; anti-embargo movement; Clinton administration, policies toward Cuba; economic performance and transitions to democracy; engagement policy
Helms, Sen. Jessie, 103, 107, 153
Helsinki Accords, 136
Herrera, William, 34, 39
Horowitz, Irving Louis, 123, 147, 148
Hufbauer, Gary, 125–127, 141–142, 146, 178
humanitarian aid, to Cuba, xxii, 8–9, 11, 46, 97–98, 139, 172. See also civil society, in Cuba: assistance to from abroad
Huntington, Samuel, xv, xxviii, 1, 43, 66, 137, 159–160

Institute for Democracy in Eastern Europe, 94, 95
international factors in transitions to democracy, xi–xii, xiv, xxiii–xxviii, 20, 57, 66, 135–136, 162–163, 168–173. See also assistance to civil society from abroad; Clinton administration, policies toward Cuba; Martí, Radio and TV; Radio Free Europe
International Foundation for Election Systems, 102
International Rescue Committee, 94

Jan Hus organizations, 93, 95, 96, 98
Jan Palach Information Research Trust, 95, 96
Javits, Jacob, 114
Johnstone, Craig, 150

Karklins, Rasma, xxx, 31, 42–43, 44–45, 57, 66, 70
Kaufman, Robert, 2–3, 178
Kellenberger, Jakob, 131
Kennedy administration, policies toward Cuba, 111–113, 115–116. See also U.S. policies toward Cuba
Kissinger, Henry, 114
Kosak, Michael, 117, 123

Lage, Carlos, 5, 15, 143
legitimacy. See Castro regime: legitimacy of
Lexington Institute, 155
Lieberman, Sen. Joseph, 103
Light, Margot, xxvi
Limongi, Fernando, 2
Linz, Juan, xi, xxix, 3–4, 13–14, 18, 30, 163–164
Lipset, Seymour Martin, 137

MacArthur Foundation, 93–94, 147, 150
Mariel exodus, 114–115, 118
Marsh, Alan, 56
Martí, Radio and TV, xii, xxvii, 64, 72–74, 76–82, 103–104, 115, 121, 171; jamming of, 74–75, 78–81. See also communication, independent
Maurice, Archbishop Pedro, 91
Menem, Pres. Carlos, 131
Mesa-Lago, Carmelo, 3–4, 129–130, 142, 178
methodological considerations, xi, xiv–xvi, xviii–xix, xxxi–xxxii

Millar, James, xxxii
Morejón Almagro, Leonel, 34, 39

National Endowment for Democracy, xii,
xxvii, 65, 92–94, 96, 98–102, 105–106
National Policy Association, 102
nationalism: and Castro regime, xix–xx, 44,
164; and Ceauşescu regime, xx, 44
Nixon administration, policies toward Cuba,
114. *See also* U.S. policies toward Cuba
non-transition to democracy in Cuba. *See*
Cuba, non-transition to democracy in

OAS. See Organization of American States
(OAS)
Oberschall, Anthony, 57
O'Donnell, Guillermo, xiii, 18, 160
Opp, Karl-Dieter, xxxii, 25–26, 43, 56, 87
Organization of American States (OAS), 114,
129
Orr, Peter, 122
Ortega, Cardenal Jaime, 88
Ostpolitik, 134

Palacio Ruiz, Hector, 34
Pan American Development Foundation, 102
Paya, Oswaldo Sardiñas, 96
Pell, Claiborne, 114
Petersen, Roger, xxx, 42–43, 57, 66
political economy of transition. *See* economic performance and transitions to democracy
political efficacy: concept of, 55, 162; in
Cuba, lack of, xiii–xiv, 31–32, 60–62, 160,
167, 170; and dangerous political behavior,
55–56; in Eastern Europe, development of,
xiv, xxii–xxiv, 22, 30–31, 56–60, 66, 69–72,
85, 160, 169–170
Pope John Paul II, 36, 88, 131
popular discontent in Cuba, signs of, xvii,
xix, xx–xxi, 4, 6, 41–42, 47, 67, 164. *See
also* civil society, in Cuba
Protestant Church, in East Germany, xxv, 20,
25, 59, 68, 87–88, 201n. 11
Przeworski, Adam, xiv, xviii, xxvi, xxix, 1, 2,
57, 159, 160

Radio Free Europe, xii, xxvii, 22, 59, 69–72,
78, 81–82, 170–171
Radio Martí. *See* Martí, Radio and TV
Ranneberger, Michael, 123
Reagan administration, policies toward Cuba,
115. *See also* U.S. policies toward Cuba
repression. *See* fear of repression, overcoming
Roberts, Churchill, xxx, xxxii, 62–64, 72,
78–79, 129, 138
Rockefeller Foundation, 93–94
Roman Catholic Church: in Cuba, 20, 68, 76,
87–92, 138, 174; in Poland, 87–88
Romania, civil society in, 20–21, 31, 32; tran-
sition to democracy in, xxii–xxiii, 19–22
Romaszewski, Zbigniew, 92
Rusk, Dean, 113
Ryan, Gov. George, 119, 151, 152, 155

Santacruz, Elizardo Sánchez, 105, 129
Saxonberg, Steven, x, xvii, xxii, xxiv, xxvi,
xxix, 57–59, 70, 169, 182n. 1
Schlesinger, Arthur M., Jr., 111–112
Schmitter, Philippe, xxviii, 160
Schott, Jeffrey, 125–127, 141–142, 146, 178
Seligson, Mitchell, 56
Shapiro, Charles, 119
social malaise, 2, 6
Soros, George (Open Society Fund), 93–94, 99
Stepan, Alfred, xi, xxix, 3–4, 13–14, 18, 30,
163–164
Stevenson, Adlai, 113
sugar. *See under* Cuban economy
Support Group to the Dissidence (GAD), 101

Tarnoff, Peter, 119
Thomas, Daniel, 135–136
Thompson, Mark, x, xiii, 1, 57, 182n. 1
Time and We, 95
Todman, Terence, 114
Torres, Rep. Esteban, 107
Torricelli, Sen. Robert, 116
tourism. *See under* Cuban economy
transitions to democracy. *See* democracy,
transitions to; economic performance and
transitions to democracy; international fac-
tors in transitions to democracy

232   *Index*

transnational network advocating democratization in Cuba, 134–135

TV Martí. *See* Martí, Radio and TV

umbrella organizations, 23, 33–35. *See also* Concilio Cubano

United States Agency for International Development (USAID), Cuba Program of, xxvii, 65, 92–93, 98–102, 105–106, 202n. 56; waste of funds, Clinton administration, 101–102

U.S.-Cuba Business Council, 102

U.S. material assistance, to anti-apartheid activists, 103; to Iraqi opposition, 103

U.S. policies toward Cuba: of the Bush (41st) administration, 17, 78, 116; of the Bush (43rd) administration, xiv, 78, 103–104, 176, 180; of the Carter administration, 114–115; of the Clinton administration, xiv, xxvii–xxviii, 80, 93, 100–102, 110, 116–124, 128, 146, 154, 175–176; of the Eisenhower administration, 110–113, 176; of the Ford administration, 114–115; of the Kennedy administration, 111–113, 115–116; of the Nixon administration, 114; of the Reagan administration, 115. *See also* American embargo; engagement policy; Helms-Burton Act

Valdés, Dagoberto, 92

Viera, Mario, 41

Volcker, Paul, 147

Voss, Peter, xxxii, 25–26, 43, 56, 87

wage confiscation, 13, 137–138

Walesa, Lech, 131

Warner, Sen. John, 147

Weinberger, Caspar, 115

Whitehead, Laurence, xxv